Developments in Soft Computing

T0239003

Advances in Soft Computing

Editor-in-chief
Prof. Janusz Kacprzyk
Systems Research Institute
Polish Academy of Sciences
ul. Newelska 6
01-447 Warsaw, Poland
E-mail: kacprzyk@ibspan.waw.pl
http://www.springer.de/cgi-bin/search-bock.pl?series=4240

Esko Turunen
Mathematics Behind Fuzzy Logic
1999. ISBN 3-7908-1221-8

Robert Fullér
Introduction to Neuro-Fuzzy Systems
2000. ISBN 3-7908-1256-0

Robert John and Ralph Birkenhead (Eds.)
*Soft Computing Techniques
and Applications*
2000. ISBN 3-7908-1257-9

Mieczysław Kłopotek, Maciej Michalewicz
and Sławomir T. Wierzchoń (Eds.)
Intelligent Information Systems
2000. ISBN 3-7908-1309-5

Peter Sinčák, Ján Vaščák, Vladimír Kvasnička
and Radko Mesiar (Eds.)
The State of the Art in Computational Intelligence
2000. ISBN 3-7908-1322-2

Bernd Reusch, Karl-Heinz Temme (Eds.)
Computational Intelligence in Theory and Practice
2001. ISBN 3-7908-1357-5

Robert John · Ralph Birkenhead
Editors

Developments in Soft Computing

With 75 Figures
and 28 Tables

Physica-Verlag

A Springer-Verlag Company

Robert John
Ralph Birkenhead
De Montfort University
Department of Computer Science
The Gateway
Leicester LE1 9BH
United Kingdom
rij@dmu.ac.uk
rab@dmu.ac.uk

ISSN 1615-3871
ISBN 3-7908-1361-3 Physica-Verlag Heidelberg New York

Cataloging-in-Publication Data applied for
Die Deutsche Bibliothek – CIP-Einheitsaufnahme
Developments in soft computing: with 28 tables / Robert John; Ralph Birkenhead (ed.). – Heidelberg; New York: Physica-Verl., 2001
   (Advances in soft computing)
   ISBN 3-7908-1361-3

Physica-Verlag Heidelberg New York
a member of BertelsmannSpringer Science+Business Media GmbH

© Physica-Verlag Heidelberg 2001
Printed in Germany

Hardcover Design: Erich Kirchner, Heidelberg

SPIN 10789622   88/2202-5 4 3 2 1 0 – Printed on acid-free paper

Preface

Soft Computing has come of age. In particular, Artificial Neural Networks, Fuzzy Logic and Evolutionary Computing now play an important role in many domains where traditional techniques have been found wanting. As this volume confirms, hybrid solutions that combine more than one of the Soft Computing approaches are particularly successful in many problem areas. This volume contains twenty seven papers that represent the activities of a number of leading researchers in Soft Computing who presented their work at the International Conference on Recent Advances in Soft Computing 2000 at De Montfort University in Leicester.

We were fortunate in that the conference coincided with a workshop on mobile robots and we were able to have a joint session on areas of mutual interest to the two groups of participants. We are particularly pleased that the volume includes a paper presented to that session by Professor Kevin Warwick, in which he gives some interesting views on the future of intelligent mobile robots and their relationship with the human race.

We would also like to thank the other writers and plenary speakers for their contributions which provide an insight into current research activities from both a theoretical and application view. We hope you find the volume interesting and, if you are a researcher, that the work here will inform your own research.

Robert John and Ralph Birkenhead
Centre for Computational Intelligence
De Montfort University
Leicester
United Kingdom

Contents

Part 2 Application Exemplars

Plenary Address

How Intelligent Can a Mobile Robot Be?

Kevin Warwick

Dept. of Cybernetics, University of Reading, Whiteknights, Reading, RG6 6AY

Summary:
A look is taken at the world of mobile robots. An argument is given for robots being not only intelligent but also conscious. Cyborg type robots are considered and the robots presently operating in the Science Museum, London are introduced.

1 Introduction

Firstly let us establish some ground rules. A robot can be alive. A robot can be conscious. A robot can be intelligent. But how intelligent can a robot be?

The whole concept of intelligence has been a major philosophical discussion piece for thousands of years. Even folk such as Plato and Cicero voiced their opinion on the topic. In the last century the debate continued and over the 40 or so years from 1960 it received a concept injection from the new field of Artificial Intelligence. When this area itself bursts into life, immediately the question was raised, what exactly is artificial intelligence? Perhaps the most famous and oft quoted answer was that Minsky (1968), 'Artificial Intelligence is the science of making machines do things that would require intelligence if done by men'. Over the years this definition has been fleshed out, e.g. by Boden (1987), but basically it has remained the same.

The Minsky definition has two major problems associated with it. Firstly it does not actually tackle the question of What is Intelligence? Secondly it links intelligence solely as a human property with Artificial Intelligence (AI) as a sort of mimicking or copying exercise. I personally do not wish to dispute the fact that humans are, by and large, intelligent in their way. However I feel that other creatures on earth are also intelligent, each in their way. Despite this the Minsky definition still seems to have entrenched itself as a basic way of life. For example, the arguments of Penrose (1994) appear to rest on the idea that the whole aim of AI is to attempt to simulate the operation of a human brain.

Perhaps the use of the world 'Artificial' has not helped things. My dictionary definition defines artificial as 'not real imitation, fake', Thompson (1995). This give the strong impression that Artificial Intelligence is not real. Just as some people might question the use of the word 'Intelligence' when describing robots, I would question the use of the word 'Artificial'. Despite this it reared its head again when 'Artificial Life' came into being at the end of the 1980's, Langton (1989) and more recently 'Artificial Evolution', Husbands et. Al (1997). Perhaps we should here and now finish with the use of the word 'artificial' when describing the intelligence or life of robots.

2   Off Target

One enormous problem in studying the intelligence of machines such as robots, is the human bias that plagues the analysis. A wonderful example of this is the Turing Test, which is based solely on human values, human nuances and human communication. To be frank, if a machine could ever categorically 'pass' the Turing test then the human race would have a major problem on its hands.

Yet recent research into the intelligence of robots has looked much more at systems that exist in their own right, living in their own way, based on their own perspective of the world. Such systems generally tend to be different from biological systems, although comparisons can be made. If creatures, other than humans, are intelligent, then so too can robots be. But we should not belittle what robots can do or how they operate.

It has been said, by Rodney Brooks (1986) of MIT, that '...insects succeed. No human-built systems are remotely as reliable.' It may well be the case that the robots built by humans at MIT fit this pattern, indeed I would not wish to take issue with that. In general however the statement is blatant rubbish. It is estimated that more than 20% of bees do not make it back to the hive on their first flight, or certain types of flies only live for a maximum of one hour, Warwick (2000a). Robots exhibit a very different form of life and intelligence, we certainly should not regard their lifestyle as worse than that of insects or, for that matter as worse than that of humans.

Yet traditional robotics appear to be aimed at trying to get robots merely to copy things done by humans or animals, the examples are numerous: Gupta and Del Pobil (1998), Arkin and Arbib (1998) and Iyengar and Eltes (1991). In an industrial or production setting such an approach obviously has its merits, due to the robots' distinct advantages. Outside that scenario however the range of possibilities is enormous.

The story of flight has been oft quoted, and it is extremely pertinent as far as the intelligence question is concerned. In 1897 Lord Kelvin, one of the most eminent scientists of his time, felt that it was not possible for heavier than air machines to fly. Yet only six years later such an event had occurred, although perhaps in a different way to that imagined by Lord Kelvin. His thought had been blinkered.

Nowadays if we look to intelligence in robots, the blinkered view is one which tries to liken, as in Minsky's definition, such intelligence with that in humans or possibly animals, as in Langton's case. We must be clear, robot intelligence is based on silicon, it is founded on different material to that of the animal world. We should therefore regard it in a different way. It would be very foolish to make statements in the same fashion as those of Lord Kelvin. A recent example is: " I can be certain that conscious intelligent robots will not appear in my lifetime", Andreae (1998).

3   Balanced Realisation and Consciousness

As pointed out in Smith and Hamilton (1998), 'the sensory, actuator and neural processes of a robot are seen to be best represented as an overall system'. Such a balanced view is as true for humans and animals as it is for robots. So the robot is viewed as a whole entity for what it can do. It nevertheless brings directly into play the environment as an important part of the feedback loop of life: brain – actuators – environment – sensors – brain. This loop is particularly pertinent for a mobile robot moving around in its environment.

As humans we tend to feel we have a good idea about what it means to be human. As well as any actions that can be carried out and witnessed as part of a feedback loop, as described, our individual innermost thoughts we classify as our consciousness. As these thoughts do not usually result in any external effects that can be witnessed, so they are difficult for us to define and measure. Hence they have become the basic foodstuff for many 'theoretical' conferences around the world.

Because other humans are, we feel, mostly like ourselves then just as I 'know' that I am conscious, so most likely are other humans conscious like me. When considering other creatures however we are faced with the problem as posed by Nagel (1974) – what is it like to be a bat? As we are not a bat, with its own sensors and actuators, we can never know what the bat is thinking and whether or not it has anything like human innermost thoughts. The bat's brain though is a complex network with something like a million or so brain cells. Many feedback loops within the bat's brain exist, passing signals which are not merely processing from sensor to actuator.

From the structure of a bat's brain we can be pretty certain that at any time signals exist that are not due to a direct input to output programmed transmission through the brain. Indeed the same is true, albeit to a much lesser extent, with sea slugs, which have 8 or 9 brain cells. It's only when we get to the amoeba that a more straightforward programmed response 'appears', to be going on. Surely it is appropriate in each case, to describe the innermost brain signals as consciousness in each of those creatures. If we cannot do so, then it is difficult to see how we can describe humans as being conscious.

This being the case, how can we apply the result to mobile robots?. The answer is clear and simple. If the central processing of the robot is merely carrying out a series of programmed instructions and the input-output path is direct, then calling this consciousness sounds ridiculous and inappropriate. If however, the robot's brain contains, in normal operation, signals passing around that are not due to direct input to output programmed transmission, then the robot must be conscious in its own way. To deny this would be unscientific and certainly biased.

A robot is conscious if, in the normal operation of its brain, active signals exist which are not due to a direct input to output process.

To qualify this description of consciousness we can look for help from a dictionary definition, Thompson (1995), where 'Consciousness' is defined as 'awareness'. On the other hand 'awareness' is in the same dictionary defined as 'consciousness'. So now we know!

4 Intelligence

Whilst consciousness deals with the innermost, 'unmeasurable' brain signals, intelligence in its entirety deals with the whole range of brain functions, including taking in sensory information and causing actuators to operate. Some of this action can be regarded as programmed, whether that be in robots, animals or humans. Breathing is a good example of a programmed response in many creatures.

Many robots, perhaps less so mobile robots though, are programmed across their potential range of operation. They therefore exhibit a basic, behavioural intelligence, but nothing more. For some reason, much schooling of humans has been aimed at achieving the same sort of results in humans – thereby removing those aspects that we relate to conscious thought or imagination.

The intelligence of an individual is an integral part of their make up. It depends inherently on that individual's physical set up, their sensors, their actuators and necessarily the environment around them. In order to describe intelligence as an all encompassing entity, we must regard it as a basic thing, perhaps 'the variety of mental processes that act together to sustain life', Warwick (2000a). This definition does not include many solely human values, but rather gives a very good ability for all. It does though 'pass the buck' into a follow on requirement for a definition of 'Life'.

So we can consider intelligence in terms of very basic elements. In the first place some behavioral responses appear to fit the bill. Such responses have often been put into the form of logical rules e.g. for a frog. If a small dot of a particular size moves quickly through my line of vision then eat it, e.g. for a robot ... If I sense something to my right then move to the left, e.g. for a University Lecturer ... If I am told to produce a journal paper every year then I produce a journal paper every year.

These basic behavioral responses apparently all indicate different aspects of an intellect associated with pond life.

Other factors of intelligence such as learning, communication, reasoning, planning etc., etc., appear to a different extent in different intelligent beings. Intelligence is a multi-facetted entity, different creatures exhibiting a different range of abilities, each range being suitable for that being. For some insects, accurate and defined sensing of water vapour is a critical factor whereas for humans we do not appear to have that particular ability at all – unless the water is flavoured (particularly with hops!). This does not make humans less intelligent than such insects, unless a water vapour IQ test is the key, but rather our intelligence has its emphasis on different abilities. Similarly if a machine does not do well on the Turing test, this does not mean it is any less intelligent than a human, it merely shows that a human is perhaps better on that particular test.

One of the most successful architectures for individual robots is the subsumption approach, Brooks (1986). This is a layered method based on priority scheduling, the lowest basic control layer having the lowest priority. Higher layers then provide/take over control of the robot as an when required. Generally though the robot goes about its lower level business. This is a sensible, straightforward approach although it does impose a sort of purely behavioural, non-conscious, intelligence on the robot.

In the subsumption method, if a signal/message is received from the outside it is treated in a 'God-like' overpowering way, such as in foraging or box-pushing collective robot behaviours, Mataric (1995). In a sense this is merely showing a pseudo-collective response as an outside body has instructed all such robots to do their stuff, an order that they obey in military fashion. The subsumption architecture is therefore perhaps best taken merely as a starting point from which: firstly communication can affect several levels, dependant on the information communicated and the robot's belief in it, and secondly a conscious state within the robot effectively fuzzifies the well structured layers – maybe the robot will obey an order but maybe not, it depends on other factors!

5 Robots by Appointment

The group of robots known as the 7-dwarfs, produced by a team of researchers in the University of Reading have been described in detail in several works and it is not intended to go into great detail here. Articles can be found in Mitchell et al (1994), Dautenhahn, McOwan and Warwick in Smith and Hamilton (1998), with a 3 chapter detailed exposition in Warwick (1998).

The wheeled robots can be programmed to move around in their environment either without bumping into, or by closely tracking a moving object. By means of reinforcement learning via trial and error they can also learn a suitable strategy that will get them by. In this respect the robots will home in on a particular behaviour that is clearly a compromise between the conflicting information that the robot has received. The robot's ultimate behaviour is different each time it learns, and is directly dependant on its environment and when and how information is obtained. It is interesting that such behaviour, arrived at by numerous compromises, even causes biologists to point to robots as being "alive". "A real organism is a mass of compromises not a finely optimised piece of machinery", Stewart and Cohen (1997). Anyone who has witnessed the 7 Dwarfs learning, with a result of making occasional mistakes by bumping into the wall, would certainly not describe their action as "finely optimised".

Some of the latest versions of the 7 Dwarfs robots have now gone on display at the Science Museum, London in the new Welcome Wing. The robots are in a pit, which was officially opened (along with the remainder of the wing) on June the 27th, 2000 by Her Majesty the Queen. With a non-subsumption based architecture however, we cannot be sure at all that the robots will obey Her Majesty!

At any point in time one of the four robots in the pit can be controlled remotely by means of a joystick, with the other robots acting autonomously. The operator can then be the predator robot and chase after the other three, which will attempt to escape. Conversely the operator can be the prey, with the other three robots chasing them, tracking them down, "Terminator" style. In testing, the prey mode was not overly popular because it is just about impossible to escape from the three robots hunting - whatever the operator does the robots can out think them! We therefore had to downgrade the speed of the response and speed of reaction in the robots, in order to give the human operator a chance.

The Welcome Wing robots can also operate in a military style group, in a couple of ways. Firstly they can play follow-my-leader, with the human operator leading a robot crocodile around the pit. Secondly they can do a "Steps" style dance routine with the operator acting as choreographer. This robot group with these abilities is now a permanent attraction in the Science Museum. Please feel free to go and try them out.

The robots have ultrasonic sensors, on front and back, in order for them to sense objects, possibly other robots, nearby, to minimise the amount of bumping. The robots also have a ring of infrared transmitters and receivers. In this way they communicate with each other essentially telling each other where they are at any time. These basic capabilities were described fully in Warwick (1998).

6 Cyborgs

In the film "The Terminator", a Cyborg is defined as a Cybernetic Organism, something that is part human and part machine. For once though a dictionary definition is perhaps better, Thompson (1995), pointing to a Cyborg as "a person whose physical abilities are extended beyond normal human limitations by machine technology". Unfortunately the dictionary definition goes on to say that as yet Cyborgs are undeveloped! See Warwick (2000b) for an alternative view.

In the world of mobile robots, perhaps we have Cybots, things that are part animal/insect and part robot technology. In 1997 in a widely publicised project at the University of Tokyo, some of the motor neurons of a cockroach were attached to a microprocessor, which the cockroach wore as a backpack. Signals sent to the neurons through electrodes then involuntarily propelled the cockroach in different directions, despite what the cockroach wanted to do itself. To all intents and purposes the cockroach was remote controlled - even to the extent of having small LED's on its backpack to indicate when it was turning left or right. A nice photograph of this cybot is given in the Robotics section of the 1999 Guiness Book of Records, on the same page as a description of an internet robot learning experiment that was carried out between Reading University and New York.

John Chapin's research at the MCP Hahnemann School of Medicine in Philadelphia is also of considerable note. As is reported on his web page, he implanted electrodes into the brains of rats. Initially the rats were taught to pull a lever in order to obtain a ratty treat. However the implants were used such that the rats merely had to "think" about pulling the lever for the treat to be released, they did not have to actually carry out the action.

Finally, as reported in the 10 June 2000 issue of New Scientist, a mobile robot has been built with its body controlled by the brain of a fish. Light sensors feed the fish brain information such that the body is caused to move in one direction or the other. With only relatively few fish neurons, complex behaviours can be achieved. Clearly the world of mobile robots is changing rapidly.

7. Conclusions

When we consider a robot with a machine body, but with a fish brain we might say that this is a conscious, intelligent being but if we give the robot a machine brain instead, then we may say it is not? What about the mixed brain of the cockroach as described in the previous section, is that conscious and intelligent as well? Drawing a line between creatures in this way because one brain is made of one substance and another is made of something else is clearly non-productive, biased and gets us absolutely nowhere.

A result of this is to understand that mobile robots can not only be intelligent, but also conscious beings as discussed in section 3. If they are then doing their own thing, in their own way I would not wish to question whether they are alive or not!

But a machine brain has oodles of advantages. Speed, memory and multi-dimensional thought being some immediate positives in comparison with biological brains as we know them at the moment. Could this result ultimately in robots far more intelligent than anything on earth at present or are we more likely to take a cyborg route and join closely with them?

References

Smith L.S and Hamilton A (eds), "Neuromorphic Systems", World Scientific, 1998.

Andreae, J.H, "Associative Learning for a Robot Intelligence", Imperial College Press, 1998.

Gupta, K and Del Pobil A.P (eds), "Practical Motion Planning in Robotics", Wiley, 1998.

Penrose R, "Shadows of the Mind", Oxford University Press, 1994.

Arkin R.C and Arbib M, "Behaviour Based Robotics", MIT Press, 1998.

Iyengar S.S and Eltes A, "Autonomous Mobile Robots: Control, Planning and Architecture", IEEE Press, 1991.

Husbands P, Harvey I, Cliff D and Miller G, "Artificial Evolution: A New Path for Artificial Intelligence?", Brain and Cognition, Vol. 34, pp.130-159, 1997.

Minsky M, (ed), "Semantic Information Processing", MIT Press, 1968.

Boden M.A, "Artificial Intelligence and Natural Man", 2nd edition, MIT Press, 1987.

Nagel T, "What is it like to be a bat?", Philosophical Review, Vol.83, pp. 435-450, 1974.

Thompson D (ed), "The Concise Oxford Dictionary", Oxford University Press, 1995.

Langton C, "Artificial Life", Addison Wesley,1989.

Warwick K, "QI: The Quest for Intelligence", Piatkus, 2000a.

Brooks R.A, "A robust layered control system for a mobile robot", IEEE Transactions on Robotics and Automation, Vol. 2, pp. 14-23, 1986.

Mataric M.J, Nilsson M and Simsarian K.T, Co-operative multi robot box pushing, Proc. IROS-95, Pittsburgh, 1995.

Mitchell R.J, Keating D.A and Kambhampati C, "Learning Strategy for a simple robot insect." Proc. Int., Conference Control 94, Warwick University, pp. 492-497, 1994.

Warwick K, "In the Mind of the Machine", Arrow, 1998.

Stewart I and Cohen J, "Figments of Reality", Cambridge University Press, 1997.

Warwick K, "Cyborg 1.0", Wired, Vol 8, No. 2, pp. 144-151, 2000b

Part 1

Theoretical Development

Hybrid Heuristics for Optimal Design of Artificial Neural Networks

Ajith Abraham & Baikunth Nath

Gippsland School of Computing & Information Technology
Monash University, Churchill 3842, Australia
{Email: Ajith.Abraham, Baikunth.Nath@infotech.monash.edu.au}

ABSTRACT: Designing the architecture and correct parameters for the learning algorithm is a tedious task for modeling an optimal Artificial Neural Network (ANN), which is smaller, faster and with a better generalization performance. In this paper we explain how a hybrid algorithm integrating Genetic algorithm (GA), Simulated Annealing (SA) and other heuristic procedures can be applied for the optimal design of an ANN. This paper is more concerned with the understanding of current theoretical developments of Evolutionary Artificial Neural Networks (EANNs) using GAs and how the proposed hybrid heuristic procedures can be combined to produce an optimal ANN. The proposed meta-heuristic can be regarded as a general framework for adaptive systems, that is, systems that can change their connection weights, architectures and learning rules according to different environments without human intervention.

Keywords: Artificial neural networks, simulated annealing, genetic algorithm, evolutionary artificial neural network and genetic annealing.

1. Introduction

Conventional design of ANNs requires the user to specify the number of neurons, their distribution over several layers and interconnection between them. Several methods have been proposed to automatically construct ANNs for reduction in network complexity that is to determine the appropriate number of hidden units, layers, etc. Topological optimization algorithms such as Extentron [7], Upstart [3], Pruning [18] and Cascade Correlation [8] etc. got its own limitations.

The interest in evolutionary search procedures for designing ANN architecture has been growing in recent years as they can evolve towards the optimal architecture without outside interference, thus eliminating the tedious trial and error work of manually finding an optimal network [1]. GA and SA, which are the most general purpose optimization procedures are increasingly being applied independently to a diverse spectrum of problem areas. For a long time theoretical investigators in SA and GA have focused on developing a hybrid algorithm that employs the good properties and performance of both GA and SA [2, 5]. In certain situations GA outperformed SA and vice versa. GAs are not designed to be ergodic and cover the space in a maximally efficient way. But the prime benefit of GAs is the parallelization capability. In contrast SA is largely sequential in moving from one optimal value to the next. States must be sampled sequentially, for acceptability and to permit identification of current local minima about which new test parameters are chosen.

2. Genetic Algorithm (GA)

GA is a process, which mimic the way biological evolution works. GAs are adaptive computational techniques that transform a set (population) of individual mathematical objects (usually fixed length character or binary strings), each with an associated fitness value, into a new population (next generation) using operations patterned after the Darwinian principle of reproduction and survival of the fittest and naturally occurring genetic operations (crossover, mutation). Not only does it produce more of the good solutions but better and better solutions. This is because it combines the best traits of parent individuals to produce superior children. The procedure may be written as the difference equation: $x[t + 1] = s(v(x[t]))$; where $x[t]$ is the population at time t under a representation x, v is a random variation operator, and s is the selection operator.

3. Simulated Annealing (SA)

SA is a global optimization algorithm with a Metropolis procedure, statistically promising to deliver an optimal solution. If the generation function of the simulated annealing algorithm is represented as [6]

$$g_k(Z) = \prod_{i=1}^{D} g_k(z_i) = \prod_{i=1}^{D} \frac{1}{2(|z_i| + \frac{1}{\ln(1/T_i(k))}) \ln(1 + \ln(1/T_i(k)))} \tag{1}$$

Where $T_i(k)$ is the temperature in dimension i at time k. The generation probability will be represented by

$$G_k(Z) = \int_{-1}^{z_1} \int_{-1}^{z_2} .....\int_{-1}^{z_D} g_k(Z)dz_1 dz_2....dz_D = \prod_{i=1}^{D} G_{ki}(z_i) \tag{2}$$

Where $G_{ki}(z_i) = \frac{1}{2} + \frac{\text{sgn}(z_i) \ln(1 + |z_i| \ln(1/T_i(k)))}{2 \ln(1 + \ln(1/T_i(k)))}$ \hfill (3)

It is straightforward to prove that an annealing schedule for

$$T_i(k) = T_{0i} \exp(-\exp(b_i k^{1/D})) \tag{4}$$

A global minimum, statistically, can be obtained. That is,

$$\sum_{k=k_o}^{\infty} g_k = \infty \tag{5}$$

Where $b_i > 0$ is a constant parameter and k_0 is a sufficiently large constant to satisfy Eq. (5), if the generation function in Eq. (1) is adopted.

4. Genetic Annealing Algorithm (GAA)

GAA is a hybrid random searching technique fusing SA and GA methodologies into a more efficient algorithm. Such hybrid algorithms can inherit the convergence property of SA and parallalization capability of GA. Each genotype is assigned an energy threshold, initially equal to the energy of the randomized bit string to which it is assigned. If the energy of the mutant exceeds the threshold of the parent that spawned it, the mutant is rejected and a new genotype is considered. However if the energy of the new genotype is less than or equal to the energy of the parent, the mutant is accepted as a replacement for its progenitor. GAA uses an Energy Bank (EB) to keep track of the energy liberated by the successful mutants. Whenever a mutant passes the threshold test, the difference between the threshold and the mutant's energy is added to the EB for temporary storage. Once the quantum of energy is accounted, the threshold is reset so that it equals the energy of the accepted mutant and move on to next member of the population. After each member has been subjected to a random mutation, the entire population is reheated by changing the threshold. The rate of reheating is directly proportional to the amount of energy accumulated in the EB (from each member of the population) as well as designer's choice of coolant rate (Section 3). Annealing results from repeated cycles of collecting energy from successful mutants and then redistributing nearly all of it by raising the threshold energy of each population member equally [17].

5. Back-Propagation (BP) Algorithm

BP [11] is a gradient descent technique to minimize some error criteria E. In the batched mode variant the descent is based on the gradient ∇E for the total training set.

$$\Delta w_{ij}(n) = -\varepsilon * \frac{\delta E}{\delta w_{ij}} + \alpha * \Delta w_{ij}(n-1)$$

ε and α are the learning rate and momentum respectively. A good choice of both the parameters are required for training success and speed of the ANN. Empirical research has shown that BP algorithm often is stuck in a local minimum mainly because of the random initialization of weights. BP usually generalizes quite well to detect the global features of the input but after prolonged training the network will start to recognize individual input/output pair rather than settling for weights that generally describe the mapping for the whole training set.

6. A Framework for Optimal Design of ANNs

An optimal design of an ANN can only be achieved by the adaptive evolution of connection weights, architecture and learning rules which progress on different time scales [1]. Figure 1 illustrates the general interaction mechanism with the architecture of the ANN evolving at the highest level on the slowest time scale. For every architecture, there is the evolution of learning rules that proceeds on a faster time scale in an environment decided by the architecture. For each learning rule, evolution of connection weights proceeds at a faster time scale in an environment decided by the problem, the learning rule and the architecture. Hierarchy of the architecture and learning rules rely on the prior knowledge. If there is more prior knowledge about the learning rules than the architecture then it is better to implement the learning rule at a higher level.

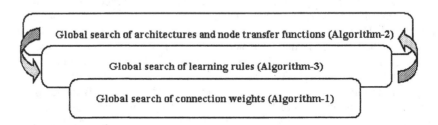

Fig 1. Interaction of various search mechanisms in the design of optimal ANN

7. Global Search of Connection Weights (*Algorithm 1*)

The shortcomings of the BP algorithm could be overcome if the training process is considered as a global search of optimal connection weights wherein the architecture and learning rules of the ANN are pre-defined and fixed during the search process. Connection weights may be represented as binary strings of a certain length or as real numbers directly [13]. The whole network is encoded by concatenation of all the connection weights of the network in the chromosome. A heuristic concerning the order of the concatenation is to put connection weights to the same node together. Figure 2 illustrates the binary representation of connection weights wherein each weight is represented by 4 bits. A real number weight representation of the ANN could be (2.0, 6.0, 5.0, 1.0, 4.0, 10.0). However proper genetic operators are to be chosen depending upon the representation used.

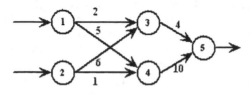

Genotype: 0010 0110 0101 0001 0100 1010

Fig 2. Genotype of binary representation of weights

Global search of connection weights using the hybrid heuristic can be formulated as follows:

1) *Generate an initial population of N weight vectors and for i =1 to N, initialize the ith threshold, $T_h(i)$, with the energy of the ith configuration.*

2) *Begin the cooling loop*
    - *Energy bank (EB) is set to zero and for i = 1 to N randomly mutate the ith weight vector.*
    - *Compute the Energy (E) of the resulting mutant weight vector.*
        - *If $E > T_h(i)$, then the old configuration is restored.*
        - *If $E \leq T_h(i)$, then the energy difference $(T_h(i) -E)$ is incremented to the Energy Bank (EB) = EB+ $T_h(i) -E$. Replace old configuration with the successful mutant*
    End cooling loop.

3) *Begin reheating loop.*
    - *Compute reheating increment $eb = \dfrac{EB * T_i(k)}{N}$, for i= 1 to N.*

    (Ti(k)=cooling constant).
    - *Add the computed increment to each threshold of the weight vector.*
    End reheating loop.

4) *Go to step 2 and continue the annealing and reheating process until an optimum weight vector is found (required minimum error is achieved).*

5) *Check whether the network has achieved the required error rate. If the required error rate is not achieved, skip steps 1 to 4, restore the weights and switch on to back propagation algorithm for fine-tuning of the weights.*

6) *End*

Proposed algorithm can be considered generally much less sensitive to initial conditions. However, performance of the algorithm by using the above approach will directly depend on the problem. Previous research [14] has shown that it is worthwhile to incorporate a gradient-based search (BP) during the final stages of the global search to enhance fine tune of local search and avoid the global search being trapped in some local minima.

8. Global Search of Optimal Architecture *(Algorithm 2)*

Evolutionary architecture adaptation can be achieved by constructive and destructive algorithms. Constructive algorithms starting from a very simple architecture add complexity to the network until the entire network is able to learn the task [3-4, 12]. Destructive algorithms start with large architectures and remove nodes and interconnections until the ANN is no longer able to perform its task [18]. Then the last removal is undone. Figure 3 demonstrates how typical neural network architecture could be directly encoded and how the genotype is represented. We assume that the node transfer functions are fixed before the architecture is decided. For an optimal network, the required node transfer function (gaussian, sigmoidal, tangent etc.) can be formulated as a global search problem, which runs at a faster time scale than the search for architectures. Scalability is often an issue when the direct coding (low level) scheme is used.

The genotype string will be very large as the ANN size increases and thus increase the computation time of the evolution.

To minimize the size of the genotype string and improve scalability, when priori knowledge of the architecture is known it will be efficient to use some indirect coding (high level) schemes. For example, if two neighboring layers are fully connected then the architecture can be coded by simply using the number of layers and nodes. The blueprint representation is a popular indirect coding scheme where it assumes that architecture consists of various segments or areas. Each segment or area defines a set of neurons, their spatial arrangement and their efferent connectivity. Several high level coding schemes like graph generation system [16], Symbiotic Adaptive Neuro-Evolution (SANE) [15], Marker Based Genetic Coding [19], L-Systems [9], Cellular Encoding [20], Fractal Representation [21] and ENZO [10] are some of the rugged techniques. Global search of transfer function and the connectivity of the ANN using the hybrid algorithm can be formulated as follows:

1) *Generate an initial population of N architecture vectors and for i =1 to N, initialize the ith threshold, $T_h(i)$, with the energy of the ith configuration. Depending on the coding schemata used, each vector should represent the architecture and the node transfer function.*

2) *and 3) are same as in Algorithm 1. Replace weight vector by architecture vector*

4) *Go to step 2 and continue the annealing and reheating process until an optimum architecture vector is found.*

5) *End*

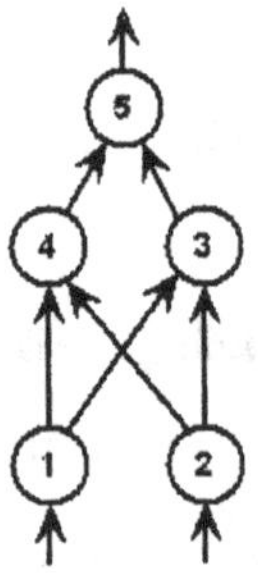

From To	1	2	3	4	5	Bias	Gene
1	0	0	0	0	0	0	000000
2	0	0	0	0	0	0	000000
3	1	1	0	0	0	1	110001
4	1	1	0	0	0	1	110001
5	0	0	1	1	0	1	001101

Complete Genotype: 000000000000110001110001001101

Fig 3. Direct coding and genotype representation of neural network architecture

9. Global Search of Learning Rules *(Algorithm 3)*

For the neural network to be fully optimal the learning rules are to be adapted dynamically according to its architecture and the given problem. Deciding the learning rate and momentum can be considered as the first attempt of learning rules [22]. The basic learning rule can be generalized by the function [1]:

$$\Delta w(t) = \sum_{k=1}^{n} \sum_{i_1,i_2,\dots,i_k=1}^{n} (\theta_{i_1,i_2,\dots,i_k} \prod_{j=1}^{k} x_{ij}(t-1))$$

Where t is the time, Δw is the weight change, $x_1, x_2,\dots x_n$ are local variables and the $\theta's$ are the real value coefficients which will be determined by the global search algorithm. In the above equation different values of $\theta's$ determine different learning rules. In deriving the above equation it is assumed that the same rule is applicable at every node of the network and the weight updating is only dependent on the input/output activations and the connection weights on a particular node. Genotypes ($\theta's$) can be encoded as real-valued coefficients and the global search for learning rules using the hybrid algorithm can be formulated as follows:

1) *Generate an initial population of N θ-vectors and for i =1 to N, initialize the ith threshold, $T_h(i)$, with the energy of the ith configuration.*
2) *and 3) are same as in Algorithm 1. Replace weight vector by θ- vector*
4) *Go to step 2 and continue the annealing and reheating process until an optimal θ-vector is obtained.*
5) *End*

It may be noted that a BP algorithm with an adaptive learning rate and momentum can be compared to a similar situation.

10. Conclusion

In this paper we have investigated the up-to-date tools available for adaptive optimum design of an ANN and presented how the optimal design of an ANN could be achieved using a 3-tier global search process. When compared to the pure genetic evolutionary search, the proposed algorithm has a better theoretical convergence and moreover by incorporating other algorithms (BP for fine tuning of weights) an optimal ANN can be designed. The real success in modeling such systems will directly depend on the genotype representation of the connection weights, architecture and the learning rules. Global search procedures are computationally expensive. As computers continue to deliver accelerated performance, the global search of large ANNs become more easily feasible.

11. References

1) Yao, X. (1999): *Evolving Artificial Neural Networks*, Proceedings of the IEEE, 87(9): 1423-1447.
2) Hart, W.E. (1996): *A Theoretical Comparison of Evolutionary Algorithms and Simulated Annealing*, Proceedings of the 5th Annual Conference on Evolutionary Programming. MIT press.
3) Frean, M. (1990): *The Upstart Algorithm: A Method For Constructing and Training Feed Forward Neural Networks*, Neural computations, pp.198-209.
4) Mezard, M., Nadal, J.P. (1989): *Learning in Feed Forward Layered Networks: The Tiling algorithm*, Journal of Physics A, Vol 22, pp. 2191-2204.

5) Ingber, L., Rosen, B., (1992): *Genetic Algorithms and Very Fast Simulated Annealing – A Comparison*, Mathematical and Computer Modeling, pp 87-100.

6) Yao, X. (1995): *A New Simulated Annealing Algorithm*, International Journal of Computer Mathematics, 56:161-168.

7) Baffles, P.T., Zelle, J.M. (1992) *Growing layers of Perceptrons: Introducing the Exentron Algorithm*, Proceedings on the International Joint Conference on Neural Networks, Vol 2, pp. 392-397.

8) Fahlman, S.E., Lebiere, C. (1990) *The Cascade Correlation Learning Architecture*, Advances in Neural Information Processing Systems, pp. 524-532.

9) Boers, E.J.W, Kuiper, H., Happel, B.L.M. and Sprinkhuizen-Kuyper; I.G. (1993): *Designing Modular Artificial Neural Networks*, In: H.A. Wijshoff (Ed.); Proceedings of Computing Science in The Netherlands, pp. 87-96.

10) Gutjahr, S., Ragg, T. (1997): *Automatic Determination of Optimal Network Topologies Based on Information Theory and Evolution*, IEEE Proceedings of the 23rd EUROMICRO Conference.

11) Schiffmann, W., Joost, M. and Werner, R. (1993) *Comparison Of Optimized Backpropagation Algorithms*, Proceedings. Of the European Symposium on Artificial Neural Networks, Brussels, pp. 97-104.

12) Mascioli, F., Martinelli, G. (1995): *A Constructive Algorithm for Binary Neural Networks: The Oil Spot Algorithm*, IEEE Transactions on Neural Networks, 6(3), pp 794-797.

13) Porto, V.W., Fogel, D.B. and Fogel, L.J. (1995): *Alternative Neural Network Training Methods*, IEEE Expert, volume 10, no.4, pp. 16-22.

14) Topchy, A.P., and Lebedko, O.A. (1997): *Neural Network Training by Means of Cooperative Evolutionary Search*, Nuclear Instruments & Methods In Physics Research, Volume 389, no. 1-2, pp. 240-241.

15) Polani, D. and Miikkulainen, R. (1999): *Fast Reinforcement Learning Through Eugenic Neuro-Evolution*. Technical Report AI99-277, Department of Computer Sciences, University of Texas at Austin.

16) Kitano, H. (1990): *Designing Neural Networks Using Genetic Algorithms with Graph Generation System*, Complex Systems, Volume 4, No.4, pp. 461-476.

17) Price, K.V. (1994) *Genetic Annealing*, Dr. Dobbs Journal, Vol.220, pp. 127-132.

18) Stepniewski, S.W. and Keane, A.J. (1997): *Pruning Back-propagation Neural Networks Using Modern Stochastic Optimization Techniques*, Neural Computing & Applications, Vol. 5, pp. 76-98.

19) Fullmer, B. and Miikkulainen, R. (1992): *Using Marker-Based Genetic Encoding of Neural Networks To Evolve Finite-State Behavior*, Proceedings of the First European Conference on Artificial Life, France), pp.255-262.

20) Gruau, F. (1991): *Genetic Synthesis of Modular Neural Networks*, In S Forrest (Ed.) Genetic Algorithms: Proc. of the 5th International Conference, Morgan Kaufman.

21) Merril, J.W.L., Port, R.F. (1991): *Fractally Configured Neural Networks*, Neural Networks, Vol 4, No.1, pp 53-60.

22) Kim, H.B., Jung, S.H., Kim, T.G. and Park, K.H. (1996): *Fast Learning Method for Back-Propagation Neural Network by Evolutionary Adaptation of Learning Rates*, Neurocomputing, vol. 11, no.1, pp. 101-106.

Efficient Image Sequence Analysis Using Fuzzy Techniques

M. J. Allen, Q. H. Mehdi, N. E. Gough and I. M. Coulson

University of Wolverhampton, United Kingdom
Email: ma@scit.wlv.ac.uk

1. Introduction

Machine Vision Systems (MVSs) used, for example in mobile robots, have to function in real-time and there is a need to develop more efficient ways of processing frame sequences. The problem can be addressed by mimicking aspects of human vision [1-4]. Previous work by Griffiths *et al* described a process for examining scenes using a camera mounted on a pan and tilt unit. This process used stochastic scanpaths that were tuned using a Fuzzy Inference System (FIS) to determine the next orientation of the camera. The development of this technique for scanning image frames, captured offline by a digital video camera, is described in Allen *et al* [6]. This paper introduces the concept of Fuzzy tuned scanpaths in Section 2. Section 3 examines the implementation and operation of an adaptive technique. Experimental work using this adaptive technique is described in Section 4 and conclusions are given in Section 5.

2. Implementation of Fuzzy-Tuned Scanpaths

A Fuzzy-Tuned Scanpath (FTS) method was proposed by Allen *et al* [6] as a low-level image processing technique that can be used when analyzing a frame sequence that changes with time. The technique works on the premise that the changes in data over all the frames in the sequence are gradual and, therefore, the changes from frame-to-frame are small. When analyzing a particular frame, FTSs use historical data to reduce the amount of processing required by identifying significant sub-regions within each frame. The historical data is a product of high-level processing and is encoded into a *saccade map* (a transition state matrix of possibility values) that is fed back to facilitate the processing of the next frame. Each element of the saccade map corresponds to a sub-region of the frame and the value of this element relates to the *possibility* that a sub-region is significant (Figure 1). The size and configuration of the sub-regions is dictated by the size and shape of the saccade map. The possibility values contained within the saccade

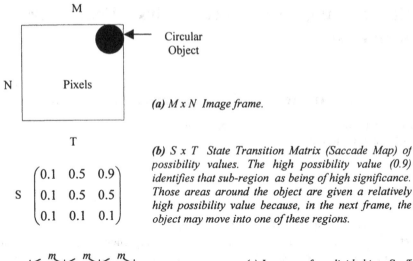

(a) M x N Image frame.

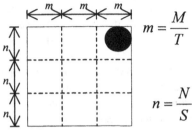

(b) S x T State Transition Matrix (Saccade Map) of possibility values. The high possibility value (0.9) identifies that sub-region as being of high significance. Those areas around the object are given a relatively high possibility value because, in the next frame, the object may move into one of these regions.

$$m = \frac{M}{T}$$

$$n = \frac{N}{S}$$

(c) Image surface divided into S x T sub-regions where each sub-region has nxm pixels. Each element of the Saccade Map relates to a corresponding sub-region on the image surface, e.g. element (2,2) on the saccade map relates to sub-region (2,2).

Fig 1: Saccade Map and Image Data Relationship

map are determined using a FIS (Figure 2). When viewing a dynamic environment with a static or mobile camera the areas of significance within each frame will change with time and, therefore, the saccade map must continuously be updated to accommodate these changes. The saccade map is used to construct the **scanpath** which identifies the sub-regions that are to be examined from each frame. The saccade map *biases* the selection towards significant sub-regions but does not control it. A **weighted roulette wheel** and the possibilities contained within the saccade map are used to direct the selection process. During each scan, once a sub-region has been selected for examination its possibility is set to zero to ensure it is not examined twice. The data contained within each sub-region is analyzed and, if the sub-region is significant its position is stored. The position of a region is represented by its centre using the pixel co-ordinate system. The position of an object is represented by the centre of the sub-region in which it is located. If the object has been detected in more than one sub-region then its position is represented by the centroid calculated from the centres of all these sub-regions. Having identified the position of the significant sub-regions, this data can then be passed on to subsequent processes and used to construct the saccade map (Figure 2).

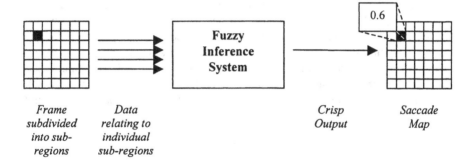

| Frame subdivided into sub-regions | Data relating to individual sub-regions | Crisp Output | Saccade Map |

Fig 2: Production of the saccade map from frame data

A saccade map is constructed at the beginning of the process. All the elements of this initial saccade map can be initialized to the same value to induce a totally random search over the whole of the image surface. Alternatively, prior knowledge regarding the environment can be applied. If a static camera is used to relay image data to the system then strategic information and/or antecedent information can be used to construct the map. Strategic information identifies areas of significance that will not change with time, e.g. the location of doorways through which agents might enter the environment, and is used throughout the process. Antecedent information identifies areas of initial significance that will change with time, e.g. the position of an agent or non static object when the MVS system is shut down. Antecedent information is transitional and, therefore, can only be used in the initial map.

A *Mamdani* FIS was used in each case to determine the possibilities contained within the saccade maps. The input metrics are: *attention, strategy, distance* and *bias*. The **attention** metric is a cumulative quantity and defines the time elapsed in terms of frame scans and is normalized between 0 and 1:

$$A_{(i,j)} = \frac{f_{current} - f_{(i,j)}}{f_{current} - f_{min}}$$

where $A_{(i,j)}$ is the attention assigned to sub-region (i,j) in $f_{current}$, $f_{current}$ is the current frame number in the sequence, $f_{(i,j)}$ is the frame number when sub-region (i,j) was last examined and f_{min} is the frame number of the sub-region that has not been examined for the longest period, i.e. has received the least attention. The input metric *attention* determines the possibilities within the saccade map for those sub-regions that are not local to a significant area. The function is to promote a systematic scan of pixels in areas of low significance in order to search for new objects. The **strategic** input metric is environmental knowledge and identifies areas of constant significance. A strategic map is created during the initialization of the system and areas of constant significance can be identified on this map, i.e. a significant sub-region(s) is assigned a 1 whereas non-significant sub-regions are assigned a 0. Sub-regions assigned strategic significance receive more attention than sub-regions of low significance. During runtime the *bias* (see below) can have an effect on the attention shown to areas of strategic significance. If an object is not identified in a particular frame the bias reduces the attention paid to sub-regions with strategic significance until the object is relocated. The input metric *distance* is a measurable quantity and is calculated in terms of map cells (sub-regions) using the *chessboard* measure [7]. The values are normalized between 0 and 1, i.e.:

$$d_{assess} = \frac{\max(| i_{object} - i_{assess} |,| j_{object} - j_{assess} |)}{D}$$

where d_{assess} is the normalized distance between the cell being assessed and the nearest object, (i_{object}, j_{object}) and (i_{assess}, j_{assess}) are the row and column dimensions of the nearest sub-region known to contain an object and the sub-region under examination, and D is the maximum distance possible. The *distance* metric aims to focus attention on those sub-regions of high significance by assigning high possibilities to those sub-regions containing or local to objects. The *bias* input metric identifies system status and is used to determine which fuzzy rules are used. Therefore, it has a direct effect on the system's behaviour. The *bias* parameter is used to reduce the possibilities in the saccade assigned to those regions not local to an object. It is activated if the system fails to identify an object on a particular iteration of the scan cycle. The consequence of invoking the bias is that more attention is paid to those sub-regions local to the objects in order to re-locate their position on the next scan.

The FIS consists of fourteen fuzzy rules in a verbose form. Each rule carries the same weighting of 1 and triangular membership functions (MFs) are used throughout. The fuzzy inputs for *distance* and *attention* are each defined using sets of four MFs. The inputs *bias* and *strategy* just act as switches which are either on or off, i.e. 0 or 1. The fuzzy output set that results from implication is defined using seven MFs.

3. Adaptive Fuzzy-Tuned Scanpaths

In Section 2, the potential importance of the inter-relationship between the size (surface-area) of an object within the image and the size of each sub-region was identified. The relative size of an object varies with respect to its distance from the camera. In this section, the inter-relationship between the size of each sub-region and the relative size of the object within the frame sequence is investigated. Using the results of this investigation an adaptive system is tested which changes the size of the sub-regions in order to optimize the accuracy with which it can identify an object's position. It does this by counting the number of sub-regions identified in each frame as containing a specific object (object-hits). A sub-region is said to contain the object if that object occupies more than 50% of the sub-region's surface area. If the number of object-hits exceeds a predetermined threshold then the size of the sub-regions are increased, i.e. the dimensionality (resolution) of the saccade map is reduced. Conversely, if the system fails to identify the object over a series of frames then the size of the sub-regions is reduced and, consequently, the resolution of the saccade map is increased.

The performance of the system over a set number of frames - its *history* - is analyzed when determining if the resolution of the saccade map should be changed. For example, if the history is set to three then the number of object-hits from the three most recent frame scans - contained in a *history vector* - are used as a measure of performance. If the mean of these results exceeds the upper threshold or falls below the lower threshold then the resolution of the saccade map is halved or doubled respectively, i.e.:

$$\text{If } \frac{1}{h}\sum_{i=1}^{H} v(i) \geq Q_{max} \text{ then } S = \frac{S}{2} \text{ and } T = \frac{T}{2}$$

or

$$\text{If } \frac{1}{h}\sum_{i=1}^{H} v(i) \leq Q_{min} \text{ then } S = S \times 2 \text{ and } T = T \times 2$$

where: h is the history, v is the history vector, Q_{min} is the minimum number of allowable hits, Q_{max} is the maximum number of allowable hits (stepping thresholds) and S and T are the dimensions of the saccade map.

The values of S and T are allowed to vary between predetermined limits. If the system attempts to change the resolution beyond the predetermined limits then the resolution remains unchanged. A number of frames are taken into account to ensure that a change is not initiated on the basis of a single unrepresentative scan, e.g. if just one scan failed to identify the position of the object. Once the dimensionality of the saccade map has been changed the most recent value contained within the history vector is changed to a value midway between the upper and lower limits of allowable hits. This ensures that the elements of the history vector are ascertained before the change in map dimensionality does not initiate another, and potentially unnecessary, change after the subsequent scan.

The area of each frame that is examined by the system, i.e. the number of sub-regions contained within a particular scanpath, is specified as a percentage of the total image surface. The percentage area is used as a measure in preference to the number of sub-regions because it is invariant to changes in the resolution of the saccade map. If the area of examination is reduced it makes the system potentially more efficient and, therefore, quicker as less processing is required. However, it can result in a reduction in the reliability of the system and less attention is paid to locating new objects. In these tests 10% of each image frame is examined.

4. Experimental Work

An artificially constructed frame sequence is used to observe and evaluate the behaviour of two non-adaptive procedures that use saccade maps of different resolutions, i.e. a 20x20 map, a 40 x 40 map, and two adaptive procedures in which the resolution of the saccade map is varied. The frame sequence contains a square black object against a white background that varies in size from frame to frame. The sequence has been constructed to simulate the effect of an object moving towards the camera and then moving away again. The aim is to test the ability of the different system configurations to accurately identify the position of the object throughout the test.

In the frame sequence the object's size starts at 6x6 pixels and gradually grows until it approaches the confines of the frame surface (each frame is 640x480 pixels). At this point the object starts to diminish in size until it finally returns to its original dimensions. The centroid of the object is always maintained at the centre of the frame (320.5, 240.5). The sequence contains 474 frames. Four different system configurations are evaluated in these tests. In each configuration the resolution of the saccade map is different but *10%* of every frame is examined. The configurations used are:

1. A *20x20* saccade map that identifies *400* equally sized sub-regions (the dimensions of each region are *32x24* pixels). *40* sub-regions are selected from each frame by the scanpath.
2. An *40x40* saccade map that identifies *1600* equally sized sub-regions (the dimensions of each sub-region are *16x12* pixels). *160* sub-regions are selected from each frame by the scanpath.
3. A saccade map the resolution of which is allowed to vary between *10x10* and *80x80* and identifies between *100* and *6400* sub-regions (the dimensions of each sub-region range from *64x48* and *8x6* respectively). *10* to *640* are selected from each frame by the scanpath.
4. A saccade map the resolution of which is allowed to vary between *20x20* and *40x40* and identifies between *400* and *1600* sub-regions (the dimensions of each sub-region range from *32x24* and *16x12* respectively). *40* to *160* are selected from each frame by the scanpath.

The stepping thresholds for the adaptive configurations 3 and 4 were set *1* and *5*, i.e. values for Q_{min} and Q_{max} respectively (see Section 4). The resolution of the saccade map in the adaptive system is intialized to 40x40 and the *history* is maintained at *3* frame scans (Section 4). All systems were provided with antecedent information which located the position of the object from the outset.

Table 1 contains data from running each of the four system configurations described above. The data in this table relates to the overall accuracy and operational efficiency of each system configuration. The data fields are:

Object Location: Represents as a percentage the number of frames in which the system positively identified the presence of the object.

Initial Location: Represents as a percentage the number of frames that pass before the system positively identifies the presence of the object.

Location Error: Represents the accuracy of the system in those frames where it positively identifies the presence of the object. The error is the Euclidean distance between the estimated centroid of the object, as determined by the system, and actual position of the object (see Section 3).

System Efficiency: Compares the computational load of the different system configurations. Computational load was represented by the average number of floating point operations performed by each system configuration during the test. The results are expressed as a percentage of the most efficient system tested.

The results represent the average values for each measure compiled after running each system configuration *20* times.

	Object Location	Initial Location	Location Error	Mean System Efficiency
Config. 1	92.82%	18 frames	16 pixels	100%
Config. 2	97.05%	7 frames	7.62 pixels	41%
Config. 3	96.01%	6 frames	27.73 pixels	79%
Config. 4	96.41%	7 frames	15.46 pixels	91%

Table 1: Summary of Results using Configurations 1, 2, 3 and 4

Interesting points observed from the experimental work are:

- Configuration 2, using the 40x40 map (the saccade map with the highest fixed resolution), was the most accurate (7.62 pixels) but least efficient in terms of floating point operations – 41% (1012187 flops).
- Configuration 1, using the 20x20 map (the saccade map with the highest fixed resolution), was the most efficient in terms of floating point operations – 100% (411787 flops) - but the least accurate.
- Configuration 1 had the lowest Object Identification (92.82%) whereas system configuration 2 had the highest (97.02%).
- Configuration 3 was the quickest to identify the presence of the object (6 frames). This figure could have been improved had the initial saccade been initialized to 80x80 (the highest resolution).
- Overall the performance of configuration 3 was the poorest (27.73 pixels). Due to the size of the object within the frame sequence the system operated for the majority of the test using a very low resolution map, i.e. 10x10, with very large sub-regions. The extensive use of this low resolution map accounts for this poor performance.
- The spread of attention shown by each configuration to the frames in the sequence is relatively constant in that all concentrate on the centre of the object area. This applied irrespective of the size of the object within the frame.

5. Conclusion

We have analyzed the behaviour of different configurations that employ FTSs to analyze frame sequences, concentrating on how these configurations react when monitoring the position of an object as it moves towards the camera. In addition, much additional information has been obtained regarding the advantages and disadvantages of using saccades maps of different resolutions. The results presented in Section 5 show that a configuration using a saccade with a fine resolution is consistently more accurate than a configuration using a saccade map with a coarse resolution, but using the high resolution map is computationally more expensive. The adaptive system approach offers an answer to this problem. Configuration 3 that employed a saccade map with a relatively coarse resolution performed poorly in relation to the other system configurations. It was the least accurate and offered no advantage in terms of efficiency. However, configuration 4, operating with a over a more restricted range, offered improvements in accuracy over configuration 1 in terms of location error and object location. This was at the expense of a marginal loss of efficiency. The trade-off between efficiency and accuracy could initially be dictated by the designer to suit the system requirements by controlling the transition between the high and low resolution maps. In future work, this adaptive method will be tested under a range of different conditions, i.e. objects displaying a wider range of movement and with a real frame sequence captured using a digital video camera. The length of the scanpath is currently predetermined based on the speed and number of object(s) contained with the frames of the sequence. A method to calculate the length of this parameter at runtime is currently under investigation.

References

[1] Hubel, D. H., *Eye, brain and vision,* Scientific American Library, p36 (1995).

[2] Henderson J. M., A. Hollingworth, Eye Movements During Scene Viewing: An Overview, *Eye Guidance in Reading and Scene Perception*, Elsevier Science Ltd., pp 269 – 293 (1998).

[3] Hacisalihzade, S., L. Stark, J. Allen, Visual Perception and sequences of eye movements: A stocahastic modelling approach, *IEEE Trans. On Systems, Man and Cybernetics,* 22(3), pp474 - 481 (1992).

[4] Griffiths I. J., Q. H. Mehdi, N. E. Gough, Fuzzy tuned stochastic scanpaths for AGV vision, *Int. Conf. on Artificial Neural Networks and Genetic Algorithms - ICANNGA '97*, Norwich, UK, pp 88-92 (1997).

[5] Allen M. J., Mehdi Q., Griffiths I. J., Gough N., Coulson I. M., Object location in colour images using fuzzy-tuned scanpaths and neural networks, *Proc. 19th SGES Int. Conf. Knowledge Based Systems and Applied Artificial Intelligence,* Cambridge, UK, pp 302-314 (1999).

[6] Jain R., R. Kasturi, B. G. Schunck, *Machine Vision,* McGraw Hill, (1995).

Automatic Generation of Fuzzy Rule-based Models from Data by Genetic Algorithms

P P Angelov, R A Buswell, V I Hanby, J A Wright

Department of Civil and Building Engineering, University of Loughborough, Loughborough, Leicestershire LE11 3TU, UK

Keywords: Fuzzy rule-based models, self-learning, genetic algorithms, structure and parameter identification.

1 Introduction

The so-called *classical* models (which are based on differential equations, energy- and mass-balance principles and neglect qualitative and subjective information) are inadequate or practically difficult to use in many cases [1]. In last decade fuzzy models have been widely used in different fields like economics, biotechnology, civil engineering etc. They have a very important advantage over neural-network-based models in that they are transparent; that they contain expressible knowledge about the object being modelled. Determination of fuzzy rules and membership functions of fuzzy sets, however, is usually based on subjective estimation. In many cases it is a complex and ambiguous process [1].

In last few years the methods for fuzzy membership functions adjustment, learning, and rule extraction have been intensively developed [2-7]. A part of them [3, 6] treat parameter identification only (adjustment of parameters of membership functions), while the model structure (rules) is supposed to be known. Another group of papers [4, 7] presents generation of a black-box model which is quite close in nature to neural networks but is considered as a fuzzy rule-based one. The model treated in these papers lacks interpretability, although it could be used for control purposes. Most approaches use encoding of the exhaustive rule-base into the chromosome of the GA [5]. The length of the chromosome there is determined on the basis of all possible combinations of linguistic variables, which is not effective and hampers solving problems with realistic dimensions. A new encoding procedure, which leads to significant minimisation of the chromosome, is proposed in this paper. Combining the new encoding mechanism with a real-coded GA permits parameter identification simultaneously with the structure identification in addition to allowing the application of the approach to realistically dimensioned problems.

One possible engineering application that may benefit from this approach is in the generation of component models for use in the simulation of air conditioning systems. The performance of some of the components of interest are too complex to describe using either classical or expert knowledge approaches. Black-box methods such as polynomial models have been used in this problem. Automatic generation of fuzzy rule based models from data by GA offers the benefits of transparency without additional expert intervention. In addition, the high dimensionality of the operating space associated with some components can simplify the initialisation of the search by allowing the GA to select and find the rules, rather than establishing them *a priori*.

2 Methodology

Fuzzy rule-based models of the so-called Mamdani type could be represented as a set of rules of the type:

$$\text{IF}(x_1 \text{ is } X_1)\text{AND...AND}(x_n \text{ is } X_n) \text{ THEN } (y \text{ is } Y) , \tag{1}$$

where x_i denotes a fuzzy linguistic input variable; y stands for the output variable; Y denotes the fuzzy linguistic term of y; $Y \in \{Y1,Y2,...,Ym0\}$; X_i denotes the fuzzy linguistic term of the i-th input variable; $X_i \in \{X, X,...,X\}$.

A fuzzy set and a membership function define each linguistic term, which could be of any allowed type (Gaussian, triangular, trapezoidal, etc.) [1]. Given the number of linguistic variables and linguistic terms, the number of all possible rules (r) can become extremely high for real problems, because of the so called *curse of dimensionality* [1]. Practically, up to 50-100 rules is used and the number of used rules is significantly smaller then the number of all possible rules, because of information redundancy. There are two main approaches for extraction of a set of rules, which describes the object of modelling with a pre-defined precision. One of them uses neural networks and gradient-based learning techniques. The other is based on GA. The second approach is used in this paper.

Appropriate encoding of the fuzzy model is very important for the effectiveness of the learning process. For problems with realistic dimensions, consideration of a chromosome which represents all possible fuzzy rules as in [5], is time consuming and can become an unsolvable problem. Therefore, we propose encoding the indices of rules, which participate into the fuzzy model only. Different encoding schemes could be applied. The main requirement is non-ambiguity in coding and decoding. We propose a simple encoding procedure, which assigns an index to every possible rule. As a result, a single non-negative integer number represents each fuzzy rule. This allows us to consider only the rules, which participate in the model. Together with their parameters (centres and spreads) they form the genotype of the chromosome considered in the our approach (Table 1):

Table 1: Genotype; left part represents indices of rules; right one - membership functions' parameters

I_1	I_2	...	I_K	c_{11}	c_{12}	...	$c_{m_i n+1}$	σ_{11}	σ_{12}	...	$\sigma_{m_i n+1}$

The coding scheme, which is adopted in this paper, could be represented as a two-stage one. First, we translate each linguistic term of a given rule into a M -based number (where $M = \max_{i=1}^{n+1}(m_i)$ is the maximal number of linguistic terms in all linguistic variables). 0 could be assigned to the one boundary linguistic term, 1 to the next etc. For example, let we have three linguistic terms *(Low, Medium* and *High)*. Then a number with a base 3 would represent the code of each linguistic term: 0 could stand for the *Low*, 1 - for *Medium* and 2 for *High*. Therefore, the code of the linguistic term *Low* will be $a_3=0$, the code of *Medium* - $a_3=1$ etc. At the second stage we transform the set of M-based numbers (codes of linguistic terms) into a single decimal integer positive number representing the index of the considered fuzzy rule:

$$I = (a_M^1, a_M^2, ..., a_M^n)_{10} + 1 , \tag{2}$$

where I denotes the index of the respective fuzzy rule; a^j, j=1,2,...,n+1 is a code of the linguistic term $a^j \in [0; m_i-1]$.

Using this effective encoding mechanism in combination with a real-coded GA makes it possible to treat parameters of fuzzy membership functions as unknowns as well. It reveals a possibility for fine-tuning of the fuzzy rule-based models generated. The process of identification became more flexible and independent of the subjectivity in structure determination. In the same time, some degree of influence on the model structure is also possible. It could be realised by choosing parameters like the number of linguistic terms (m), the maximal number of fuzzy rules considered (K), the pre-defined level of mean root square error (*E*) and the type of the membership functions as well as using *a priori* knowledge during the initialisation.

Learning procedure realises numerical solution of both parameter and structural identification problems. The identification problem could be formulated as:

To determine the fuzzy rules (represented by their indices) and their parameters such that to minimise the deviation between the model and the experimental outputs (E → min):

{subject to (1)}; (3)

$$(j-1)\delta \le c_{lj} \le (j+1)\delta; \quad l = 1, 2, ..., n+1; \quad \text{where,} \quad \delta = \frac{\overline{LV} - \underline{LV}}{m_l + 1};$$

$$\underline{parc}_{lj} < \sigma_{ij} < \overline{parc}_{lj};$$

where $\underline{LV}_l$ and $\overline{LV}_l$ are the lower and upper bounds of the l-th linguistic variable; $j=1,2,...m_l$; $1 \le I_i \le r$; $i = 1, 2, ..., K$. Note that fuzzy model (1) is considered as one of the constraints. The values of $\underline{par}$ and $\overline{par}$ determine the shape of the Gaussian membership functions. Practically, its spread could be fixed to $\sigma_{ij} = \delta c_{lj}$ minimising the number of unknowns without significantly sacrificing the flexibility of the fuzzy model.

For numerical solution of this problem we used real-coded GA [8], which matches better the specifics of the considered problem:

1. indices of fuzzy rules and parameters of the membership functions (unknowns) are integer values and parameters are real values respectively, not binary ones;

2. shorter chromosome allows simultaneous parameter and structure identification as well as solving real problems (with some tens of unknowns).

3 Method Implementation

The algorithm is realised in the Matlab environment making use of both dedicated code and the Matlab Fuzzy Toolbox. The principle programme modules are the operational parameter selection, the GA, the fuzzy inference and the search criterion function. The relationships between these are demonstrated in Figure 1.

A population of chromosomes, which represent a set of fuzzy rules including their parameters, is set-up initially. The algorithm could start either by a set of pre-defined fuzzy rules, which are based on the a priori knowledge and previous experience either by a random set of fuzzy rules if such knowledge does not exists. New populations are produced in an iterative fashion using modified recombination (real-coded crossover), mutation and selection operation. Due to the specifics of the problem (a part of chromosomes represents indices of the rules and consists of integer values while the other part represents the parameters of fuzzy sets and consists of real values) the recombination and mutation operations are performed separately for both parts (Table 1).

For a given set of search characteristics, the parameters of the GA need to be selected. These control the crossover, selection and mutation operations and select the population size.

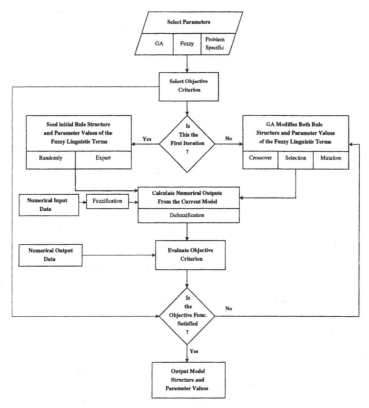

Figure 1: The Principle Program Modules

For simplicity, the number of fuzzy linguistic terms (FLT) for each input variable is chosen to be the same. The input variable membership functions type are all Gaussian, with the spread selected as a percentage of the input space dictated be the data (3). The output membership functions are triangular with the same number of FLT as the inputs and the maximal number of rules used to describe the process is also set. The number of rules should be high enough to allow the likelihood covering of every possible value of each input variable by at least one rule in the final rule set. This ensures good coverage of the model. All of the parameters associated with the FLT have the potential to be optimised as part of the procedure. In addition to these parameters, there are a number of problem specific parameters that need to be established; the number of input variables; size of data files; and proportion of total operating space to be modelled. At present these are chosen based on experience with both the problem and with the method.

Trials using the mean squared error as the criterion function found a tendency to generate results that produced an uneven distribution of the magnitude of the model errors. This is undesirable where *all* data are considered equally appropriate for describing the system characteristics. To improve the optimisation, a criterion function based on the mean squared error has been developed. The termination of the optimisation is made a function of the reduction of the error between the model prediction and the data *and* the maximal error:

$$E = (y - \hat{y})^2 + \max |y - \hat{y}|,$$ (4)

where $\hat{y}$ is the experimental output.

This results in some priority to averaging out the error so that there are fewer 'very poor' points at the expense of spreading the error more evenly over the whole range. There is much scope for variation. The example given below, as with many processes, are 'smooth' functions and so some improvement could be gained by adding a smoothing penalty in the search criterion such as demonstrated by Cho *et al*[9]. In addition, convergence checks on the rule structure and estimated parameters could be incorporated to terminate the search without falling into over fitting.

The initialisation of the rule structure and parameter values is made randomly, although they have the potential to be selected by an expert or from previous models derived from data from similar processes. Subsequent iterations involve the GA generating the next model.

The Matlab Fuzzy Toolbox is utilised to carry out the fuzzification of the input data, then the calculation of the current model output and finally defuzzification to yield a numerical output. The vector of model predictions and of the measured data is then used to evaluate the model quality against the objective criterion. If the model is unacceptable the optimisation process is repeated until it is acceptable or until the number of generations exceeds a predetermined limit.

4 Experimental Results

One application of models originally developed for Heating Ventilating and Air-Conditioning (HVAC) simulation is on-line condition monitoring, in which the model output represents the system performance operating under correct conditions. If there is a change in the system performance, a difference between the model prediction and measured output will occur. Various modelling approaches have been investigated [10]. Models usually need some data from the target system to tune the models in order to predict the performance to an acceptable degree of accuracy. An approach to the estimation of the parameters associated with a classical model approach has been demonstrated by *Buswell et al* [11]. One disadvantage of this approach is the length of time and special testing regime required generating a rich enough data set to allow the parameters to be estimated. The principle advantage of the classical model approach is the accuracy of extrapolation, which has been proven to be quite good over typical operating conditions experienced by HVAC plant [12].

The evolving FRB approach can make use of data from normal operating conditions, negating the requirement for special testing in addition to the advantages over black-box models discussed earlier. Here, the FRB models are demonstrated on real data from a cooling coil subsystem of and air-conditioning unit [12]. In the example, a *single* FRB model represents *all* of the components used to form the subsystem depicted in Figure 2.

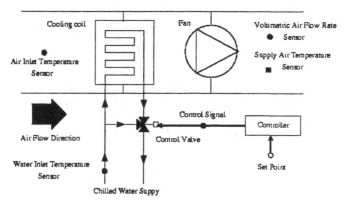

Figure 2: The Test Subsystem

Under normal operation, the supply air temperature is controlled to some predetermined set point by regulating the mass flow rate of chilled water through the coil. This is achieved via a control signal that commands an electrically driven actuator which operates the control valve diverting the water flow from one port to the other.

The measurements of air and water inlet temperatures, volumetric flow rate of air and the control signal to the control valve are used as inputs to the model. The model is then used to predict the supply air temperature. Samples were taken at one minute intervals for two 24 hour periods, a few days apart. Some model simplifications have been affected:

- The model is based on the static data alone and so the data that exhibits dynamic characteristics have been filtered using a 'steady-state detector' developed by Salsbury [13].

- Dehumidification is not explicitly modelled. Cooling coil performance is affected by air moisture content. When the conditions allow, condensation forms on the surface of the coil, reducing the moisture content in the supply air. This additional latent heat exchange reduces the sensible heat exchange and therefore affects the supply air temperature.

- Heat losses (to the environment through the duct wall) and gains (across the fan) to the supply air between the inlent and supply air sensors have not been explicitly modelled. These are, however, expected to be fairly constant over the test and validation data.

One complication for the modelling of the system is the highly non-linear characteristics associated with the output of heat exchangers. The cooing coil gives an exponential response to an increase in water mass flow. The control valve and actuator is designed to counter these effects leaving a linear water mass flow/heat output response. Practically, these criteria are seldom met and highly non-linear characteristics, often with some 'dead-bands' at either end of operation are typical. The example used here is no exception.

The FRB model used 9 fuzzy linguistic terms in each of the input and the output membership functions, and a maximum of 30 rules. The GA search used a population size of 80 and the probabilities of mutation and crossover set to 8% and 80% respectively. Figure 3 depicts the plots of the measured and predicted supply air temperature for both the training and validation data.

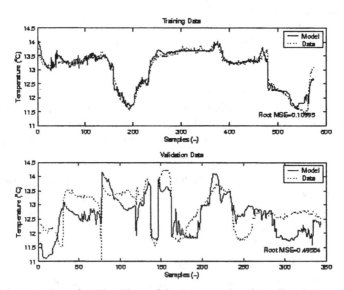

Figure 3: Sample Wise Plots of the Measured and Predicted Output.

The coil was dehumidifying at times during both test days. At the observed conditions therefore, this will affect the sensible coil performance and hence the supply air temperature. It can be expected that this simplification comes at the expense of some model precision.

Using the product moment correlation coefficient, r, as a measure of the goodness of fit of the model predictions to the measured data, the training data yielded a value for r in excess of 0.97. The validation data yields a value of $r=0.69$. This is reflected in the root mean square errors giving 0.11°C and 0.50°C for training and validation data respectively, noted on Figure 3. In addition, the majority of the errors associated with the validation data are less than ±1.0°C.

5 Conclusions

An approach to the automatic generation of fuzzy rule-based models has been presented. The encoding/decoding procedure that allows the optimisation of the model structure and parameters by genetic algorithm has been described. The learning procedure has been discussed and an enhancement on the mean square error as the search criterion function has been introduced resulting in better convergence. The implementation of the approach has been described and an application example of HVAC modelling based on real system data has been demonstrated.

The validation of the approach in this paper was based of data collected from a real cooling coil subsystem comprising of numerous components. The results demonstrate the ability of the method to derive a model of a highly dimensioned problem using relatively few rules. The low number of rules increases the interpretability of the model. The accuracy of the model on the validation data is reasonable, and may be improved by adding the air moisture content as an input. Using the trained model for simulation is straightforward. The approach has been implemented as a Matlab program and extensive validation with a variety of data types has been successfully carried out.

References

1   Yager R., D. Filev, Essentials of Fuzzy Modeling and Control, John Willey and Sons, NY (1994).

2   Angelov P.P., V.I.Hanby, J.A.Wright, HVAC Systems Simulation: A Self-Structuring Fuzzy Rule-Based Approach, International Journal of Architectural Sciences, v.1, pp.30-39 (2000).

3   Bastian A., A Genetic Algorithm for Tuning Membership Functions, Proc. of the 4th European Congress on Fuzzy and Intelligent Technologies EUFIT'96, Aachen, Germany, 1, 494-498 (1996).

4   Chiang C. K., H.-Y. Chung, J.J. Lin, A Self-Learning Fuzzy Logic Controller using Genetic Algorithms with Reinforcements, IEEE Trans. on Fuzzy Systems, 5, 460-467 (1996).

5   Lim M. H., S.Rahardja, B.H.Gwee, A GA Paradigm for Learning Fuzzy Rules, Fuzzy Sets and Systems, 82, 177-186 (1996).

6   Nozaki K., T. Morisawa, H. Ishibuchi, Adjusting Membership Functions in Fuzzy Rule-based Classification Systems, Proc. of the 3d European Congress on Fuzzy and Intelligent Technologies, EUFIT'95, Aachen, Germany, 1, 615-619 (1995).

7   Takagi H., M. Lee, Neural Networks and Genetic Algorithm Approaches to Auto-Design of Fuzzy Systems, In: Lecture Notes on Computer Science, Springer Verlag: Proc. of FLAI'93, Linz, Austria, 68-79 (1994).

8   Michalewicz Z., Genetic Algorithms + Data Structures = Evolution Programs, Springer Verlag, Berlin (1996).

9   Cho H.-J., Wang B.-H, Smoothness Cost of Genetic Algorithms Applied to Ruke Generation for Fuzzy Controllers, IEEE Transactions on Systems, Man and Cybernetics, (2000), Submitted.

10 Hyvarinen, J., IEA Annex 25 Final Report, Volume I - Building Optimization and Fault Diagnosis Source Book, VTT, Espoo, Finland, (1997).

11 Buswell, R., A. Haves, P. and Salsbury, T. I., A model-based approach to the commissioning of HVAC systems, Proceedings of Clima 2000, Prague, The Czech Republic, (1997).

12 Norford, L., K., Wright, J., A. and Buswell, R. A., and Luo, D., Demonstration of Fault Detection and Diagnosis Methods in a Real Building (ASHRAE RP1020), (Final report of ASHRAE Research Project 1020), (1999).

13 Salsbury, T,. I., Fault Detection and Diagnosis in HVAC Systems using Analytical Models, Loughborough University, UK, PhD Thesis, (1996).

Acknowledgements

The authors acknowledge financial support for this work under EPSRC grant GR/M97299 and use of the data courtesy of ASHRAE; generated from the ASHRAE funded research project RP1020.

Resemblance Relations and Fuzzy Weak Orderings

D. Boixader * and J. Recasens **

Sec. Matemàtiques i Informàtica, E.T.S. Arquitectura del Vallès, Pere Serra 1-15, 08190 Sant Cugat. Spain.
boixader@ea.upc.es, recasens@ea.upc.es

Abstract. In this paper we clarify the relation between two different kinds of fuzzy relations: Fuzzy Weak Orders [Bodenhofer, 99] and Resemblance Relations [Bouchon-Meunier & Valverde, 92]. The main idea to relate them is that any Fuzzy Weak Ordering defined on a set X can be isomorphically embedded into a Resemblance Relation on the fuzzy power set $[0, 1]^X$ by means of the Duality Principle for Fuzzy Sets [Ovchinnikov, 94]. In this way, Resemblance Relations can be seen as a generalization of Fuzzy Weak Orders.
Keywords: fuzzy relation, t-norm, fuzzy preorder, fuzzy equivalence relation, similarity relation, fuzzy weak ordering, resemblance relation, T-indistinguishability operator.

1 Introduction

In [Zadeh,71] Similarity Relations and Fuzzy Orderings were introduced with the aim of extending classical equivalence relations and preorders to the fuzzy framework. The key idea to do this is to generalize the notion of transitivity by using a t-norm, as follows:

Definition 1.2. Let T be a t-norm. A fuzzy relation $R : X \times X \to [0,1]$ is transitive w.r.t. T (or T-transitive) if $T(R(x,y), R(y,z)) \leq R(x, z)$ for all $x, y, z \in X$.

Being t-norms the conjunction connectives in the setting of Fuzzy Logic, it is obvious that T-transitivity turns into classical transitivity when a crisp relation R is considered.

Fuzzy T-transitive relations have generated lots of research, mainly two special kinds of them: Fuzzy T-Preorders and Fuzzy T-Equivalence Relations.

Definition 1.3. A fuzzy relation $R : X \times X \to [0, 1]$ is Reflexive if $R(x, x) = 1$ for all x in X.

---

* Corresponding author
** Partially supported by DGICYT PB98-0924.

Definition 1.4. *A fuzzy relation* $R : X \times X \to [0,1]$ *is Symmetric if* $R(x,y) = R(y,x)$ *for all x,y in X.*

Definition 1.5 *A Fuzzy Preorder w.r.t. a given t-norm* T *(or a Fuzzy T-preorder) is a Reflexive and T-Transitive fuzzy relation.*

Definition 1.6 *A Fuzzy Equivalence Relation w.r.t. a given t-norm* T *(or a Fuzzy T-equivalence Relation) is a Reflexive, Symmetric and T-Transitive fuzzy relation.*

Fuzzy Equivalence Relations appear under many different names in the literature, depending on the authors and on the chosen t-norm T. We have **Similarity Relations** in a narrow sense $(T = MIN)$ [Zadeh 71, Jacas 90] or in abroad sense (every t-norm T) [Klawonn & Kruse 94, Dubois & Prade 94, Esteva et. al. 97], **Likeness Relations** $(T = L$, the Lukasiewicz t-norm)[Ruspini,82], **Probabilistic Relations** $(T = PROD)$[Ovchinnikov,], **T-indistinguishability Operators** [Trillas & Valverde 84, Jacas & Recasens 94,95] or simply **Fuzzy Equivalence Relations** [Boixader 99].

Recently, in [Bodenhofer, 99] the so-called Fuzzy Weak Orderings - a special kind of Fuzzy Preorders - were introduced. These relations can be seen as the natural extension to a fuzzy framework of those crisp preorders $\leq$ such that, for every x,y in X, $x \leq y$ or $y \leq x$.

Definition 1.7. *A fuzzy relation* $R : X \times X \to [0,1]$ *is Strongly Linear if* $max(R(x,y), R(y,x)) = 1$, *for all x,y in X.*

Definition 1.8. *A Fuzzy Weak Order w.r.t. a given t-norm* T *(or a Fuzzy Weak T-Order) is a Fuzzy T-Preorder that is strongly linear.*

Example 1.9. *Let* T *be a left continuous t-norm. Then*

$$\hat{T}(x|y) = \sup\{\alpha \in [0,1] \mid T(x,\alpha) \leq y\}$$

defines a Fuzzy T-Preorder on $X = [0,1]$ *that is also a Fuzzy Weak T-Order.*

Note. $\hat{T}$ is usually called the pseudo-inverse of T, and from a logical point of view, it is the residuated implication associated to the conjunction T.

Example 1.10. *Let* T *be a left continuous t-norm. Then*

$$E_T(x,y) = \hat{T}(Max(x,y)) \mid Min(x,y))$$

is a Fuzzy T-Equivalence on $[0,1]$.

The importance of these two previous examples lies on Valverde's representation theorems [Valverde 85]. Roughly speaking, these theorems state that every Fuzzy T-Preorder and every Fuzzy T-Equivalence Relation may be constructed by inducing P_T (res. E_T) into a set X by means of some family of applications $h : X \to [0,1], h \in H$.

Theorem 1.11.(Representation Th.) *A fuzzy Relation P (res. E) on a set X is a Fuzzy T-Preorder (res. a Fuzzy T-Equivalence Relation) on a set X if and only if there exists a family of fuzzy sets $H \subseteq [0,1]^X$ such that $P(x,y) = \inf_{h \in H} P(h(x), h(y))$ (res. $E(x,y) = \inf_{h \in H} E(h(x), h(y))$), for all x, y in X.*

It is clear that fuzzy weak orders can also be obtained from such families H, because they are instances of fuzzy preorders. In [Bodenhofer 99] necessary and sufficient conditions are given over a family H of fuzzy sets in order to generate a fuzzy weak order instead of just a Fuzzy Preorder. The following representation theorem for fuzzy weak orders results.

Theorem 1.12. *A fuzzy relation L on a set X is a Fuzzy Weak T-Order if and only if there exists a linear order $\preceq$ on X, and a family H of non-decreasing w.r.t. $\preceq$ fuzzy sets, such that $L(x,y) = \inf_{h \in H} P_T(h(x), h(y))$ for all x, y in X.*

The families H of fuzzy sets appearing in both representation theorems are called *generating families*, and are in no way intended to be unique. Actually, given a Fuzzy Preorder P (res. a Fuzzy Equivalence Relation E) there is always an infinite set of generating families for it.

In another different setting, Resemblance Relations [Bouchon & Valverde 92] were introduced to modelise some kind of analogical reasoning patterns. Unlike the relations we have been considered until now, Resemblance Relations are defined on sets of fuzzy sets. Given two fuzzy sets $g, h : X \to [0,1]$, we will note $g \leq h$ when $g(x) \leq h(x)$ for all $x \in X$ (the pointwise order for fuzzy sets).

Definition 1.13 *A Resemblance Relation w.r.t. a t-norm T is a reflexive and T-transitive fuzzy relation $R : [0,1]^X \times [0,1]^X \to [0,1]$ such that $R(x,y) = 1$ when $g \leq h$.*

Note. Sometimes it is also required that $R(h,g) = 0$ when $h \wedge g = 0$.

From the above definition it is clear that Resemblance Relations are instances of fuzzy T-preorders, $(X = [0,1])$. What we are going to show in the following section is that every Fuzzy Weak Order may be seen as a subset of a suitable Resemblance Relation, in the sense that it can be isomorphically embedded into this relation.

2 Duality and Models

Firth of all, let us introduce a systematic way of obtaining models of fuzzy T-transitive relations based on the Duality Principle for fuzzy sets [Ovchinnikov 94, Boixader & Jacas 94]. For a model of a given fuzzy relation R on a set X we will understand just an example of it, i.e. another fuzzy relation S on a set Y having the same structure as F.

Definition 2.1. *Let $R : X \times X \to [0,1]$ and $S : Y \times Y \to [0,1]$ be Fuzzy Relations. We will say that S and R are isomorphic if there exists a bijective map $\varphi : X \to Y$ such that $S(\varphi(x_1), \varphi(x_2)) = R(x_1, x_2)$, for all x_1, x_2 in X.*

Definition 2.2. *A fuzzy relation S on a set Y is a model for a given fuzzy relation R on a set X if R and S are isomorphic.*

We are interested in obtaining models of such structures made up by fuzzy sets. In order to do this, let us introduce the Duality Principle for fuzzy sets. Roughly speaking, this principle states that every fuzzy set on a universe may be thought either as an application (as it is) or as a point. (This is a quite common idea in the fuzzy literature, when fuzzy sets are represented by points in the unit cube of $\Re^n$).

Definition 2.3. *A family H of fuzzy subsets of X ($H \subseteq [0,1]^X$) is a separating family on X if for any $x, y \in X$ there exists $h \in H$ such that $h(x) \neq h(y)$.*

Given a family $H \subseteq [0,1]^X$ there is an associated map B_H that allows us to think of elements in X as fuzzy subsets of H, (i.e. H is the Universe of Discourse for such fuzzy sets).

$$B_H(x) : H \longrightarrow [0,1]$$
$$h \longmapsto B_H(x)(h) = h(x)$$

It is clear that B_H is an injective map when H is a separating family. In this case, we can identify elements in X with fuzzy subsets of H and, if there is no ambiguity about H, we will note $B_H(x) = x^{**}$, and thus $B_H(x)(h) = x^{**}(h) = h(x)$ for all x in X.

In general, the Duality Principle for fuzzy sets leads to dual structures that, in the case of Fuzzy Equivalence Relations were extensively investigated in [Boixader & Jacas 95, Boixader 97]. For our pourposes in this paper, just a few easy results will be enough.

Definition 2.4. *Given $H \subseteq [0,1]^X$, the Natural T-Preorder on H is*

$$\overline{P}_X(h_1, h_2) = \underset{x \in X}{INF} \hat{T}(h_1(x)|h_2(x))$$

Definition 2.5. *Given $H \subseteq [0,1]^X$, the Natural T-Equivalence on H is*

$$\overline{E}_X(h_1, h_2) = \underset{x \in X}{INF} E_T(h_1(x), h_2(x))$$

Of course, the Natural T-Preorder $\overline{P}_X$ is a Fuzzy T-preorder and the Natural T-Equivalence $\overline{E}_X(h_1, h_2)$ is a Fuzzy T-Equivalence Relation. This is a consequence of the Representation Theorems that we can easily obtain by identifying every element $x \in X$ with x^{**} through the Duality Principle.

Going farther, this identification allows us to construct as many models for a given Fuzzy T-Preorder P (res. a Fuzzy T-Equivalence E)as generating families it has.

Theorem 2.6. *Let H be a (separating) generating family of a Fuzzy T-preorder P (res. a Fuzzy T-equivalence Relation E) on a set X. Then the Natural Fuzzy Preorder $\overline{P}_X$ (res. the Natural Fuzzy Equivalence) on X^{**} is a model for P (res. for E).*

Proof: H is a separating family and then $B_H : X \to X^{**}$ is a bijective map. Furthermore,

$$\begin{aligned} \overline{E}_{H_E}(x_1^{**}, x_2^{**}) &= \underset{h \in H_E}{INF} E_T(x_1^{**}(h), x_2^{**}(h)) = \\ &= \underset{h \in H_E}{INF} E_T(h(x_1), h(x_2)) = E(x_1, x_2), \end{aligned}$$

for any x_1, x_2 in X. ∎

Obviously, the same approach can be taken with fuzzy weak orderings.

Theorem 2.7. *Let H be a generating (separating) family of a Fuzzy Weak Ordering L on a set X. Then the Natural Fuzzy Preorder $\overline{P}_X$ on X^{**} is a model for L.*

Proof: Like proof in Th.2.6. ∎

At this point, we have obtained models for fuzzy preorders, fuzzy equivalences and fuzzy weak orders that are made up of fuzzy sets, and the relations on such fuzzy sets are introduced in a very similar way, namely taking infima of implication or equivalence degrees over all points in their domains. These models allow us to compare fuzzy weak orders with resemblance relations, which are also defined on a set of fuzzy sets.

Definition 2.7. *The pointwise order in fuzzy sets is defined by $h_1 \leq h_2$ if and only if $h_1(x) \leq h_2(x)$ for all x in X.*

Proposition 2.8. *A fuzzy relation L is a Fuzzy Weak Ordering if and only if it has a model consisting of the Natural Preorder on a linearly ordered chain of fuzzy sets.*

Proof: Trivially follows from the identification made between points x and fuzzy sets x^{**} in presence of a generating family H. ∎

In fact, there are as many models for L in the sense of Prop.2.8 as generating families it has.

Corollary 2.9. *Every Fuzzy Weak Ordering can be isomorphically embedded into a Resemblance Relation.*

Proof: Trivial. ∎

In this way, fuzzy weak orderings can be seen as an special case of Resemblance Relations, namely, the one when such relations are defined on linearly ordered chains of fuzzy sets. Given a generating family H, the model $\{x^{**}\}_{x \in X} \subseteq [0,1]^H$ endowed with the Natural Preorder satisfies that for all x, y in X we have either $x^{**} \leq y^{**}$ or $y^{**} \leq x^{**}$.

3 Conclusions and Future Works

This paper has presented a first step into a more ambitious research concerned with the construction of a unified framework for all T-transitive relations. We have just showed that two different kinds of such relations are in fact isomorphic, and thus the same thing from a mathematical point of view. We are confident that the investigation we are addressing will lead to explain the theory of fuzzy T-transitive relations in a more rational and understandable way.

References

1. Bodenhofer, U. (1999) Representations and Constructions of Strongly Linear Fuzzy Orderings. In: Proc. 1999 EUSFLAT-ESTYLF Joint Conference 215-218. Palma (Mallorca).

2. Boixader, D. (1999) On the Unidimensional Fuzzy Equivalence Relations, Int J Int Systems.

3. Boixader, D., Jacas, J. (1994) Generators and Dual T-Indistinguishabilities, in: Fuzzy Logic and Soft Computing. Bouchon-Meunier,B., Yager, R.R. and Zadeh, L. eds. World Scientific. Singapore, 283-291.

4. Bouchon-Meunier, B., Valverde, L. (1992) Analogical Reasoning and Fuzzy Resemblance, in: Uncertainty in Intelligent Systems. Bouchon-Meunier et al. eds. Elsevier Science Pub.

5. Jacas, J. (1990) Similarity Relations - The Calculation of Minimal Generating Families. Fuzzy Sets & Systems **35**, 151-162.

6. Jacas, J., Recasens, J. (1994) Fixed points and generators of fuzzy relations. J Math Anal Appl **186**, 21-29.

7. Jacas, J., Recasens, J. (1995) Fuzzy T-transitive relations: eigenvectors and generators. Fuzzy Sets & Systems **72**, 147-154.

8. Ruspini, E. (1982) Recent Developments in Fuzzy Clustering,in: Fuzzy Sets and Possibility Theory: Recent Developments. R.R. Yager (Ed.) Pergamon Press, New York, 133-147.

9. Trillas, E., Valverde, L. (1984) An Inquiry on Indistinguishability Operators, in: Aspects of Vagueness H. Skala et al. (Eds.) Reidel, Dordrecht, 231-256.

10. Valverde, L. (1985) On the structure of F-indistinguishability operators. Fuzzy Sets & Systems **17**, 313-328.

11. Zadeh, L.A. (1971) Similarity Relations and Fuzzy Orderings. Information Sciences **3**, 177-200.

Fuzzy Control System with $\mathcal{B}$-operations

Bohdan S. Butkiewicz

Institute of Electronic Systems, Warsaw University of Technology
Nowowiejska 15/19, 00-665 Warsaw, Poland. Tel: (+48) 22 6605314
Fax: (+48) 22 8252300 E-mail: bb@ise.pw.edu.pl

Abstract. Fuzzy systems are described by rules using conjunctions "and", "or", "also". Different mathematical operations are used during approximate reasoning for interpretation of these conjunctions. New interesting theorem about steady-state behavior of the system is presented and proofed. If $\mathcal{B}$-operations, defined in the paper, are applied in reasoning steady-state of the system is independent on the type of $\mathcal{B}$-operations. Examples of system with PD and PI fuzzy controllers are presented with different $\mathcal{B}$-operations and linear and nonlinear plants. Properties of the system are discussed. All triangular operations, used typically for approximate reasoning, are $\mathcal{B}$-operations. Thus, these properties are important in practice. It was shown that system is very robust against to changes of reasoning methods.

1 Introduction

There are many methods of approximate reasoning. In fuzzy control Mamdani method is very often used in practice. It is called sometimes min-max method because minimum is used for interpretation of "and" and maximum is applied for "or". However, not only these logic operations can be used for reasoning. Other triangular norms [1] give also good results. Moreover, Larsen [4] idea, where membership function of conclusion set is multiplied by the weight of rule, may be used too. Mizumoto [5] are introduced product-sum method profiting this idea. He compared some of typically exploiting approximate reasoning and defuzzification methods considering simple example of PI controller with linear first order plant with delay.

This paper presents some generalization of fuzzy control system property discovered by author of the paper and published in IEEE Transactions [2]. It was proofed that if system is stable and steady-state exists then output signal of a system with fuzzy PD or PI controller and linear or nonlinear plant tends in steady-state to same value independent on the mathematical interpretations of sentence conjunctions "and" "or". The property is true for all triangular norms used as mathematical interpretations of "and", "or". Therefore, steady-state step error of PD controller, and velocity error of PI controller, are independent on this interpretation. Here, the property is generalized and more complex system than fuzzy PD and PI controllers are considered. Also, usefulness of some other operations than triangular norms is discussed. They are called here basic ($\mathcal{B}$) operations.

2 Description of Rules

Consider a fuzzy system described by input linguistic variables X_1, X_2, ... , X_n output linguistic variable U and rules

R_1: if x_1 is A_{11} and x_2 is A_{12} and ... and x_n is A_{1n} then u is U_1
also R_2: if x_1 is A_{21} and x_2 is A_{22} and ... and x_n is A_{2n} then u is U_2
....
also R_i: if x_1 is A_{i1} and x_2 is A_{i2} and ... and x_n is A_{in} then u is U_i
....
also R_m: if x_1 is A_{m1} and x_2 is A_{m2} and ... and x_n is A_{mn} then u is U_m

Values A_{ik} $i = 1, ..., m$ $k = 1, ..., n$ are fuzzy sets describing variables X_k. Some of them can be identical. Rules may contain not all terms "and x_k is A_{ik}". Values x_k are crisp. Some of output conclusion sets $U_1, ..., U_m$ can be also identical. In this case rules with identical conclusion can be aggregated in one rule by sentence conjunction "or". Sometimes, in the place of "or", conjunction "also" is used. In the paper for both "or" and "also" the same mathematical meaning, $\mathcal{B}_{or}$-operation is applied. For "and" operation $\mathcal{B}_{and}$ is used.

Definition (Basic operations)
Basic operations $\mathcal{B}_{and}$, $\mathcal{B}_{or}$ for fuzzy system satisfy for $x, y \in X$

$\mu_x \mathcal{B} \mu_y = \mu_y \mathcal{B} \mu_x$ commutativity condition for both $\mathcal{B}_{and}$, $\mathcal{B}_{or}$
$\mu_x \mathcal{B} (\mu_y \mathcal{B} \mu_z) = (\mu_x \mathcal{B} \mu_y) \mathcal{B} \mu_z$ associativity condition for both $\mathcal{B}_{and}$, $\mathcal{B}_{or}$
$\mu_x \mathcal{B}_{and} 1 = \mu_x$ $\mu_x \mathcal{B}_{and} 0 = 0$ boundary condition for $\mathcal{B}_{and}$ operation
$\mu_x \mathcal{B}_{or} 1 = 1$ $\mu_x \mathcal{B}_{or} 0 = \mu_x$ boundary condition for $\mathcal{B}_{or}$ operation
and moreover for both $\mathcal{B}_{and}$, $\mathcal{B}_{or}$
$\mu_x \mathcal{B} \mu_y \leq \mu_z \mathcal{B} \mu_y$ when $x \leq z$ local monotonicity for $x, y \in X_s \subset X$

It can be seen that basic operations are enough similar to triangular operations, but they are more general. Monotonicity condition may not be satisfy in all real space X, but only for subset X_s. This subset will be interpreted later as neighborhood of system set point.

3 Fuzzy System in Boundary Conditions

Consider situation when one of input values, example x_1 attains value where $\mu_{i1}(x_1) \neq 0$ and other input values x_k $k = 2, ..., n$ approach to such values that $\mu_{ik}(x_k)$ tend to 0 or to 1.
This situation occurs when a system is in a special state which occurs only in some conditions, for exapmple in steady-stae. Here, these conditions are called boundary conditions, because boundary conditions for $\mathcal{B}$-operations will be used for system inputs.

Theorem (Fuzzy system in boundary conditions)
Let fuzzy system is described by set of rules of the type

$$R_i : \quad if\ (S_1)\ and\ (S_2)\ and\ ...\ and\ (S_{ni})\ then\ u\ is\ U_i$$

joined by sentence conjugation "also", where $S_j\ j = 1, ..., n_i$ are sentences of the type "x_j is A_l". Values x_j are crisp, set A_l is any fuzzy set, defined on x_j axis, of linguistic variable X_j. If all crisp values x_j except one, say x_1, attain such values that appropriate membership functions $\mu_j(x_j)$ are equal to 0 or 1 then result of approximate reasoning, basing on $\mathcal{B}$-operations, is independent on the pair of $\mathcal{B}$-operations used for mathematical interpretation of "and", "or". If same mathematical interpretation of "or" "also" is applied then the result is also independent on aggregation, i.e. if aggregated or not aggregated form of rules is used. The result of approximate reasoning can depend on defuzzification method.

Proof
Let we have a rule R_i where $\mu_{i1}(x_1) = a_i$ and $\mu_{ik}(x_k) = 1$ for $k = 2, ..., n$. Then, the weight w_i of rule R_i is equal to

$$w_i = \mu_{i1}(x_1)\mathcal{B}_{and}\mu_{i2}(x_2)\mathcal{B}_{and}\ ...\ \mathcal{B}_{and}\mu_{in}(x_n) = a_i\mathcal{B}_{and}1\mathcal{B}_{and}1\ ...\ \mathcal{B}_{and}1 = a_i$$

Now, consider a rule R_j where at least one of the x_k values $k = 2, ..., n$ attains such value that $\mu_{jk}(x_k) = 0$. From boundary conditions follows immediately that weight w_j of the rule R_j is equal

$$w_j = a_i\mathcal{B}_{and}1\mathcal{B}_{and}1\mathcal{B}_{and}0\mathcal{B}_{and}1\ ...\ \mathcal{B}_{and}1 = 0$$

Thus, rules R_j are not active and output u depends only on a_i values. This output value is independent on the type of $\mathcal{B}_{and}$-operation used for approximate reasoning because any $\mathcal{B}$-operation must satisfy boundary conditions. Same mathematical meaning is aplied for "or" and "also", so result not depend on the way of rule aggregation.

$$\square$$

It is typical situation when system with one input x tends to steady-state. All derivatives of input tend to zero.

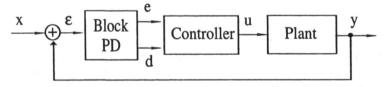

Fig. 1. System with fuzzy controller of PD type

Example (Fuzzy PD control)

Let system consists with fuzzy PD controller and a plant linear or nonlinear (Fig. 1). There are two input variables e (proportional to error ε), d (proportional to derivative of ε) and one output variable u. Suppose linguistic values for all variables are (from negative to positive values) NL, NM, NS, ZE, PS, PM, PL with appropriate, ex. triangular, shape of membership functions. Let the system is stable (for limited input the system response is limited) near set point where derivative $\dot{\varepsilon} \to 0$ and e is ZE. Suppose that behavior of the system near set point is described by rules (full aggregated form, see Fig. 2)

if (e is PS and d is (ZE or PS)) or (e is ZE and d is PS) then u is PS

if (e is NS and d is (ZE or NS)) or (e is ZE and d is NS) then u is NS

if (e is NS and d is PS) or (e is ZE and d is ZE) or (e is PS and d is NS) then u is ZE

Applying properties of triangular norms [1], it is possible to establish some typical range for our system responses with triangular operations. Of course "upper limit", obtained using minimum as t-norm and drastic sum as s-norm, may be surpassed in some time instants. Also "lower limit", obtained using drastic product as t-norm and maximum as s-norm, is not always minimal value of response for given time. Basic operations give very similar responses as triangular operations.

If triangular norms are used for "and", "or", "also" then system error in

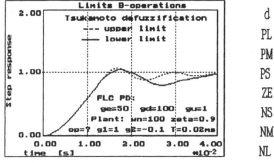

d \ e	NL	NM	NS	ZE	PS	PM	PL
PL	ZE	PS	PM	PL	PL	PL	PL
PM	NS	ZE	PS	PM	PM	PL	PL
PS	NM	NS	ZE	PS	PS	PM	PL
ZE	NL	NM	NS	ZE	PS	PM	PL
NS	NL	NM	NS	NS	ZE	PS	PM
NM	NL	NL	NM	NM	NS	ZE	PS
NL	NL	NL	NL	NL	NM	NS	ZE

Fig. 2. "Upper" and "lower" limits for triangular operations and rule matrix

steady-state is independent on the pair of relations used for approximate reasoning. System dynamic is also similar. Differences between step responses are very small, graphically indistinguishable. In the author papers [3] figures with system responses for many triangular norms (logic, algebraic, bounded, Hamacher, etc.), mean operations (arithmetic, geometric, harmonic), and some others are shown. Here, other examples are presented. Output gain of controller is chosen to obtain same overshoot of 15%. The results for logic, algebraic, and modified drastic operations with different defuzzification methods are shown in the Fig. 3.

Here, for approximate reasoning three pairs of $\mathcal{B}$-operations are used.

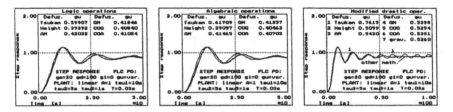

Fig. 3. System response with 15% overshoot for triangular operations

Examples of $\mathcal{B}$-operations are shown below

$$\mathcal{B}1_{and} = \begin{cases} \mu_x \mu_y & \text{for } \mu_x, \mu_y < 0.1 \\ \min(\mu_x, \mu_y) & \text{for } \mu_x, \mu_y \in [0.1, 0.2] \\ \mu_x + \mu_y - 1 & \text{for } \mu_x, \mu_y > 0.2 \end{cases}$$

$$\mathcal{B}1_{or} = \begin{cases} \max(\mu_x, \mu_y) & \text{for } \mu_x, \mu_y < 0.1 \\ \mu_x + \mu_y - 1 & \text{for } \mu_x, \mu_y \in [0.1, 0.2] \\ \min(\mu_x + \mu_y, 1) & \text{for } \mu_x, \mu_y > 0.2 \end{cases}$$

If result is negative $\mathcal{B}_{and} = 0$ is put, so $\mathcal{B}1_{and}$ is algebraic, logic or bounded product. If result is greater than 1 it is put $\mathcal{B}_{or} = 1$, so $\mathcal{B}1_{or}$ it is logic, bounded or cut sum. These operations are not monotonic and not continuous.

$$\mathcal{B}2_{and} = \begin{cases} \max(0, \mu_x + \mu_y - 1) & \text{for } \mu_x < 0.1, \mu_y < 0.05 \\ \mu_x \mu_y / (\mu_x + \mu_y - \mu_x \mu_y) & \text{for } \mu_x \in [0.1, 0.2], \mu_y \in [0.05, 0.1] \\ 1 - \min(1, [(1 - \mu_x)^p + (1 - \mu_y)^p]^{1/p}) & \text{for } \mu_x > 0.1, \mu_y > 0.2 \end{cases}$$

$$\mathcal{B}2_{or} = \begin{cases} \min(1, [\mu_x^p + \mu_y^p]^{1/p}) & \text{for } \mu_x < 0.05, \mu_y < 0.1 \\ \min(1, \mu_x + \mu_y) & \text{for } \mu_x \in [0.05, 0.1], \mu_y \in [0.1, 0.2] \\ (\mu_x + \mu_y - 2\mu_x \mu_y)/(1 - \mu_x \mu_y) & \text{for } \mu_x > 0.1, \mu_y > 0.2 \end{cases}$$

Operations $\mathcal{B}2_{and}$ and $\mathcal{B}2_{or}$ are combination of bounded, Hamacher, and Yager operations but in different order, so they are not continuous.

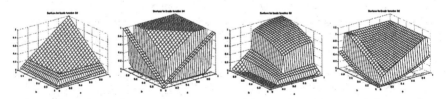

Fig. 4. Examples of $\mathcal{B}$-operations from left to right: $\mathcal{B}1_{and}$, $\mathcal{B}1_{or}$, $\mathcal{B}2_{and}$, $\mathcal{B}2_{or}$

Third $B3$ operation is like $B1$, but modified sinusoidally

$$B3_{and} = [1 + sin(20\pi\mu_x)sin(20\pi\mu_y)/5]B1_{and}$$

$$B3_{or} = [1 + sin(20\pi\mu_x)sin(20\pi\mu_y)/5]B1_{or}$$

Triangular logic operations minimum, maximum, and three pairs of B-

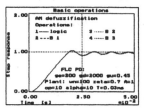 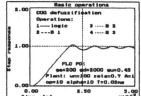 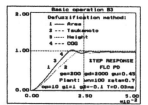

Fig. 5. System response for basic operations

operations, presented as examples, were used for fuzzy control of three different plants.

Linear plant 1 of first order with delay, same as Mizumoto [5] used for simulations, was described by transfer function

$$K(s) = \frac{A e^{-st_0}}{\tau s + 1}$$

with parameters $A = 1$, $\tau = 20$ s, $t_0 = 2$ s. Controller of PI type had parameters $g_e = 30$, $g_i = 0.05$. Sampling period $T = 0.03$ s.

Nonlinear plant 2 of second order with saturation and delay was described by equation

$$\frac{d^2y}{dt^2} + 2\zeta\omega_n\frac{dy}{dt} + \omega_n^2 = g_1u(t - t_0) + g_2u(t - t_0)|u(t - t_0)|$$

with parameters $\zeta = 0.7$, $\omega_n = 100$ rd/s, $g_1 = 1$, $g_2 = -0.1$, $t_0 = 0.3$ ms. Controller scale parameters were equal $g_e = 200$, $g_d = 2000$, $g_u = 0.45$, and it was suboptimal chouse. Sampling period $T = 0.03$ ms.

Linear plant 3 of third order was described by transfer function

$$K(s) = \frac{A}{(\tau_1 s + 1)(\tau_2 s + 1)(\tau_3 s + 1)}$$

with parameters $A=1$, $\tau_1 = 10$ s, $\tau_2 = 5$ s, $\tau_3 = 1$ s. Controller parameters: $g_e = 20$, $g_d = 100$. Sampling period $T = 0.03$ s.

Membership functions for the controllers were symmetrical, triangular, with trapezes at the end, equally placed every 2.5 in the [-10,10] section. Results are shown in the Fig. 5 and Fig. 6. Response parameters are shown in the Tables, where abs err denote absolute error, sqr err square error, t*err product time* error, y_{st-st} steady-state in observed time. Controllers parameter g_u was chosen to obtain same overshoot 15%. Its value is shown in the Figures.

54

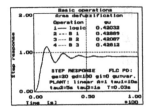 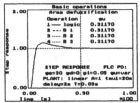 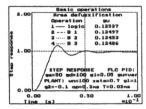

Fig. 6. System response with PD, PI, and PID controllers with basic operations

Table 1. Response parameters for system with plant 2

Operat.	Rise time $y = 0.9$ $y = 1.0$	y_{1max} time [ms] abs err	y_{1min} time [ms] sqr err	y_{2max} time [ms] t*err	y_{2min} time [ms]	y_{st-st} Ampl. os.
logic	17.576 19.184	1.150000 24.24 480.1419	0.910600 37.32 313.6207	1.015527 50.85 47.5341	0.973591 63.84	0.990021 0.003688
$B1$	17.599 19.219	1.150001 24.27 482.1848	0.908969 37.32 314.1382	1.015963 50.88 47.7363	0.972596 63.96	0.989551 0.003791
$B2$	17.635 19.257	1.150000 24.30 484.4734	0.907162 37.35 314.7160	1.016506 50.91 47.9629	0.971397 64.02	0.989102 0.004034
$B3$	17.608 19.230	1.150016 24.30 483.3342	0.907453 37.35 314.3379	1.016456 50.94 47.8501	0.971722 64.11	0.989470 0.003963

Table 2. Response parameters for system with plant 3

Operat.	Rise time $y = 0.9$ $y = 1.0$	y_{1max} time [s] abs err	y_{1min} time [s] sqr err	y_{2max} time [s] timerr	y_{2min} time [s]	y_{st-st} Ampl. os.
logic	8.5604 9.3602	1.150002 12.00 535.2367	0.749918 20.04 194.4255	0.962499 28.05 52988.44	0.851450 36.00	0.886748 0.001003
$B1$	8.4536 9.2435	1.150117 11.85 526.2907	0.747094 19.77 191.7706	0.976569 27.69 52102.78	0.847778 35.64	0.889047 0.002941
$B2$	8.5521 9.3492	1.149998 11.97 530.5267	0.742051 19.89 194.2588	0.982601 27.93 52522.14	0.842929 35.97	0.887814 0.003811
$B3$	8.4646 9.2574	1.150007 11.88 527.8916	0.745059 19.80 192.5657	0.977937 27.72 52261.27	0.836840 35.52	0.889243 0.003634

Table 3. Response parameters for system with plant 1

Operat.	Rise time $y = 0.9$ $y = 1.0$	y_{1max} time [s] abs err	y_{1min} time [s] sqr err	y_{2max} time [s] timerr	y_{2min} time [s]	y_{st-st} Ampl. os.
logic	8.5604	1.150002	0.749918	0.962499	0.851450	0.886748
$B1\ B2\ B3$	9.3602	12.00	20.04	28.05	36.00	0.001003
		535.2367	194.4255	52988.44		

4 Conclusions

In the paper some examples of B-operations are presented. It is shown that very different operations give similar responses, very often graphically undistinguishable. The values of parameters obtained for plant 1 were the same for logic and all B-operations. Thus, the system is very robust to changes of approximate reasoning methods. Also, the response not depends strongly on defuzzification method, especially for typical area (AM), height, and center of gravity (COG) methods. Only Tsukamoto defuzzificatin gives different results.

References

1. Bloch, I. (1996) Information combination operators for data fusion: A comparative review with classification. IEEE Transactions on System, Man, and Cybernetics—Part A: Systems and Humans. **1**, 52-67
2. Butkiewicz, B. S. (1998) Steady-State Error of a System with Fuzzy Controller. IEEE Transactions on System, Man, and Cybernetics —Part B: Cybernetics, **6**, 855-860
3. Butkiewicz, B. S. (1998) Behavior of Fuzzy PD Controller under Different Reasoning Methods. Proc. Int. Conf. Soft Computing and Measurements, St. Petersburg, v. **1**, 250-259
4. Larsen, P, M, (1980) Industrial Applications of Fuzzy Logic Control. Int. J. Man Machin Studies, **12**, No. 1, 3-10
5. Mizumoto, M. (1995) Improvement of Fuzzy Control Method. In book Li, H. Gupta, M. (ed.) Fuzzy Logic and Intelligent Systems, Kluwer Acad. Publishers, 1-16

Roughness Indicator Fuzzy Set

Kankana Chakrabarty

School of Mathematical and Computer Sciences, The University of New England, Armidale 2351, New South Wales, Australia

Abstract. In the present paper, the author presents the idea of Roughness Indicator Fuzzy set, which is a fuzzy set associated with an approximation space, capable of indicating the amount of roughness present in the elements and thus she describes how fuzzy membership can be used as as a measure of roughness. The relationships between the different types of indices of fuzziness and the roughness measures are established. It is also observed that nearest ordinary sets play important roles in this case. Consequently, the concept of Roughness Indicator Fuzzy class is also proposed.

1 Introduction

The ability to operate in uncertain environments is an essential and crucial component of any intelligent system because many applications involve human expertise and knowledge which are invariably imprecise and incomplete. Therefore, the intelligent sytem should combine knowledge-based techniques for gathering and processing information with the methods of approximate reasoning. Fuzzy set theory, as proposed by Zadeh[12], allows us to uncertain conflicting propositions and makes it possible to deal with different types of uncertainty within a single conceptual framework. Classes with unsharp boundaries, in which the transition from membership to non-membership is gradual, rather than abrupt, can be represented by using the notion of fuzzy sets.

Pawlak's rough sets[8] embody the idea of indiscernibility among the objects in a set, and the underlying assumption is that knowledge has granular structure which is caused by the situation when some objects of interest can not be distinguished. The formal recognition of the fact that the ability to describe a set of objects is constrained by our limitation in distinguishing individual members of the set explains the significance of the notion of rough sets in which we first of all assume that any vague concept is characterized by a pair of precise concepts called the lower and the upper approximations of the concerned vague concept. The lower approximation is the set of objects surely belonging to the concept and the upper approximation is the set consisting of all objects possibly belonging to the concept. The boundary region of the vague concept is merely the difference between the upper and the lower approximations of it.

In this paper, the author proposes the notion of the Roughness Indicator Fuzzy Set (RI- Fuzzy Set) which is a fuzzy subset of the power set of the universal set in case of an approximation space, and shows that how its membership function can be used to measure the roughness of the concerned elements. For this fuzzy set, the indices of fuzziness are considered and interesting relationships between the linear and quadratic indices of fuzziness and measure of roughness are establised, it is observed that in those cases the nearest ordinary sets play important roles. Consequently, the notion of Roughness Indicator Fuzzy Class is also introduced.

2 Preliminaries

Let $\mathcal{U}$ be a set called universe and let $\mathcal{R}$ be an indiscernibility relation defined on $\mathcal{U}$. The pair $A = (\mathcal{U}, \mathcal{R})$ is called an approximation space. For any non-null subset X of $\mathcal{U}$, the sets

$$\underline{Apr}_A(X) = \{x \in \mathcal{U} : [x]_\mathcal{R} \subseteq X\},$$

$$\overline{Apr}_A(X) = \{x \in \mathcal{U} : [x]_\mathcal{R} \cap X \neq \phi\}$$

are respectively called the lower and the upper approximation of X in A, where $[x]_\mathcal{R}$ denotes the equivalence class of the relation $\mathcal{R}$ containing the element x.

$Apr_A(X) = (\underline{Apr}_A(X), \overline{Apr}_A(X))$ is called the rough set of X in A. For a fixed approximation space $A = (\mathcal{U}, \mathcal{R})$ and for a fixed non-null subset X of $\mathcal{U}$, $Apr_A(X)$ is unique.

Let $A = (\underline{A}, \overline{A})$ and $B = (\underline{B}, \overline{B})$ be any two rough sets in the approximation space $A = (\mathcal{U}, \mathcal{R})$. Then,

$$(i) \quad A \cup B = (\underline{A} \cup \underline{B}, \overline{A} \cup \overline{B})$$

$$(ii) \quad A \cap B = (\underline{A} \cap \underline{B}, \overline{A} \cap \overline{B})$$

$$(iii) \quad A \subset B \Longleftrightarrow A \cap B = A$$

We say that A is a rough subset of B or B is a rough superset of A. Thus in the case of rough sets A and B , $A \subset B$ if and only if $\underline{A} \subset \underline{B}$ and $\overline{A} \subset \overline{B}$. The natural inverse rough set of A denoted by $-A$ is defined by

$$(iv) \quad -A = (U - \overline{A}, U - \underline{A})$$

This $-A$ is also called the rough complement of A in (U, R).

$$(v) \quad A - B = A \cap (-B) = (\underline{A} - \overline{B}, \overline{A} - \underline{B})$$

Let $A = (\mathcal{U}, \mathcal{R})$ be an approximation space and let $X \subseteq \mathcal{U}$. The accuracy of approximation of X in A is given by

$$\eta_A(X) = \frac{\underline{\nu}_A(X)}{\overline{\nu}_A(X)}$$

where $\underline{\nu}_A(X)$ and $\overline{\nu}_A(X)$ represents the numbers of atoms in $\underline{Apr}_A(X)$ and $\overline{Apr}_A(X)$ respectively. Obviously, for any approximation space $A = (\mathcal{U}, \mathcal{R})$, and any $X \subseteq U$, $0 \leq \eta_A(X) \leq 1$. For any set X in a discrete approximation space $A = (\mathcal{U}, \mathcal{R})$, $\eta_A(X) = 1$, and this is the greatest possible accuracy. Here $\eta_A(X)$ expresses the roughness of the set X.

3 Roughness Indicator Fuzzy Set

Let $A = (U, R)$ be an approximation space and let $\pi(U)$ be the power set of U. Define a fuzzy subset $\mu^R_{\pi(U)}$ of $\pi(U)$ such that

$$\mu^R_{\pi(U)}(X) = 1 - \frac{\nu_A(X)}{\overline{\nu}_A(X)}$$

for each X in $\pi(U)$, where $\mu^R_{\pi(U)}(X)$ indicates the measure of roughness of X in A and $0 \leq \mu^R_{\pi(A)}(X) \leq 1$ for any X in $\pi(U)$. Greater the value of the ratio $\frac{\nu_A(X)}{\overline{\nu}_A(X)}$, the lower is the roughness of X. Clearly $\mid \pi(U) \mid = 2^{|U|}$, where $\mid \pi(U) \mid$ denotes the cardinality of $\pi(U)$. Thus, $\mu^R_{\pi(U)}$ is a fuzzy set having $2^{|U|}$ supporting points.

The index of fuzziness of $\mu^R_{\pi(U)}$ is given by

$$\xi(\mu^R_{\pi(U)}) = \{2/(2^{|U|})^\sigma\} \delta(X, \tilde{X}) \tag{1}$$

where $\delta(X, \tilde{X})$ denotes the distance between the fuzzy set X and its nearest ordinary set $\tilde{X}$. The number 2 in the numerator and the positive constant σ appear in order to make $\xi(\mu)$ lie between 0 and 1. The value of σ depends on the type of distance function used, e.g. $\sigma = 1$ for a generalized Hamming distance whereas $\sigma = 0.5$ for an Euclidean distance. The corresponding indices of fuzziness are called the linear index of fuzziness denoted by $\xi_l(\mu^R_{\pi(U)})$, and the quadratic index of fuzziness denoted by $\xi_q(\mu^R_{\pi(U)})$.

Therefore,

$$\xi_l(\mu_{\pi(U)}^R) = \{2/(2^{|U|})\}.\delta(X, \tilde{X}) \tag{2}$$

$$\xi_q(\mu_{\pi(U)}^R) = \{2/(2^{|U|})^{1/2}\}.\delta(X, \tilde{X}) \tag{3}$$

Let $\mu_{\pi(U)}^R$ be the fuzzy subset of $\pi(U)$ indicating the measure of roughness of its elements and let $\zeta_{\pi(U)}^R$ be another arbitrary fuzzy subset of $\pi(U)$. Then the Hamming distance between $\mu_{\pi(U)}^R$ and $\zeta_{\pi(U)}^R$ is given by

$$\delta(\mu_{\pi(U)}^R, \zeta_{\pi(U)}^R) = \sum_{i=1}^{2^{|U|}} \mid \mu_{\pi(U)}^R(X_i) - \zeta_{\pi(U)}^R(X_i) \mid$$

$$= \sum_{i=1}^{2^{|U|}} \mid 1 - \frac{\nu_A(X_i)}{\overline{\nu}_A(X_i)} - \zeta_{\pi(U)}^R(X_i) \mid \tag{4}$$

If $\tilde{\mu}_{\pi(U)}^R$ be the nearest ordinary set of the fuzzy set $\mu_{\pi(U)}^R$, then from equation(2)

$$\xi_l(\mu_{\pi(U)}^R) = \{2/(2^{|U|})\} \sum_{i=1}^{2^{|U|}} \mid \mu_{\pi(U)}^R(X_i) - \tilde{\mu}_{\pi(U)}^R(X_i) \mid$$

$$= \{2/(2^{|U|})\} \sum_{i=1}^{2^{|U|}} \mid 1 - \frac{\nu_A(X_i)}{\overline{\nu}_A(X_i)} - \tilde{\mu}_{\pi(U)}^R(X_i) \mid$$

$$= \{2/(2^{|U|})\} \sum_{i=1}^{2^{|U|}} \mid 1 - \eta_A(X_i) - \tilde{\mu}_{\pi(U)}^R(X_i) \mid \tag{5}$$

Equation(5) represents a relationship between the linear index of fuzziness $\xi_l(\mu_{\pi(U)}^R)$ and the measures of roughness of X_i's.
Similarly,

$$\xi_q(\mu_{\pi(U)}^R) = \{2/(2^{|U|})^{1/2}\} \sqrt{\sum_{i=1}^{2^{|U|}} \{\mu_{\pi(U)}^R(X_i) - \tilde{\mu}_{\pi(U)}^R(X_i)\}^2}$$

$$= \{2/(2^{|U|})^{1/2}\} \sqrt{\sum_{i=1}^{2^{|U|}} \{1 - \frac{\nu_A(X_i)}{\overline{\nu}_A(X_i)} - \tilde{\mu}_{\pi(U)}^R(X_i)\}^2}$$

$$= \{2/(2^{|U|})^{1/2}\} \sqrt{\sum_{i=1}^{2^{|U|}} \{1 - \eta_A(X_i) - \tilde{\mu}_{\pi(U)}^R(X_i)\}^2} \tag{6}$$

Equation (6) represents a relationship between $\xi_q(\mu_{\pi(U)})$ and $\eta_A(X_i)$'s.

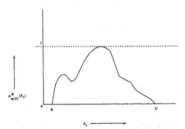

Fig. 1. The Membership Curve

Clearly, $\tilde{\mu}_{\pi(U)}^{R}(X_i)$ can take up either of the two values 0 and 1. If the nearest ordinary set is ϕ, then

$$\xi_l(\mu_{\pi(U)}^{R}) = \{2/(2^{|U|})\} \sum_{i=1}^{2^{|U|}} |\mu_{\pi(U)}^{R}(X_i)|$$

$$= \{2/(2^{|U|})\} \sum_{i=1}^{2^{|U|}} |1 - \frac{\nu_A(X_i)}{\bar{\nu}_A(X_i)}|$$

$$= \{2/(2^{|U|})\} \sum_{i=1}^{2^{|U|}} |1 - \eta_A(X_i)| \tag{7}$$

$$\xi_q(\mu_{\pi(U)}^{R}) = \{2/(2^{|U|})^{1/2}\} \sqrt{\sum_{i=1}^{2^{|U|}} \{\mu_{\pi(U)}^{R}(X_i)\}^2}$$

$$= \{2/(2^{|U|})^{1/2}\} \sqrt{\sum_{i=1}^{2^{|U|}} \{1 - \eta_A(X_i)\}^2} \tag{8}$$

Evidently, the support set $Supp\{\mu_{\pi(U)}^{R}\}$ of $\mu_{\pi(U)}$ does not contain ϕ and $\pi(U)$, hence, $Supp\{\mu_{\pi(U)}^{R}\} \subset \pi(U)$.

The entropy of the fuzzy set $\mu_{\pi(U)}$ is given by

$$\vartheta\{\mu_{\pi(U)}\} = \{-1/ln(2^{|U|})\} \sum_{i=1}^{2^{|U|}} \left[\frac{\mu_{\pi(U)}^{R}(X_i)}{\sum\limits_{i=1}^{2^{|U|}} \mu_{\pi(U)}^{R}(X_i)}\right] .ln \left[\frac{\mu_{\pi(U)}^{R}(X_i)}{\sum\limits_{i=1}^{2^{|U|}} \mu_{\pi(U)}^{R}(X_i)}\right] . \tag{9}$$

Every approximation space $A = (U, R)$ is associated with a fuzzy subset $\mu^R_{\pi(U)}$ which indicates the roughness of the elements of $\pi(U)$. We call $\mu^R_{\pi(U)}$ the Roughness Indicator Fuzzy Set (or, RI-Fuzzy Set) of A.

For any approximation space $A = (U, R)$, the RI-Fuzzy set of A is unique. If $A_1 = (U, R_1)$, $A_2 = (U, R_2)$,.........,$A_n = (U, R_n)$ be n approximation spaces and if $\mu^{R_1}_{\pi(U)}$, $\mu^{R_2}_{\pi(U)}$,............,$\mu^{R_n}_{\pi(U)}$ be the corresponding RI-Fuzzy Sets of $A_1, A_2, ..., A_n$ respectively, then each $\mu^{R_i}_{\pi(U)}$ $(i = 1, 2, ..., n)$ is a fuzzy subset of $\pi(U)$. We call $\{\mu^{R_1}_{\pi(U)}, \mu^{R_2}_{\pi(U)}, ..., \mu^{R_n}_{\pi(U)}\}$ the RI-Fuzzy Class of U over the set of indiscernibility relations $\{R_1, R_2, ..., R_n\}$.

4 Conclusion

This paper introduces the notion of Roughness Indicator Fuzzy Sets associated with an approximation space which can be used to measure the amount of roughness present in the elements. The method of utilizing fuzzy membership as a tool to measure roughness is discussed. The relationships between the linear and quadratic indices of fuzziness and the roughness measures are established and consequently the concept of Roughness Indicator Fuzzy Class is proposed.

References

1. Banerjee, M., Pal, S.K. (1996) Roughness of a fuzzy set. Info. Sc. **93**, 235-246
2. Chakrabarty,K., Biswas,R., Nanda, S. (1999) Fuzziness in Rough Sets. Fuzzy Sets and Systems. **110/2**, 247-251
3. Chakrabarty,K., Biswas,R., Nanda, S. (1998) Nearest Ordinary Set of a Fuzzy Set: A Rough Theoretic Construction. Bulletin of Polish Academy of Sciences Technical Sciences. **46(1)**, 103-112
4. Chakrabarty,K., Biswas,R., Nanda, S. (1998) On Rough Relations. Foundations of Computing and Decision Sciences. **23(4)**, 241-252
5. Dubois, D. and Prade, H. (1980) Fuzzy Sets and Systems -Theory and Applications. Academic Press
6. Novak, V. (1986) Fuzzy sets and their Applications. Adam Hilger.
7. Pawlak, Z. (1981) Rough sets basic notions. ICS PAS Reports. **436**, Warsaw Univ. of Tech
8. Pawlak, Z. (1982) Rough sets, Int.J.Inf.Comp.Sc. **11**, 341-356
9. Pawlak, Z. (1985) Rough sets and fuzzy sets. Fuzzy Sets and Systems. **17**, 99-102
10. Pawlak, Z.(1991) Rough sets, Theoretical Aspects of Reasoning about Data. Kluwer Academic Publishers
11. Slowinski, R., Ed. (1992) Intelligent Decision Support Handbook of Applications and Advances of the Rough Sets Theory. Kluwer Academic Publishers
12. Zadeh, L.A. (1965) Fuzzy sets, Information and Control. **8** 338-353
13. Zimmermann, H.-J. (1991) Fuzzy set theory and its applications. 2nd Ed. Kluwer Academic Publishers

Dynamic Recognition States for Chaotic Neural Networks

Nigel Crook and Tjeerd Olde Scheper

School of Computing and Mathematical Sciences

Oxford Brookes University

Headington

Oxford

Abstract: Chaos offers several advantages to the Engineer over other non-chaotic dynamics. One is that chaotic systems are often significantly easier to control than other linear or non-linear systems, requiring only small, appropriately timed perturbations to constrain them within specific Unstable Periodic Orbits (UPOs). Another is that chaotic attractors contain an infinite number of these UPOs. If individual UPOs can be made to represent specific internal states of a system, then a chaotic attractor can be turned into an infinite state machine. In this paper we investigate this possibility with respect to chaotic neural networks. We present a method by which a network can self-select UPOs in response to specific input values. These UPOs correspond to network recognition states for these input values.

1   Introduction

This research is inspired by the discovery that the firing behaviour in biological neural networks is fundamentally chaotic (Freeman, 1985, 1994; Guevara et al, 1983; Olde Scheper, 1995). Although there is little doubt about the presence of chaos in such networks, there is far less certainty about its role. Some have suggested that biological networks use this chaotic behaviour as a means of storing and retrieving memories (Freeman, 1994; Lourenco & Babloyantz A., 1996; Tsuda et al., 1987; Tsuda, 1992, 1996). These memories correspond to dynamic "states" which are embedded within the chaotic attractor followed by the network. The use of chaos to store and retrieve memories in an artificial neural network offers a number of significant advantages over alternative models. Among them are a dramatically increased capacity for memory storage, and an ability to "control" the network using only small perturbations (Crook, Dobbyn and olde Scheper, 2000).

A chaotic system can be described by a set of dynamic variables. An *n*-dimensional plot of an *n* variable system is called a "state space". Each point in the state space corresponds to a unique set of values for the dynamic variables. As the system changes states a continuous trajectory is described through the state space. Chaotic systems that can be modelled by a set of continuous dynamic variables are constrained to a specific sub-area of state space called an "attractor". An example of an attractor is given in Figure 1. This attractor is followed by Rössler system of equations (Rössler, 1976) which is modelled by three dynamic variables.

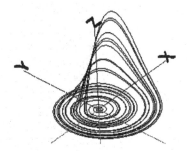

Figure 1. The attractor for the Rössler system

By definition, a chaotic system can never be in the same state twice on a continuous run. In other words, a single trajectory in state space can never intersect itself. However, as the system follows its attractor it will come very close to points in state space which it had previously visited. Such trajectories are called Unstable Periodic Orbits (UPOs). A chaotic system following a UPO would describe an orbit in state space which almost repeats itself. However, under the influence of chaos, the trajectory would drift away from this almost periodic orbit and continue to track the surface of the attractor. An example of a UPO is illustrated in Figure 2.

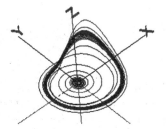

Figure 2. An Unstable Periodic Orbit embedded in the Rössler attractor

Techniques have been developed in Non-linear Dynamical Systems Theory for controlling a chaotic system so that it will remain on a periodic orbit until the control is removed (Ditto et al., 1990; Garfinkel et al, 1992; Pyragas, 1992; Shinbrot et al., 1992, 1993). These techniques can be divided into two categories: those that rely on some knowledge of the local dynamics of the attractor around the UPO to be stabilised, and those which use delayed feedback as a method of control. With the first category, the control waits for the system state to fall in the neighbourhood of the desired UPO. Once this has happened, the control makes small temporary adjustments to local dynamics of the attractor so that the system trajectory will come back to the same point when it returns to that neighbourhood, thereby stabilising the orbit. The second category of control method uses a feedback mechanism with a delay proportional to the period of the orbit to be stabilised. The control makes small temporary modifications to the dynamics of the system so that the trajectory will return close to a point in state space which it previously visited. This point is determined by the delay.

Within the context of chaotic neural networks, delayed feedback is the most appropriate method of control. There are three main reasons for this that are based on the biological plausibility of the method in question. The first is that the delay feedback method does not rely on a priori knowledge of the local dynamics of the attractor around the UPO to be stabilised. It seems extremely unlikely that biological neural networks are aware of the local dynamics in every UPO. The second is that the delayed feedback method does not specify which UPO is to be stabilised, it simply specifies the period of the required orbit. This suggests an element of self-organisation which is more biologically appealing than the first method. The third reason is that delays are inherent in biological neural networks: the nerve impulse takes time to travel the length of the axon to its target neurons, these neurons, in turn, take time to summate their inputs and produce their response. Consequently, we consider the delayed feedback method to be best suited to the control of chaos in neural networks.

Our approach has been to study small networks consisting of two or three interconnected neurons. We use systems of chaotic equations to model the activation functions of the neurons. Our method for the control of chaos is based on that presented by Kittel *et al* (1996) and Pyragas (1992).

2   Controlling Chaos Using Delays

Pyragas' delayed feedback method of controlling chaos assumes that we have a continuous time system which has an output variable, say $y(t)$, that can be measured, and an input signal, $F(t)$:

$$\frac{dy}{dt} = P(y, \mathbf{x}) + F(t)$$
$$\frac{d\mathbf{x}}{dt} = \mathbf{Q}(y, \mathbf{x})$$

(1)

Here, $P(y,x)$ and $Q(y,x)$, which govern the chaotic dynamics of the system, and **x**, which denotes all of the remaining system variables, are assumed to be unknown. When the control signal $F(t)$ is zero, the system (1) is governed by a chaotic attractor.

The input signal $F(t)$ is proportional to the difference between the value of y at time t and the value of y at time $t - \tau$, where τ is a fixed delay:

$$F(t) = K[y(t) - y(t-\tau)] \tag{2}$$

Input signal $F(t)$ attempts to nudge the system back to a state in which output variable y repeats the same value it had at the earlier time specified by the delay τ. In this way, $F(t)$ encourages the system to follow a periodic trajectory with periodicity τ (Figure 3).

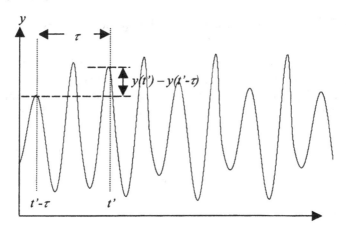

Figure 3 A sample time series in y with the time delay τ superimposed

As the system approaches the periodic trajectory, $F(t)$ will become very small. Figure 4 shows a time series for the Rössler system. The controlling input signal is initially zero and the system follows its chaotic attractor for a period of time. When the input signal is activated the system quickly converges to a period one UPO. Figure 4 shows a burst of activity in $F(t)$ which the system is brought under control. Subsequently, as the system moves into the UPO, $F(t)$ becomes very small.

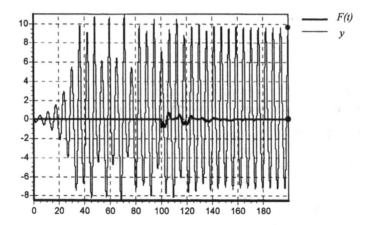

Figure 4 Time series plot for one of the Rössler equation variables, superimposed on a plot of $F(t)$

UPOs of varying periods and periodicities can be controlled by this method. Some UPOs are very unstable and require a greater amount of control than others, resulting in an input signal which does not tend towards zero. Furthermore, this control method is sensitive to the choice of τ and K: UPOs cannot be stabilised for several sub-ranges of values of these control variables.

We have adapted this method of delayed feedback control so that the time delay τ is not constant, but is a variable of the system whose value is determined in a self-organised manner. Before describing in detail this method of dynamically adapting the delay time, we will consider the Biological justification for adopting such an approach.

3   Biological Rationale for Adaptive Delays

In Biological neuronal systems, the action potentials generated by the soma of a neuron travel the length of the axon and are transmitted to other neurons via synaptic connections. In most cases these synapses are located on the dendritic trees of the receiving neurons. Impulses from synapses will cause a sharp rise in the intercellular voltage of the receiving neuron which spreads along the dendritic tree towards the soma. If the voltage rise is sufficiently high at the soma as a result of integrating all inputs on the dendrite, an action potential is generated to travel down the axon of this neuron. Therefore, whenever an action potential is generated, it takes time for the impulse to travel to the soma of the receiving neurons. Figure 5 illustrates this schematically.

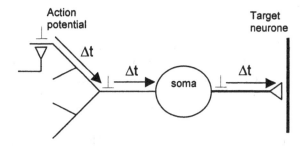

Figure 5 A schematic diagram of the delay between the initiation of an action potential, and its arrival a the target neuron

Typically, a neuron will have many synaptic connections with the dendritic tree of a receiving neuron. Since each of these connections will be located at a different point on the dendrite, and so each will result in a different time delay for the signals between the sending and receiving neuron (Figure 6). According to Hebb (Hebb, 1948), those synapses which result in an action potential in the receiving neuron are strengthened, those which do not are weakened. A single impulse from a synapse is rarely sufficient to cause a cell to fire. It is more often the case that several coincident impulses from synapses are needed to provoke a response. This means that those synapses which result in impulses that are appropriately timed will be strengthened. In other words, the adaptive process involves not only the selection of synapses, but also the selection of impulse delays. The method of chaos control we present below is based on this principle of adaptation of delays.

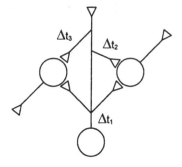

Figure 6 A schematic diagram of multiple delayed connections between neurons

4   Adaptive Delays

We have modified Pyragas' method of chaos control so that the length of the feedback delay τ is a variable of the system. We have made τ proportional to the amount of effort needed to control the system in its current orbit. If the amount of control is small, then no change is required in τ, since an orbit with a suitable delay has been successfully stabilised. However, if the system is struggling to control an orbit, then τ needs to be modified so that the length feedback delay is commensurate with an existing UPO of the system. The equation for adapting τ is as follows:

$$\frac{d\tau}{dt} = \alpha F \frac{dy}{dt} \qquad (3)$$

Where a is a constant. Equation (3) will be minimised when F becomes small and dy/dt is periodic.

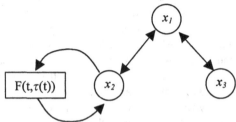

Figure 7. A three unit model with delayed feedback and external input.

We have applied this method to the Rössler system of equations (Rössler 1976). We have modelled these equations using a small network of neurons (Figure 7) whose activations are defined as follows:

$$\frac{dx_1}{dt} = w_{12}x_2 + w_{13}x_3 \qquad (4)$$

$$\frac{dx_2}{dt} = w_{21}x_1 + w_{22}x_2 + F(t, \tau) \qquad (5)$$

$$\frac{dx_3}{dt} = v + x_3 x_1 + w_{33}x_3 \qquad (6)$$

Where w_{ij} is the weight to unit i from unit j. The weights prior to adaptation in this system are given in Table 1 and correspond to the constants used in the Rössler system.

Weight	Value
w12	-1
w13	-1
w21	1
w22	0.2
w33	-5.7
v	0.2

Table 1 Weights for the Rössler system

The control of this systems is achieved through the rightmost term in equation (5), as defined by equations (2) and (3).

In this paper we present the results of a set of experiments we ran the model on a range of initial values for τ. The purpose of these experiments was to see if equation (3) would be able to adapt τ towards a nearby controllable orbit. In each experiment, the model was allowed to follow its chaotic attractor until $t = 100$, at which point the control was activated using one of the initial values of τ. The results of these experiments are given in Table 2. The initial values for τ range from 4 to 20, increasing in steps of 2. In 6 out of 9 of these initial values the system managed to adapt τ to a delay value which corresponded to a UPO. Apart from experiment 4 in which τ went negative, the final values of τ for these stabilised UPOs were ~5.83 for a period 1 UPO and ~11.72 for a period 2 UPO. These values are in close agreement with the results obtained by Pyragas (1992) which were 5.9 for a period 1 UPO and 11.75 for a period 2 UPO.

Experiment No.	Initial tau	Final tau	Max F	Min F	UPO Period
1	4	5.83	0.01	-0.01	1
2	6	17.46	1.0	-1.1	-
3	8	5.84	0.01	-0.01	1
4	10	-25.60	0.9	-0.9	1
5	12	11.66	0.01	-0.01	2
6	14	11.76	0.03	-0.03	2
7	16	17.54	0.8	-0.8	-
8	18	23.53	0.8	-0.8	-
9	20	11.72	0.06	-0.04	2

Table 2 Results for Experiment 1

Table 2 shows the maximum and minimum values of $F(t, \tau)$ when a UPO was stabilised. Small values of Max F and Min F indicate that very little effort was required to keep the system in that UPO. Note that for those experiments which did not result in a stabilised orbit (experiments 2, 7 and 8) $F(t, \tau)$ fluctuates over a

70

relatively wide range of values, indicating that the system is struggling to gain control of the orbit. Graphs 1, 3 and 5 show time series plots of $F(t, \tau)$ and τ for experiments 1, 5 and 7 respectively. Graphs 2, 4 and 6 show the state space in the x_1 vs. x_2 plane.

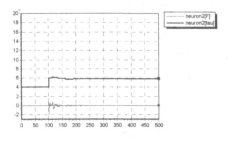

Graph 1 $F(t, \tau)$ and τ for experiment 1

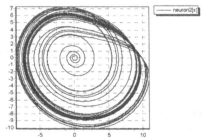

Graph 2 state space for experiment 1

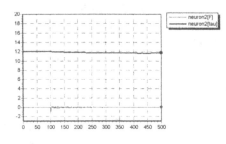

raph 3 $F(t, \tau)$ and τ for experiment 5

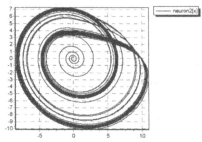

Graph 4 state space for experiment 5

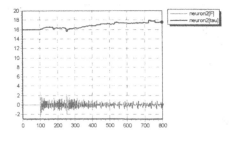

Graph 5 $F(t, \tau)$ and τ for experiment 7

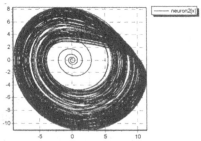

Graph 6 state space for experiment 7

Graph 1 shows that τ immediately jumps from 4 to a value close to 5.9 as soon as the control is activated at $t = 100$. This is in response to large fluctuations in $F(t, \tau)$. Once τ is close to the periodicity of the UPO at 5.9, only small adjustments are made to its value until it reaches a steady state at 5.83 where the period 1 orbit has been stabilised. Graph 3 shows τ starting at a value of 12 and dropping steadily to the nearby UPO at 11.66. $F(t, \tau)$ does not need to exert much control over the system to maintain this period 2 orbit. Graph 5 shows the time series for $F(t, \tau)$ and τ for experiment 7, where the delayed feedback was not able to bring the system under control for any orbit, even on an extended run up to $t = 800$. As this graph shows, τ does not show any signs of approaching a steady state.

5   Discussion

We have presented a first step towards developing a chaotic neural network which is able to select internal dynamic states in response to external input in a self-organised manner. Our results indicate that for the Rössler system it is possible to devise a method of chaos control which self-selects values for τ corresponding to the nearest UPO which can be stabilised with relatively small fluctuations in the feedback signal $F(t, \tau)$. If the initial value of τ is made proportional to the "value" of the external input signal, then the system would move into a UPO corresponding to a recognition state for that input value.

The results for the Rössler system show some promise. However, we have tried the same method on other chaotic models with less success. We have experimented with both Lorenz (1963) and Duffing equations, and have found that $F(t, \tau)$ does not reduce to a small range of values around 0. In both cases it seems that a strong feedback signal is required to maintain a UPO within the attractor. Furthermore, equation (3) is unable to find a steady state and continues to wander over a wide range values. It is possible that the reason that our experiment worked so well had more to do with the specific properties of the Rössler equations than of chaos in general. However, we believe that the underlying principle of adaptive feedback delay periods is a promising area of research in the context of chaotic neural networks. We are currently experimenting with other models which use adaptive feedback delay periods to select UPOs. These models focus on the adaptation of the K parameter, which is the weighting of the delayed feedback signal.

72

References

Ditto, W.L., Rauseo, S.N. & Spano, M.L. (1990). Experimental control of chaos. *Physical Review Letters* **65**, 3211-3214.

Freeman, W.J. (1985). Strange attractors in the olfactory system of rabbits. *Electroencephalography And Clinical Neurophysiology* **61**, S155-S155

Freeman, W.J. (1994). Neural networks and chaos. *J.Theor.Biol.* **171**, 13-18.

Garfinkel, A., Spano, M.L., Ditto, W.L. & Weiss, J.N. (1992). Controlling cardiac chaos. *Science* **257**, 1230-1235.

Guevara, M.R., Glass, L., Mackey, M.C. & Shrier, A. (1983). Chaos in neurobiology. *IEEE Transactions on systems, man and cybernetics* **SMC-13**, 790-798.

Hebb, D.O. (1948). *The Organization of Behaviour: A Neurophysiological Theory,* John Wileym New York.

Kittel, A., Popp, M., Parisi, J. and Pyragas, K. (1996) Control of Chaos by Self-Adapted Delayed Feedback. Lect. Notes Phys. 976: 239 – 247.

Lorenz, E.N. (1963). Deterministic nonperiodic flow. *J. Atmos. Sci.* **20**, 130-41.

Lourenco C. & Babloyantz A. (1996). Control of spatiotemporal chaos in neuronal networks. *Int.J.Neural Syst.* **7**, 507-517.

Olde Scheper, T. (1995) Application of Chaos analysis on patient EEG. 1995. University of Utrecht. 9-30-1995. Ref Type: Thesis/Dissertation

Pyragas, K. (1992). Continuous control of chaos by self-controlling feedback. *Phys. Lett.*, **170A**, 421-428.

Rössler, O.E. (1976). *Phys. Lett. A 57 397.*

Shinbrot, T., Ditto, W.L., Grebogi, C., Ott, E., Spano, M.L. & Yorke, J.A. (1992). Using the sensitive dependence of chaos (the "butterfly effect") to direct trajectories in an experimental chaotic system. *Physical Review Letters* **68**, 2863-2866.

Shinbrot, T., Grebogi, C., Ott, E. & Yorke, J.A. (1993). Using small perturbations to control chaos. *Nature* **363**, 411-417.

Tsuda, I., Koerner, E. & Shimizu, H. (1987). Memory dynamics in asynchronous neural networks. *Progress Of Theoretical Physics* **78**, 51-71.

Tsuda, I. (1992). Dynamic link of memory - chaotic memory map in nonequilibrium neural networks. *Neural Networks* **5**, 313-326.s

Tsuda, I. (1996). A new-type of self-organization associated with chaotic dynamics in neural networks. *International Journal Of Neural Systems* **7**, 451-459..

A Neural Network Phoneme Classification Based on Wavelet Features

O. Farooq & S. Datta

Department of Electronic and Electrical Engineering

Loughborough University

Loughborough LE11 3TU UK

o.farooq@lboro.ac.uk & s.datta@lboro.ac.uk

Summary

This paper presents the use of discrete wavelet transform for feature extraction of phoneme. Instead of using the conventional wavelet coefficients, energy per sample is calculated in different frequency bands and used as features. Training and test samples of the phonemes were obtained from the TIMIT database from the dialect region DR1 and DR2. Features extracted were updated every 8ms to account for the non-stationary property of the speech signal. For the classification of the phonemes two different classifiers were used based on Linear Discriminant Analysis (LDA) and Multi-Layer Perceptron (MLP). The results obtained show high speaker independent recognition rate by both the classifiers. The recognition rates obtained by using MLP classifier were found to be about 3-10% higher than the LDA for different number of features.

Keywords: Feature extraction, Wavelet transform, Multi-Layer Perceptron

1   Introduction

Automatic speech recognition has made considerable progress from its early days. Today they are capable of recognising tens of thousands of words and fast decoding algorithms allow continuous speech recognition in near real time. Major part of this success is due to the recent advances in language modelling and search techniques. However, not much progress has been made in the area of feature extraction. A number of feature extraction techniques such as filter bank amplitude, linear prediction followed by perceptual weighting, Fast Fourier Transform (FFT) power spectrum etc have also been used, but the cepstral analysis and its time derivative still remains the most commonly used. These features are calculated by taking the Discrete Cosine Transform (DCT) of the log of energy at the output of a mel filter. As the features are based on Fourier Transform, they inherit its time frequency limitation as well. Due to this reason classification of some phonemes is difficult using these features. More recently Discrete Wavelet Transform (DWT) [1], [3], [6], [7] has been tried for feature extraction owing to its multi-resolution capabilities. The features offer advantage of picking up high frequency from a slowly varying signal but it also suffers with a problem of shift variance. A small shift in the signal causes large difference in the features extracted. In this paper we propose a feature extraction technique based on DWT which is shift invariant and test its performance by using LDA and MLP classifiers.

2 Wavelet Transform

Fourier analysis assumes that the signal is stationary during the entire time, however, for the case of speech signal it is not true. Thus for the speech signal a windowed version of data is used for processing with the assumption of stationarity during this period. This is known as Short Time Fourier Transform (STFT). If the window duration is chosen small then the frequency resolution is poor (although high time resolution is achieved); increasing the window duration gives an opposite effect. Since the window size is fixed the time frequency resolution achieved by STFT is also fixed. To overcome the problem of fixed resolution Wavelet Transform uses an adaptive window size which allocates more time to the lower frequencies and less time for the higher frequencies [5]. The filters used for Wavelet Transform have higher time resolution at higher central frequency of the filter. By using these filters, two very short bursts can be separated in time by going to the higher frequency. Therefore, this analysis can be used for the signals, which have short duration high frequency components and long duration low frequency components (e.g. speech signal). All the filters are scaled version of a prototype filter $\psi(t)$ (also known as the mother wavelet) given by:

$$\psi_a(t) = a^{-1/2}\psi(t/a) \qquad \psi \in L^2 \ (L^2 \text{ is a finite energy space}) \qquad (1)$$

where 'a' is the scaling factor and $a^{-1/2}$ is used for energy normalisation. The Continuous Wavelet Transform (CWT) of a signal $x(t)$ (where $x \in L^2$) is given by:

$$CWT(\tau, a) = a^{-1/2}\int x(t).\psi^*((t-\tau)/a)dt \qquad (2)$$

The parameter 'τ' and '**a**' is called translation and scaling parameters respectively. The scaling parameter '**a**' gives the width of the wavelet and τ gives the position.

Typically CWT is over-complete and an appropriate sampling may be used to eliminate the redundancy. A Dyadic DWT can be obtained as:

$$C(j,k) = 2^{-j/2} \sum_{i} x(i)\psi(2^{-j}i - k) \tag{3}$$

$$x(i) = 2^{-j/2} \sum_{j} \sum_{k} C(j,k)\psi(2^{-j}i - k) \tag{4}$$

where i, j and k are integers.

3 Feature Extraction

Earlier techniques have also used wavelet transforms for feature extraction [1], [6], [7]. In these techniques only the wavelet coefficients were used as features. However, as the DWT is shift variant, these features are not very reliable and would require additional processing for shift adjustment. Here in this work we assume that the phonemes are available after the segmentation of the speech samples. By decomposing the segmented phoneme once using a dyadic DWT the frequency spectrum is split into two equal halves (a lower frequency band and a higher frequency band). To start with a three level decomposition of the phoneme is done by using 'Daubechies 6' wavelet filter [2]. As the sampling frequency of the speech signal is 16kHz the frequency bands obtained after decomposition are 0-1kHz, 1-2kHz, 2-4kHz and 4-8kHz. A frame of 32ms (512 samples for 16 kHz sampling) is formed for the analysis of the phoneme. As the speech signal is stationary for the duration of about 10ms (due to physical limitation in the movement of articulators for speech production), thus to have details of variation in the signal the frame is further divided into sub-frames. Since the signal of dyadic length is more suitable so sub-frames of 8ms duration are used [1]. This results into four sub-frames in 32ms duration. Wavelet decomposition of the sub-frame samples is then carried out and energy of the wavelet coefficients in each frequency band is calculated. This energy is normalised by the number of samples in the band thereby giving an average energy per sample in each band [3]. The normalisation is essential because each band will have different number of samples. A three level decomposition of a sub-frame will give four features, thus over the 32ms phoneme duration there will be a total of 16 features. The level of decomposition was increased to 7 giving the lowest frequency band of 0-62.5Hz. Any further decomposition is not expected to improve upon the recognition performance, as very low frequency content will be insignificant. The features extracted on a sub-frame basis not only gives the energy in band but also gives an idea of how the energy in each band varies with time (temporal variation).

4 Experiments and Results

TIMIT [4] database was used and three vowel phonemes (/aa/, /ax/ & /iy/) from the dialect region DR1 (New England region) and DR2 (Northern part of USA) were extracted for training and testing the classifier. A total of 151 speakers were used out of which 114 were used for training and the rest for testing the classifier. There were 49 female speakers in all, out of which 37 speakers were used for training the classifier. As there is no overlap in the data for training and testing the recognition achieved is essentially speaker independent. For the classification a Linear Discriminant Analysis (LDA) [7] and Multi-layer Perceptron (MLP) classifier were used. LDA is a transform-based method, which tries to minimise the ratio of within-class scatter to the between-class scatter. A simple MLP classifier with one hidden layer and an output layer was simulated. The number of nodes in the output layer was chosen to be equal to the number of classes (three) and eight hidden nodes were chosen. More than 2000 phoneme samples were used for training the network using the Levenberg–Marquardt backpropagation. The performance was tested by using about 900 phoneme samples. The recognition performance achieved by using the energy coefficients per sample is found to be quite high even for a very small number of features. Also by using these features the phonemes can be better recognised even in the presence of time shift. To have finer resolution the phonemes were further decomposed by discrete wavelet transform to level 4, 5, 6 and 7, thereby, giving 5, 6, 7, and 8 features per sub-frame respectively. The percentage recognition obtained by having four sub-frames in a 32ms duration with 4, 5, 6, 7, and 8 features per sub-frame is shown in Figure 1.

The recognition rate improved initially with the increase in number of features for the LDA classifier but it reduced later (see Figure 1). This may be attributed to the fact that larger features result into a higher dimensional space that may not be very well linearly separable. Due to this fact the linear decision boundary in LDA cannot classify effectively for large number of features, while MLP which can have a non-linear decision boundary has an improvement in the performance with the increase in the features.

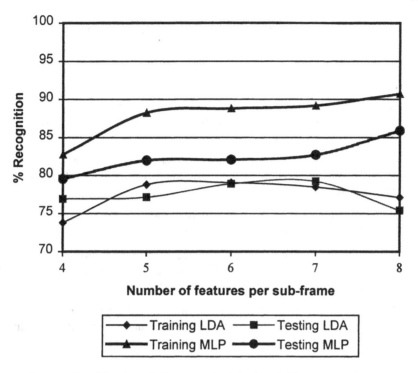

Figure 1 Classification of phonemes /aa/, /ax/ & /iy/ by LDA and MLP

5   Conclusion

The features obtained by using the wavelet transform show higher recognition rate using a MLP classifier for all set of features as expected. The results also show that wavelet transform can be effectively used for the extraction of features for speaker independent phoneme recognition. Partitioning the frames into sub-intervals takes care of the dynamic nature of speech. A good recognition rate can be achieved for a very small number of features.

6   References

1.   Beng T. Tan, Minyue Fu, Andrew Spray & Phillip Dermody, "The use of wavelet transform for phoneme recognition", Proceeding of 4th Int. Conf. of

Spoken Language Processing Philadelphia, USA Oct. 3-6 1996, Vol. 4, pp. 2431-2434.

2. Stéphane Mallat, "A wavelet tour of signal processing", Academic Press, 1998.

3. Sungwook Chang, Y. Kwon & Sung-il Yang, "Speech feature extracted from adaptive wavelet for speech recognition", Electronic Letters, Vol. 34, No. 23, 12th Nov. 1998, pp. 2211-2213.

4. TIMIT Acoustic-Phonetic Continuous Speech Corpus, National Institute of Standards and Technology, Speech Disc 1-1.1, Oct. 1990, NTIS Order No. PB91-505065.

5. Olivier Rioul & Martin Vetterli, "Wavelet and signal processing", IEEE Signal Processing Mag., Oct. 1991, pp. 14-38.

6. C. J. Long & S. Datta, "Wavelet based feature extraction for phoneme recognition", Proc. of 4th Int. Conf. of Spoken Language Processing Philadelphia, USA Oct. 3-6 1996, Vol. 1, pp. 264-267.

7. C. J. Long & S. Datta, "Discriminant wavelet basis construction for speech recognition", Proc. of 5th Int. Conf. of Spoken Language Processing Sydney, Australia 30th Nov-4th Dec. 1998, Vol. 3, pp. 1047-1049.

Fuzzy Symptoms and a Decision Support Index for the Early Diagnosis of Confusable Diseases

P. R. Innocent

Centre for Computational Intelligence
Computer Science Department
De Montfort University
Leicester, UK

Abstract: This paper describes an extension to a computationally fast and simple procedure that produces an index of support for the diagnosis of diseases. The extension allows the specification of fuzzy symptoms by using fuzzy relations to determine a symptom's strength based on observed intensity and certainty of duration. We begin by briefly considering the context of use of the process and then go on to formally describe the fuzzy approach and the algorithm that produces the improved index. Finally, we show how the improved index values relate to two confusable diseases given a range of symptom strengths.

Keywords: Lightweight, Fuzzy , Medical Diagnosis

1 Introduction

In primary health care, a medical physician may have to deal with a small but important number of cases where relatively rare life threatening diseases (such as meningitis) can be confused with relatively common non-threatening diseases (such as the common cold) in their early stages. In such cases, it is dangerous to let a disease progress to a point where it can be unambiguously diagnosed or to wait for the results of detailed clinical tests. There are a number of non-exclusive approaches to decision support in these situations.

The general problem with building decision support systems is data acquisition. We would like to have exact or crisp knowledge of well defined symptoms relating to all patients with well defined confirmed diseases. There are a number of problems with this on both a theoretical and practical basis. First, the actual occurrence or non-occurrence of a symptom is not in reality a crisp event. Patients suffer from a symptom to some degree (e.g. severe, mild, etc.) over an ill defined period (e.g. 'for about 2 days last week'). Secondly, the degree to which a patient suffers a disease is to some extent dependant on the patient's state of health and the cause(s) of the disease. Clearly, somehow a physician takes these into account when making a diagnosis using a hypothetico-deductive method.

In these circumstances, a fuzzy approach is better suited to a decision support process than a crisp one and in our earlier work [2] we presented a simple algorithm which processed crisp symptom information using a fuzzy knowledge base. In this paper we extend this work to allow fuzzy symptom information to be processed using the algorithm. We therefore start by reviewing the basis of the support index presented in [2], then presenting our new algorithm and finally showing some results of applying it.

1.1 Overview Of Knowledge Representation

In our approach, the temporal knowledge base relating the class of disease (D) to the general symptom set (S) uses fuzzy representations of time information [5] since we commonly find linguistic descriptions such as :
'fever usually develops between the 3rd and 4th day of influenza and lasts for approximately 3 days'.
By using a linguistic translation, we use the causal relevance term 'always' to be synonymous with 'usually' and use fuzzy sets for the time information. This may be represented using fuzzy set notation as:
'Influenza (always) causes fever at time "fever_set" '
where "fever_set" is a convex fuzzy set represented in Fig. 1 in discrete form over a 14 day period since onset of a disease.

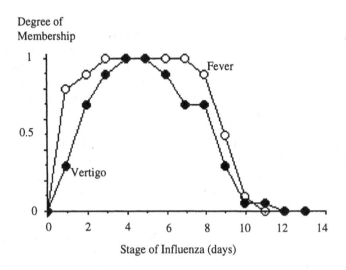

Fig. 1. Fuzzy Sets for 2 symptoms of Influenza.

The interpretation of these sets is that they define the possibility distribution of the intervals of time within which a symptom may be observed assuming that onset is on day zero. They should not be interpreted to mean that a symptom occurs to a particular degree at a particular time. Thus a symptom observation is crisp in its duration and starting time. For example, a graphic representation of the fuzzy sets for influenza with example common symptoms of vertigo and fever is shown in Fig 1. The degree of membership of the set of possibilities for the observation of vertigo when the patient has influenza at day 1 after onset is 0.3. These values have been estimated after interaction with medical expertise as an exercise to demonstrate the approach. The first and last indices of the non-zero membership grade of the fuzzy set, Q, has special significance for the computation of our support index and is denoted by ^{low}Q (e.g. day 1 in Fig.1 for vertigo) and ^{high}Q (e.g. day 11 in Fig.1 for vertigo) respectively.

1.2 Fuzzy Temporal Inference

Diseases (which are not fuzzy) are said to start on day 0 (onset) although a symptom may not be observable until after this day. The basic goal of the inference engine is to establish the stage of a disease at the current day given observations of symptoms in the crisp form:

'Symptom occurred from M days ago up to and including N days ago'.

where M>N>=0. A value of 0 is interpreted to mean the current day.

e.g. 'fever started 3 days ago and is still present' is represented as :

'fever occurred during time interval (3,0)'

We place the observed symptom into the history and estimation of the current disease by checking to see if the observed symptom duration is possible in Q and, if so, determining the lower and upper boundaries of the position of the current day in Q for each symptom expected for each disease. The lower boundary is set to be ^{low}Q. The upper boundary is the result of a simple search for the best fit of the observed symptom interval into the full range of possible intervals. Observation of another causally relevant symptom for the disease under test produces another set of boundaries and these are combined with the older estimate using fuzzy min/max operators. If this combination results in a null interval, then we assume that the temporal dependencies for that disease are not fulfilled. Otherwise, we have a revised estimate of the upper and lower boundaries of the current day for that disease. This is repeated for all observed symptoms for each disease. The outcome of this process is an estimate of the stage of each disease presented as the interval $T_{stage}^{D_j} = [null_{low}^{D_j}, null_{high}^{D_j}]$, where $null_{low}^{D_j}$ is the lower bound and $null_{high}^{D_j}$ is the upper bound for the day of the jth disease, D_j, since onset. This information is then used together with the known disease/symptom profiles to provide clinical decision support information.

2 Clinical Decision Support Information

In order to provide diagnostic information, we now use the estimated stages of each disease and the causal relevance labels (always, normally, often, sometimes, never) to compute an estimate of 'goodness of fit' called an index of support (Support) for each disease. This uses a centre of gravity (cog) approach applied to all the sets of all the symptoms causally associated with a disease.

2.1 Computation of a Decision Support Index

Suppose the ith symptom, S_i, was observed in time interval $\Delta T_s = [t_i^{low}, t_i^{high}]$, and is causally related to the disease D_j. We now use ΔT_s in the appropriate temporal fuzzy set, $Q_i^j[t]$, (which is diagrammatically represented in Fig. 1 for example) for calculating the support for the particular disease, D_j. The causal relevance (CR) of the symptom, S_i, to the disease D_j is a linguistic term.

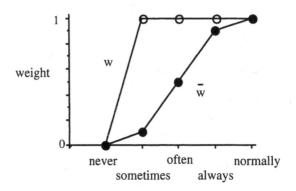

Fig.2. Causal relevance to weight relation.

For our computational purposes, we translate CR into a numeric weight, w_i^j, for symptoms which have been observed and are expected (see Fig. 2). The non-observation of an expected symptom, S_k, implies that the disease is not supported.

For each disease, we now compute an index based on the centre of gravity ('cog') of the combined sets derived from the expected symptoms for that disease and the observed symptom information. For a particular disease, D_j, we take each causally relevant symptom associated with it in turn and compute a weighted sum from the possibility distributions using time interval and causal relevance weightings. The index, F_j^+, is computed using all the expected symptoms which have been observed (denoted by 'm') and hence support D_j. F_j^+ is computed using (1) where Δt_i is the interval $[(\text{null}_{low}^{Dj}+t_i^{low})$, $(\text{null}_{high}^{Dj}+t_i^{high})]$.

$$F_j^+ = \frac{\sum_{i=1}^{m} \left(w_i^j * \frac{\int Q_i^j(t)dt}{\Delta t_i} \right)}{\sum_{i=1}^{m} w_i^j} \tag{1}$$

Similarly, the index for evidence against, F_j^-, a particular disease D_j is given in (5) where there are 'n' unobserved but expected symptoms. As before, for our computational purposes, we translate CR into a numeric weight, $\overline{w}_i^j$, for symptoms which have not been observed (see Fig. 2). F_j^- may be computed using (2) where ΔT_k is the interval from $\min(\text{null}_{low}^{Dj}, {}^{low}Q_k^j)$ up to $\min(\text{null}_{high}^{Dj}, {}^{high}Q_k^j)$.

$$F_j^- = \frac{\sum_{k=1}^{n} \left(\overline{w}_k^j * \frac{\int Q_k^j(t)dt}{\Delta T} \right)}{\sum_{k=1}^{n} \overline{w}_k^j} \tag{2}$$

where the integration of the possibility distributions, $Q(t)$, is evaluated within the appropriate boundaries using discrete set form.

F_j^+ is clearly analogous to the conditional probability for D_j given the observation of the set of m symptoms $\{S_i(\Delta T_s)\}$. F_j^- is clearly analogous to the conditional probability for $\overline{D}_j$ given the absence of set of n symptoms $\{S_k(\Delta T)\}$. F_j^+ and F_j^- do not obey the laws of probability, however, and are now weighted, combined and normalised into an index, 'Support$_j$', using (3) which indicates the overall degree of support for a particular disease D_j given 'm' observed symptoms and 'n' unobserved symptoms expected for that disease. The computation of Support$_j$ is analogous to combining the conditional probabilities.

$$\text{Support}_j = \frac{(\sum_{i=1}^{m} w_i^j)*F_j^+ + (\sum_{k=1}^{n} \bar{w}_k^j)*(1-F_j^-)}{(\sum_{i=1}^{m} w_i^j) + (\sum_{k=1}^{n} \bar{w}_k^j)} \tag{3}$$

2.2 Extending the index to include fuzzy symptom observations

There are a number of possible ways to introduce the idea of fuzzy observed symptoms into our work. The simplest method is to allow the symptoms to be defined at a higher linguistic granularity, such as:

'(high) fever occurred during (approximate) time interval (3,0)'

This must then be treated as a different symptom from:

'(mild) fever occurred during (exact) time interval (3,0)'

If we use this approach, then for every disease, and for all variations of fever and duration, there must be a set of temporal possibilities ($Q(t)$) and causal relevance's generated as in Fig. 1. This is a major knowledge acquisition and user interface problem and we propose an alternative approach.

In this paper we propose introducing the concept of the 'strength' (P_i) of the ith observed symptom. We allow our strength values to be in the range [0,1] and use particular strength values of particular observed symptoms to modify the computation of F_j^+ as given in (4).

$$F_j^+ = \frac{\sum_{i=1}^{m} (w_i^j * P_i * \int_{\Delta t_j} Q_i^j(t)dt)}{\sum_{i=1}^{m} w_i^j} \tag{4}$$

The computation of the index of support then continues as before using (3).

3 Estimating Symptom Strength

The strength of an observed symptom depends on a number of factors. In this paper we define strength in terms of an assumed relationship with the observability (O) of a symptom as in Fig 3. Thus weakly observable symptoms have a low strength. The relationship between O and P is assumed linear above a particular threshold in this work. Future work can tune this relationship appropriately using feedback from actual cases.

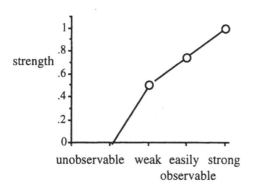

Obervability of a symptom

Fig.3. The assumed relationship between strength and observability of a symptom

Observability is assumed to be dependant on the intensity(I) and the certainty of the duration(D) of the observed symptom. We assume that both of these attributes are fuzzy in nature since they are usually reported from the recollections of patients. If crisp information from test results is known, it would have a maximum strength value.

To determine the observability (and hence strength) we propose simple fuzzy relations of the form shown in Fig. 4 where I ={low, medium, high} and D ={ low, medium, high} and O={weak, easy, strong}.

Thus, for a given symptom, we require the user to provide an estimate of the intensity and duration certainty as well as the duration. e.g.

(high) fever occurred during (low certainty) interval (3,0)

This statement is treated as if it were:

(easily observable) fever occurred during interval (3,0)

and hence translated as:

fever occurred during interval (3,0) with strength 0.75

Clearly this method requires development of the appropriate relations and it may be possible to develop Type 2 rules from these relations which would allow greater precision in estimating the strength of a symptom.

		easy	strong	strong
	high			
Intensity	medium	weak	easy	strong
	low	weak	weak	easy
		low	medium	high

Duration certainty

Fig.4. Observability as a function of the intensity and certainty of duration of a symptom

4 Results

A series of simple tests was made with the prototype which implemented the ideas presented above for the diseases of influenza and scarlet fever since the disease histories are well known and readily available in, for example, [6].

This results in about 60 different symptoms and about 90 different symptom descriptions in a data base where each symptom is related to a temporal fuzzy set description for each disease. We wished to show how the support index changes as symptom information is collected in the early stages (i.e. the first few days since onset) of a disease and then how the symptom strength affects the index.

In all the tests, we entered symptom observations in the same order and with the same temporal details (all symptoms started X days ago and are still present where X varied from 1 to 3). The symptoms and ordering was based on what would be ideally expected for the disease of influenza as shown in Table 1 for that disease.

Symptom		Causal relevance to:	
Index	Description	Influenza	Scarlet Fever
1	fever	always	always
2	headache	always	sometimes
3	vertigo	always	never
4	hills	always	sometimes
5	back pains	always	sometimes
6	muscle pains	normally	never
7	collapse	sometimes	never
8	cough	often	never
9	running eyes	often	never
10	running nose	often	never
11	sore throat	often	normally

Table 1. Symptom descriptions and ordering

4.1 Time Sensitivity Test

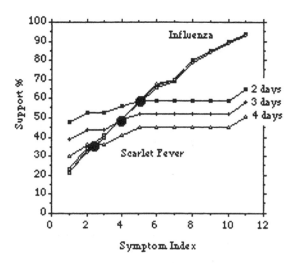

Fig. 5 Confusability as a function of symptom duration

Fig. 5 shows the sensitivity of the support index values for influenza and scarlet fever to full strength (high intensity, zero uncertainty) symptoms when the duration is varied from 2 to 4 days. The graphs indicate that influenza support is less sensitive than scarlet fever and that as the duration of the symptom increases, so the support for scarlet fever is reduced. Fig. 5 also shows we get single crossover points indicating when the support for a particular disease exceeds the other. For example, if the symptoms have been present at full strength for 4 days, we can predict that influenza is the most likely disease (has more support) after the presentation of just 3 symptoms. If the symptoms are present for 3 days, then we require 4 symptoms and for just 2 days then we require 5 symptoms. However, the values of the support index do not approach maximum for influenza until all causally relevant symptoms are present. Before these minimal numbers of symptoms are observed, we may infer incorrectly that the disease is likely to be scarlet fever. i.e. The diseases are confused with each other. However, because the symptoms are all at full strength and the same duration, the pattern is linear with one cross over point for each duration.

4.2 Strength Sensitivity Test

We fix the duration so all symptoms started 3 days ago and are still present and fix the strength of all the symptoms to be the same. Figures 6 and 7 shows the results of computing the support index for influenza and scarlet fever with different fixed strengths of 0.5 (weakly observable), 0.75 (easily observable) and 1.0 (strongly observable).

It is clear that the strength of an observed symptom has a large effect on influenza support since every observed symptom is deliberately causally relevant in this test whereas this is not true for scarlet fever. The effect is to move the crossover points from 4 symptoms at full strength (1.0) so that they are at 5 symptoms (0.75 strength) and 8 symptoms (0.5 strength). This is a larger effect than for time differences and has to be validated in a real context.

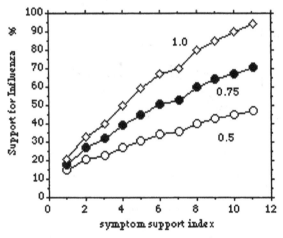

Fig. 6 Support for influenza as a function of symptom strength

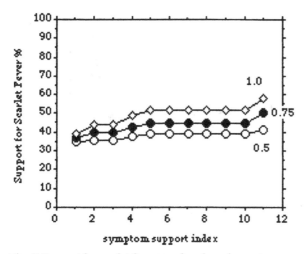

Fig. 7 Support for scarlet fever as a function of symptom strength

Fig. 9 shows perhaps a more realistic possibility for a differential diagnosis based on the support index. It is constructed from an artificially generated pattern of symptoms of different strength (see Fig. 9). Fig. 9 shows that up to symptom 5, we prefer scarlet fever over influenza, then from symptom 6 to 8 the reverse is true. At symptom 9, there is no difference, then for one symptom we marginally favour scarlet fever before symptom 11 tells us that we should prefer influenza. Since the observer has control over the order and how many symptoms are observed and their strength, the pattern is likely to be complicated and reinforces the notion that the method proposed here should be embedded in an expert system which provides suitable context and advice for its use.

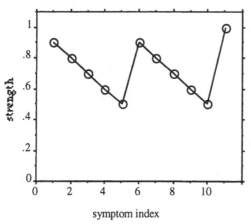

Fig. 8   Possible profile of symptom strength

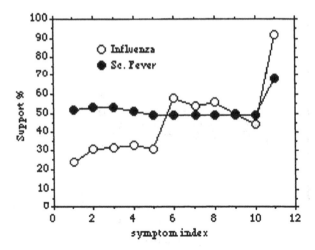

Fig. 9 Support for diseases given strength profile from Fig. 8

5 Conclusion

This paper has outlined the principles, existing work and possible future research and development of soft computing in a clinical diagnostic application. We have successfully demonstrated our simple approach although we have yet to formally evaluate it in context. There are obvious problems such as the exact definitions of the fuzzy relations between symptom observability and intensity and duration uncertainty and the relation between observability and strength. There is a great deal of exploration necessary in this area relating to knowledge acquisition which may be enhanced by recent advances in Soft Computing especially Type 2 fuzzy sets and learning algorithms.

Finally, we are aware of the difficulties of explanation of the index and guidance in assessing symptom observability for a physician. We would expect this lightweight fuzzy process to be embedded within a larger system (expert system or similar) within which some explanation and guidance capability exists and which would make use of the closure information.

Acknowledgement

Mr. T. Goeckler, for developing prototype temporal fuzzy reasoning programs and implementing the basic ideas in this paper.

References

1. F. Steimann "Fuzzy set theory in Medicine". *Artificial Intelligence in Medicine,* Vol. 11, pp1-7,. 1997.

2. P.R.Innocent A Lightweight Fuzzy Process to support Early Diagnosis of Confusable Diseases Using Causation and Time Relationships. FUZZIEEE2000, May 2000, San Antonio, Texas. In Press.

3. E.T. Keravnou "Temporal Reasoning in Medicine". *Artificial Intelligence in Medicine*, Vol. 8, pp 187-191. 1996.

4. J.Gamper and W. Nejdl "Abstract temporal diagnosis in medical domains". *Artificial in Medicine*, Vol. 10, pp209-234, 1997.

5. H. Thiele and S. Kalenka. "On Fuzzy Temporal Logic". *Proceedings of. of the 2nd International Conference on Fuzzy Systems*, San Francisco, Vol., pp1027-1032, 1993.

6. E.J. Condon (Editor) "Virtues Family Physician" published by Virtue and Company, London and Coulsdon, 1977)

Finding Diverse Examples Using Genetic Algorithms

Colin G. Johnson.

Computing Laboratory.
University of Kent at Canterbury.
Canterbury, Kent, CT2 7NX, England.
Email: C.G.Johnson@ukc.ac.uk

1 Introduction

The problem of *finding qualitative examples* is an interesting yet little studied machine learning problem. Take a set of objects, $\mathcal{O}$ and a set of classes $\mathcal{C}$, where each object fits into one and only one class. Represent this classification by a total function $f : \mathcal{O} \to \mathcal{C}$. We assume that $|\mathrm{range}(f)| \ll |\mathcal{O}|$.

Sometime this problem is fairly trivial, e.g. is the classification is represented as a database or if there is an easy way to calculate a pseudo-inverse of f. Also in some cases range(f) is a small subset of $\mathcal{C}$, so targeting members of $\mathcal{C}$ is infeasible. One promising approach is to search $\mathcal{O}$.

Clearly in doing this we are assuming that there some kind of underlying structure to f. One approach would be to attempt to uncover this structure in an explicit, symbolic form. However in this paper we use heuristic search methods which search this space without using explicit representations of which areas of the search space are fruitful, et cetera.

There are a number of variants on this problem. In some.problem areas we will know in advance how many classes there are, which will give us a stopping criterion, otherwise we will have to use traditional stopping criteria such as GA convergence. In some problem areas the classes will be defined with respect to some metric on $\mathcal{C}$ rather than defined in advance.

2 Motivations

The main motivation for studying this problem is that it occurs in a wide variety of situations, and that a general heuristic for problems of this type would benefit many different problems (Johnson, 2000). Here are some examples.

Consider creating test data for computer programs. We would like to create one example of a set of data that tests each point in a computer program, for example a set of data that ensures coverage of all lines in a program, or one which ensures that all branches in a program are visited.

A problem with text-based information retrieval systems (Belew, 2000; van Rijsbergen, 1979) is that a single search term can match a number of qualitatively different kinds of object. If we search for a particular person's name, then we might get lots of information about other people with the same name. Careful specification of additional search terms can help, but it can be difficult to find terms or they can over-restrict the search. One idea is to guide the search by looking for pages which are diverse in comparison to currently found documents, and then present the user with a number of distinct examples of documents satisfying their search criteria.

Knot theory is a topic in mathematics which studies the topology of closed loops in space (Adams, 1994; Murasugi, 1996). One common way to study these objects is to investigate the properties of 2D diagrams which are projections of the 3D loops (figure 1). A well-known problem in this subject is finding an example diagram for each of the topologically distinct 3D structures (Hoste, Thistlethwaite, & Weeks, 1998).

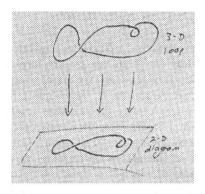

Fig. 1. A knot diagram from a three-dimensional loop.

Another scientific problem occurs in bioinformatics (Attwood & Parry-Smith, 1999). Imagine that we have a large set of rules which tell us how 3D chemical structures of some type are formed from their primary structure. We are interested only in the shape that the molecule presents to the outside world, and we would like to do some experiments in the lab with these chemicals. However there are many possible primary structures for each shape, and we would like to find one of each.

A final application is in the CAD in the broadest sense. Evolution can be used to search a space of designs, including geometrical design, design of networks, architecture and design of sound (Bentley, 1999). One way in which qualitative example finding could be used would be to give the user an overview of the design space by picking out a wide diversity of examples.

3 Review

In this paper we shall use a genetic algorithm (GA) to search for structured examples. Structured diversity which exploits qualitatively distinct niches in a population is a feature which evolution is good at producing, so GAs are a promising basis for developing qualitative example finding algorithms.

Note that this is different from multimodal optimization using GAs (as surveyed in (Mafoud, 1997)). In multimodal optimization the majority of the effort is in improving solutions within the classes, whereas in our problems moving between the classes is the most important part of the algorithm. There is some common ground with work in AI on computational creativity (Boden, 1990; Partridge & Rowe, 1994), however in our system novelty is a predefined characteristic, not something that needs to be ascertained by the system.

4 Requirements for an algorithm

In this problem there is no way to extrinsically assign a measure of quality to a solution, i.e. the individual solutions do not have a *fitness*. In order to find solutions to these kinds of problems we might choose to assign a fitness, either by setting intermediate targets or by assigning fitness "on the fly" in each generation, or we might change the selection scheme entirely.

This lack of an external fitness measure means that asking how the algorithms presented below compare with "traditional" GAs is not a meaningful question. GAs are not in themselves optimizers—instead they are robust adaptive systems, variants of which (GA function optimizers—GAFOs) can be used for optimization (De Jong, 1993; Harvey, 1997). This kind of robust adaptivity can be used to apply GAs to problems where the idea of an optimum is absent.

Some basic features of an algorithm for solving such problems:

- Some "substructures" will be capable of being built upon to form objects from many different classes. The algorithm must be able to exploit the fruitful substructures that it "finds", either symbolically or subsymbolically
- The algorithm must be capable of moving quickly onto other areas of search space once an area has been mined out.
- Similarly, the algorithm must recognize when it is in an unproductive area of the search space and move onto other areas.
- The algorithm should not return to unproductive or mined out areas of the search space.

A basic scheme that we can adopt is to use the traditional GA recombination and mutation operators but to create new selection scheme. This is based on an on-the-fly scheme which gives a fitness value to each individual in each generation, based on whether that individual has given evidence that it contains fruitful substructures on which novel solutions can be built.

5 Some test problems

In this paper we present results from two test problems. In the first problem (the *grid problem*) the solutions consist of strings of letters chosen from the set $\{L, R, U, D\}$. The classification is based around a 100×100 grid of numbers (figure 2), where most of the grid is filled with the number 1, except for four 21×21 regions, each square of which is filled with a different number. For a given solution string we begin by at the point $(50, 50)$ in the grid, and move [L]eft, [R]ight, [U]p or [D]own as we read along the string. The square in which we end up is the class to which that string belongs. If the string ends up outside of the grid it is assigned the class 1.

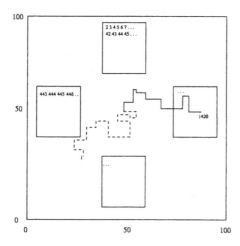

Fig. 2. The grid, with two sample solution paths.

The second problem is a variant on the knot problem described earlier. In this problem we construct knots by *braids*, i.e. sets of strings which run downwards and which cross each other at a finite number of points. We can turn these into knots by joining up the strings with loops (figure 3). Genetic operators are recombination by cutting and rejoining two braids, and mutation by replacing one crossing by a random other crossing at the same position (figure 3). We can associate a polynomial (the *Jones polynomial*) to each braid (Adams, 1994), and search for one example of a braid for each valid polynomial[1].

---

[1] Thanks to Hugh Morton, University of Liverpool, for supplying computer programs for the calculation of knot invariants.

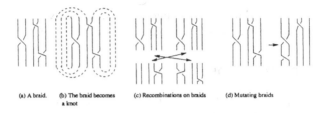

(a) A braid.   (b) The braid becomes   (c) Recombinations on braids   (d) Mutating braids
a knot

Fig. 3. Operations on braids.

6 Results

We have been experimenting with a number of variations of genetic algorithms for the test problem. As discussed above there is no extrinsic fitness function, therefore we create a fitness measure on the fly in each generation.

6.1 On the fly fitness allocation

The simplest way to do this is to give a score of 1 to those members of the current population which are "novel", defined to mean that their classifications have not occurred in any previous generations, and 0 otherwise. We have also investigated a variation on this, which attempts to strengthen those individuals which have fruitful substructures within them by assigning a higher score to those solutions which come from parent solutions that have produced a diverse range of solutions. Firstly we create a new population by crossover and mutation, using the fitness values generated in the previous generation. We then tally up the total number of novel children had by each parent, and then assign this total score to each of their children (figure 4). This is then used as a fitness measure in a traditional GA framework. Comparisons are given in figure 5(c).

6.2 Crossover with random strings

In some experiments we introduced a number of random strings into the population at each generation. The aim of this was to see whether these strings would crossover with other strings which contain good substructures but help to exploit those substructures. This was tried for a number of problems and proved unsuccessful—see figure 5(a) for the results for the grid problem.

6.3 Mutation rates

Experiments have been carried out with a number of different mutation rates (figure 5(b)). Over a number of experiments, including the one outlined here, the most successful mutation rate was typically much higher than the mutation rate for GAs used for optimization, with a mutation rate of 0.1 being

Stage 1. Identify the novel solutions

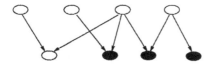

Stage 2. Pass fitness back to parents

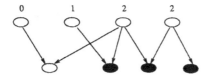

Stage 3. Pass the accumulated fitness back to the children

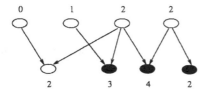

Fig. 4. An algorithm for enhancing fruitful substructures. Those structures which come from parents which have the most number of novel children receive the highest fitness.

best contrasted with rates of 0.01–0.001 (Mitchell, 1996) or the reciprocal of bitstring-length (Bäck, 1996) for GAFOs. This is likely to be caused by the mutation being a major source of the ability of this algorithm to find novel solutions based around existing ones, rather than being a "background operator" to prevent convergence as with GAFOs.

6.4   Comparisons with random search

Figures 5(d) and 5(e) present comparisons against random search for these two test problems. One difficulty here is that random search gives a good performance anyway for the grid problem, so a major next step in this kind of work is finding better test problems which are harder to solve by brute force methods. There is a more general difficulty in presenting results on problems such as these. An aim of the research is to demonstrate that general heuristics can be used for these kinds of problems, but criteria for success are problem dependent, but for test problems we have no criteria for success and comparison with random search is not ideal.

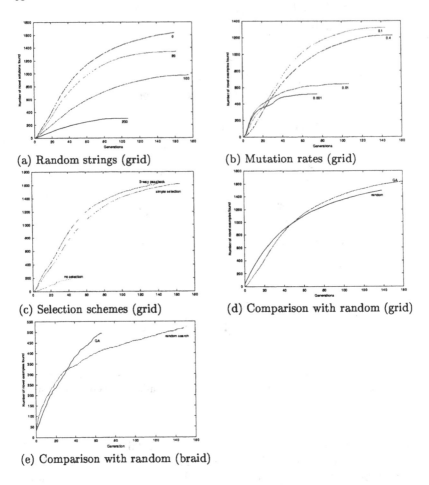

(a) Random strings (grid)

(b) Mutation rates (grid)

(c) Selection schemes (grid)

(d) Comparison with random (grid)

(e) Comparison with random (braid)

Fig. 5. Results.

7 Future work

Other variants on the algorithm are worthy of further investigation, e.g. preliminary experiments on using hypermutation to prevent the algorithm getting stuck when the number of novel solutions is small have proven fruitful. Future work will include looking for rigourous, tunable test problems, e.g. analogies with royal road functions (Mitchell, Forrest, & Holland, 1992), and deceptive problems (Goldberg, 1987); theoretical analyses, e.g. investigating how Holland's schema theorem (Holland, 1975) might explain the discovery and exploitation of fecund substructures; and application to real-world problems.

References

Adams, C. A. (1994). *The knot book.* W.H. Freeman.

Attwood, T., & Parry-Smith, D. (1999). *Introduction to bioinformatics.* Addison Wesley Longman.

Bäck, T. (1996). *Evolutionary algorithms in theory and practice.* Oxford University Press.

Belew, R. K. (2000). *Finding out about : information retrieval and other technologies for seeking knowledge.* Cambridge University Press. (In preparation)

Bentley, P. J. (Ed.). (1999). *Evolutionary design by computers.* Academic Press.

Boden, M. (1990). *The creative mind: Myths and mechanisms.* Abacus.

De Jong, K. (1993). Genetic algorithms are NOT function optimizers. In L. Whitley (Ed.), *Foundations of genetic algorithms 2* (pp. 5–17). Morgan Kauffmann.

Goldberg, D. E. (1987). Simple genetic algorithms and the minimal deceptive problem. In L. D. Davis (Ed.), *Genetic algorithms and simulated annealing.* Morgan Kaufmann.

Harvey, I. (1997). Cognition is not computation: Evolution is not optimisation. In W. Gerstner, A. Germond, M. Hasler, , & J.-D. Nicoud (Eds.), *Proceedings of the seventh international conference on artificial neural networks* (pp. 685–690). Springer-Verlag.

Holland, J. H. (1975). *Adaptation in natural and artificial systems.* MIT Press. (Second edition 1992)

Hoste, J., Thistlethwaite, M., & Weeks, J. (1998). The first 1,701,936 knots. *The Mathematical Intelligencer, 20*(4), 33-48.

Johnson, C. G. (2000). Understanding complex systems through examples: a framework for qualitative example finding. In P. A. Gelepithis (Ed.), *Complex intelligent systems.* Kingston University.

Mafoud, S. W. (1997). Niching methods. In T. Bäck, D. B. Fogel, & Z. Michalewicz (Eds.), *Handbook of evolutionary computation* (pp. C6.1.1–C6.1.4). Oxford University Press / Institute of Physics.

Mitchell, M. (1996). *An introduction to genetic algorithms.* Bradford Books/MIT Press.

Mitchell, M., Forrest, S., & Holland, J. (1992). The royal road for genetic algorithms : Fitness landscapes and GA performance. In F. Varela & P. Bourgine (Eds.), *Towards a practice of autonomous systems : Proceedings of the first european conference on artificial life.* MIT Press.

Murasugi, K. (1996). *Knot theory and its applications.* Birkhäuser.

Partridge, D., & Rowe, J. (1994). *Computers and creativity.* Intellect Books.

van Rijsbergen, C. J. (1979). *Information retrieval.* London: Butterworths.

Evolving User Profiles to Reduce Internet Information Overload

John Pagonis[1] and Mark C. Sinclair[2]

[1] Personal Area Networking, Communication Technology Group,
Symbian Ltd., 16, Harcourt Street, London W1H 1DT.
Email: john.pagonis@symbian.com
[2] Dept. of Electronic Systems Engineering, University of Essex,
Wivenhoe Park, Colchester, Essex CO4 3SQ.
Tel: 01206-872477; Fax: 01206-872900; Email: mcs@essex.ac.uk

Abstract. This paper discusses the use of Evolving Personal Agent Environments as a potential solution to the problem of information overload as experienced in habitual Web surfing. Some first experimental results on evolving user profiles using speciating hybrid GAs, the reasoning behind them and support for their potential application in mobile, wireless and location aware information devices are also presented.

1 Information Overload

In everyday life, the Internet user is faced with the ever increasing problem of information overload, whether this occurs at home, at the workplace, or as will soon be happening, everywhere [1] [2]. The overwhelming information feed that computer users face leads to anxiety, strain, inefficiency and finally results in uninformed (or misinformed) and frustrated users [3] [4]. Continuously and increasingly Internet users are confronted with laborious and difficult tasks of information filtering and/or gathering, which are inherently computer-oriented processes and need not involve human labour. Moreover, the efficiency and speed with which computer systems may retrieve and process massive amounts of data actually exacerbates the problem of ineffectiveness in information filtering without user intervention.

In our research programme, which we first presented in [5], we aim to solve the information overload problem arising from *habitual surfing*, with a focus on mobility, Wireless Information Devices (WIDs) and privacy. Therefore moving away from the model of *what is of interest to the user* to the model of *what is of interest to the user here and now*. In [5], we surveyed recent efforts at tackling the problem of information overload. Our view is that, as a means of achieving our goal, we need to research Evolving Personal Agent Environments (EPAE).

The focus in this paper is on evolving individual user profiles, which form a vital part of the EPAE research. Thus we aim to describe and explain our definition of user profiles in personal agent environments, and to support the motivation behind it. We also include an overview of our proposed research programme on EPAE and present some early experimental work on user profile evaluation and evolution.

2 Evolving Personal Agent Environments

Our means of dealing with the problem of information overload, particularly in the domain of the World Wide Web, is geared towards the use of personal and adaptive agent-based systems. The driving ideas behind such a system and an early outline of it, are presented below.

Central to the design of the suggested system are the use of evolutionary algorithms, agent technologies, collaborative filtering, privacy, agent-society trust relationships, location awareness and mobility, as well as continual adaptation [5]. Our belief is that through employing an evolutionary-algorithm-based multi-agent environment, where the 'fitness' of each individual is determined by an estimate of user satisfaction, the system should more closely adapt to the user's personality and preferences, thereby yielding increasingly better results. However, while selection of appropriate measure(s) to estimate user satisfaction will form part of our research programme, which is geared towards minimising user intervention, nevertheless it remains outside of the scope of this paper.

The system which we aim to produce will focus on transparently assisting in the filtering and presentation of information. This will be based on observation of the user's individual behaviour, enhanced through adaptation and mobility. As its major target, the proposed system will aim to constantly and continuously evolve and adapt to the locational and behavioural changes of the user. Our goal is to architect, and subsequently implement, this system which will ease the information overload problem and closely follow the individual user's interests. Our experimental work towards designing the system commenced with the evolution of basic user profiles, and is presented in the following sections.

3 User Profiles to Reduce Information Overload

We envisage that user profiling in the near future will be more and more coupled with the actual location where the user encounters information overload. Moreover active user profiles and browsing behaviour will depend upon location, and also possibly on schedule. Location awareness (or context sensitivity [6]) comes as a direct result of the use of portable computers, personal data assistants, wearable and WIDs, plus other enabling technologies, like mobile IP, GPRS, GPS and others. This ability of the mobile device, and hence of the agent environment, to discover its location, will enable new ways of following the user's behaviour, habits and interests, thus adapting and evolving more closely to them. Context sensitivity and mobility will doubtless introduce continual change and development of the users' interests yielding many profiles belonging to the same user.

In our research we define the *user profile* as a set of subjects and interests that are relevant and useful at a given location and time. For example, this could mean that a different view[1] onto the Web might be presented to the user, according to different profiles, throughout the day, *e.g.* when in the office, when at home, when on the bus. All the user satisfaction feedback, behavioural and locational changes could then be recorded. Then, when evolution next occurs, it will include all these different individual profiles. In addition, statistical behaviour could be analysed to anticipate the next locational/calendar profile change, in order to be in a position to present the user with the desired and relevant information digest. To probe further, the user could confirm creation of each different profile to allow the agent system to 'legitimately' evolve them. Though the system, based on statistical inferences, could simply make the user realise such profile changes by asking the right questions: "I see that you are on the bus quite often on Monday mornings, do you feel like reading the morning news then?"

4 Evolving User Profiles

We anticipate our approach to representing user profiles in the computer domain will be based on speciating genetic algorithms (GAs) according to location and time. In this approach, a user may have a number of domains of interest (or interest pools) which may or may not be relevant and/or useful across time and space.

Hybrid GAs were chosen to ensure that the properties of the algorithms developed would be well matched to the problem domain, and also because recent work by Moukas [7] [8] [9], Chen *et al.*[10] [11], Chen & Sycara [12] and others has shown that GAs can offer promising solutions. Moukas has demonstrated that GAs acting as filters (part of a wider ecosystem) can be very responsive in adapting to changing user behaviour [7] [8] [9]. Moreover Chen's research suggests that filtering using GAs is effective and can actually perform better than conventional techniques if the search criteria or the interest domain is vague or with no well defined starting point [10] [11].

Hence we can employ hybrid GAs with individuals consisting of variable vectors of (initially) words and their weights, within a given Web page. These individuals will merely describe subjects of interest or simply WWW content. They can then be separated into sets according to their significance in the user's everyday life, thus establishing the context within which they are valid. This context, which characterises their species, can be defined in terms of location, time and possibly date.

---

[1] Termed 'personal portal' in [5].

Traditionally a user's profile was described by modelling his/her interests regardless of context, whereas our proposal augments this with information about space and time [9] [13] [10] [12] [14]. Effectively then, the representation of a user profile becomes the collection of individuals that belong, using GA terminology, to the same species, although only the fittest of these will influence the eventual views presented to the user. Moreover, because profiles are time and location sensitive, a user can have many different profiles.

Following the assumption that a user will be interested, according to context, in a finite number of 'interests', we seek to discover whether the separation of the species can speed and enhance the selection and presentation of relevant information. In this approach, utilising contextual information, the user profile becomes a collection of the interests (species) that satisfy the active context's requirements. Thus when the system is called to filter an offering of documents, rather than just employing the fittest 'filters' to decide on those most relevant for the user to read, instead not only the most fit, but also the most *relevant* filters will be used to pick the documents. Therefore, as has been said, parting from the model of what is of interest to the user towards the model of what is of interest to the user *here and now*.

4.1 The Experiment

For simplicity, in this experiment we considered the case where a user has only one active profile at any time, of a set of two, which we conveniently divided between office hours and the user being at home. Moreover each of these two profiles encapsulates a single interest (thus being a simple profile). We first evolved the profiles and they were then evaluated by the user.

To seed the initial population, a number of recent documents was selected which had been stored as links from the user's WWW browser's bookmarks under the same bookmark category, relevant to the active profile at the given time and location (*i.e.* home). Each such document would be used to generate a single individual.

Then we randomly picked from the same category another set of documents (the training documents) which would be used to evolve the population created from the former set. Each generation, the fitness of each individual from the evolving population was evaluated against a randomly picked document from this latter set.

GA Features The genotype of the individuals resulted from representing the documents as weighted keyword vectors (which we aim to augment with the contextual information as the system is developed). The Java framework which we used to build the GA application employs a design from previous work by one of the authors [15] [16], and is intended to be generic enough to accommodate any encoding that may be needed in our future work. Based on the current encoding, the fitness function was taken to be the cosine of the angle between the multidimensional vectors representing the training and evolving individuals. This technique has been successfully used elsewhere [9]. The crossover operator used was a random two-point crossover which exchanged a part of one genotype of random length with a part of the other genotype also of random length. Moreover, the mutation operator randomly changes the value of a gene's allele in the genotype. Both of these operators were assigned a low probability of 20% and 5%, respectively, and the remainder was allocated to a reproduction operator which would clone the fittest individuals.

Results and Observations The decision to assign a relatively small probability to the crossover operator was based on the observation that a high crossover probability eventually seemed to harm the population after some generations. This appeared to be the case because the operator could potentially change the size and structure of an individual considerably and since that individual represented a document filter, the filter itself could be changed to match very different documents.

We also experimented with having adaptive operator probabilities, where the probability of selecting an operator would increase with greater improvements in population fitness. That technique proved to be very unfruitful, in this case, as the population regressed rapidly, apparently due to the effects of the increased mutation. On the contrary, by keeping the operator probabilities constant and low, better results were obtained. With such operator probabilities, our experiments showed that each profile's population (representing in effect niche filters) could be rapidly evolved to a fitter population in a matter of few generations.

Moreover that population could reliably be used to select documents of interest out of a wider set of documents. To verify this, the user selected from the Web a small set of documents of interest, in alignment with his active profile. These documents were injected into a larger set of randomly selected documents, not matching that profile. The best filters were then called to sort these documents in order, ranking the most 'interesting' documents at the top of the list.

Problems and Future Directions The problem in validating and measuring the success of such experiments is that the user is involved in deciding the validity and effectiveness of the information filters, represented by the fitter individuals. The challenge is to make the objective fitness assigned to the profile population match, what is in effect, the subjective fitness given by the user. It is also very difficult to statistically build an experiment large enough as to guarantee impartiality and non-bias by the subjects participating in the experiment. Therefore we will be looking into this difficult area in the future in order to establish an appropriate methodology for grading such experiments.

On the technical side, we are looking for further improvements in many areas of the GA, such as the operators and fitness function. In particular the crossover operator, which seemed to damage the population if assigned high probability, could be re-implemented to take account of individuals' size. That change could possibly allow for more crossover operations to take place, since it would alter the embedded structure and size of the individuals less.

Moreover we wish to experiment with other fitness functions, and possibly improve the one used by normalising the alleles of the 'genes' in the two chromosomes according to their relative values. Such a fitness function would then allow two documents of different sizes to be compared for similarity with no loss of accuracy.

Another area of improvement is to apply better pre-processing to the documents, before they are encoded as chromosomes, so as to eliminate noise. Currently prepositions, articles, conjunctions and pronouns all make up the 'noise' in the evolved individuals and need to be removed from their genotypes.

As was said above, to judge whether a population (*i.e.* a species of a single interest) can successfully filter documents and suggest those of interest, its best individuals are used to sort documents in order of relevancy. This is a useful approach, but the inherent problem in applying it, is that a 'global' threshold above which documents are relevant, cannot be predicted. Thus if the system is to present only the most relevant documents to the user, it must determine how many to select, based on how many are really relevant, which is an unknown. Estimation of such thresholds is another topic for future work.

5   Conclusions

Our motivation behind classifying user profiles according to location and time is not only based on the realisation that information overload may arise when a user has to retrieve and filter useful information from a vast offering, but also that people may now simply have interests in too many things. Moreover, that these are not always necessarily useful or relevant to their activities.

User profiling, in the most general context (of the Web domain), involves recording and somehow modelling users' preferences in viewing and navigating through webs of hyper-linked documents. However, both content preference and navigation describe people's behaviour and interests, and hence raise privacy and confidentiality issues. We will consider these in our research, and in the future we hope to examine how they can be addressed. This requirement of privacy will be even more critical if our research on modelling users' preferences, as described, proves to be a success.

The early work presented here indicates that we can obtain rapid evolution of species(*i.e.* small populations) which provide effective niche contextual filtering. It is to be hoped that eventually the system will allow us to:

- evolve newly discovered profiles on-the-fly;

- quickly apply the niche filters/populations representing interests to documents;
- give user satisfaction with minor computational overhead;
- employ a small memory footprint for both storing and processing;
- require minimal overhead in encrypting profiles;
- effectively transport the personal profile information over low bandwidth, unreliable or Personal Area Networks (PAN)

Although our research aims may seem futuristic, it is apparent that mobile platforms like WIDs will soon be able to support environments allowing research systems like ours to be realised. Evolving user profiles may then become commonplace in a fast moving information-device-laden society, where adaptability and mobility are as ubiquitous as telephony and mobile phones are today.

References

1. Halla, B. (1998): How the PC will Disappear, IEEE Computer 31, 136–138
2. Kleinrock, L. (1999): Nomadic Computing and Smart Spaces, IEEE Internet Computing 4, 52–53
3. Ireland, P. (1999): Management Paradigm to Reduce Information Overload, Computing & Control Engineering Journal 10, 29–32
4. Bowman, C.M., Danzig, P.B., Manber, U. & Schwartz, F. (1994): Scalable Internet Resource Discovery: Research Problems and Approaches, Commun. ACM 37, 98–107
5. Pagonis, J. & Sinclair, M.C. (1999): Evolving Personal Agent Environments to Reduce Internet Information Overload: Initial Considerations. In: IEE Colloquium on Lost in the Web: Navigation on the Internet, Digest No. 1999/169, London, UK, 2/1–2/10
6. Billinghurst, M. & Starner, T. (1999): New Ways to Manage Information, Computer 32, 57–64
7. Moukas, A.G. (1996): Amalthaea: Information Discovery and Filtering using a Multiagent Evolving Ecosystem. In: Conf. on Practical Application of Intelligent Agents and Multi-Agent Technology, London, UK
8. Moukas, A. (1997): Amalthaea: Information Discovery and Filtering Using a Multiagent Evolving Ecosystem, Applied Artificial Intelligence 11, 437–457
9. Moukas, A. & Maes, P. (1998): Amalthaea: An Evolving Multi-agent Information Filtering and Discovery System for the WWW, Autonomous Agents and Multi-Agent Systems 1, 59–88
10. Chen, H.C., Chung, Y.M., Ramsey, M. & Yang, C.C. (1998): An Intelligent Personal Spider (Agent) for Dynamic Internet/Intranet Searching, Decision Support Systems 23, 41–58
11. Chen, H.C., Houston, A.L., Sewell, R.R. & Schatz, B.R. (1998): Internet Browsing and Searching: User Evaluations of Category Map and Concept Space Techniques, Journal of the American Society for Information Science 49, 582–603
12. Chen, L. & Sycara, K. (1998): WebMate: A Personal Agent for Browsing and Searching. In: 2nd Intl. Conf. on Autonomous Agents and Multiagent Systems, Minneapolis, USA, 132–139

13. WebMate, http://www.cs.cmu.edu/~softagents/webmate.html
14. Autonomy, Technology White Paper, http://www.autonomy.com/tech/wp.html
15. Sinclair, M.C. (1998) Operator-probability Adaptation in a Genetic-algorithm/Heuristic Hybrid for Optical Network Wavelength Allocation. In: IEEE Intl. Conf. on Evolutionary Computation (ICEC'98), Anchorage, Alaska, USA, 840–845
16. Sinclair, M.C. (1998): NOMaD: An Optical Network Optimisation, Modelling and Design Toolset. In: IEE Colloquium on Multiwavelength Optical Networks: Devices, Systems and Network Implementations, Digest No. 1998/296, London, 6/1–6/6

Learning Fuzzy Classification Rules from Data

Hans Roubos[1], Magne Setnes[2], and Janos Abonyi[3]

[1] Delft University of Technology, ITS, Control Laboratory,
P.O. Box 5031, 2600 GA Delft, The Netherlands, hans@ieee.org
[2] Heineken Technical Services, R&D, Burgemeester Smeetsweg 1,
3282 PH Zoeterwoude, The Netherlands, magne@ieee.org
[3] University of Veszprem, Department of Process Engineering,
P.O. Box 158, H-8201 Veszprem, Hungary, abonyij@fmt.vein.hu

Abstract. Automatic design of fuzzy rule-based classification systems based on labeled data is considered. It is recognized that both classification performance and interpretability are of major importance and effort is made to keep the resulting rule bases small and comprehensible. An iterative approach for developing fuzzy classifiers is proposed. The initial model is derived from the data and subsequently, feature selection and rule base simplification are applied to reduce the model, and a GA is used for model tuning. An application to the Wine data classification problem is shown.

1 Introduction

Rule-based expert systems are often applied to classification problems in fault detection, biology, medicinem etc. Fuzzy logic improves classification and decision support systems by allowing the use of overlapping class definitions and improves the interpretability of the results by providing more insight into the classifier structure and decision making process [13]. The automatic determination of fuzzy classification rules from data has been approached by several different techniques: neuro-fuzzy methods [6], genetic-algorithm based rule selection [5] and fuzzy clustering in combination with GA-optimization [12]. Traditionally, algorithms to obtain classifiers have focused either on accuracy or interpretability. Recently some approaches to combining these properties have been reported; fuzzy clustering is proposed to derive transparent models in [9], linguistic constraints are applied to fuzzy modeling in [13] and rule extraction from neural networks is described in [8].

In this paper we describe an approach that addresses both issues. Compact, accurate and linguisticly interpretable fuzzy rule-based classifiers are obtained from labeled observation data in an iterative fashion. An initial model is derived from the observation data and subsequently, feature selection and rule base simplification methods [10] are applied to reduce the model. After the model reduction, a real-coded GA is applied to improve the classification accuracy [7,11]. To maintain the interpretability of the rule base, the GA search-space is restricted to the neighborhood of the initial rule base.

2 Fuzzy Models for Classification

2.1 The Model Structure

We apply fuzzy classification rules that each describe one of the N_c classes in the data set. The rule antecedent is a fuzzy description in the n-dimensional feature space and the rule consequent is a crisp (non-fuzzy) class label from the set $\{1, 2, \ldots, N_c\}$:

$$R_i : \quad \text{If } x_1 \text{ is } A_{i1} \text{ and } \ldots x_n \text{ is } A_{in} \text{ then } g_i = p_i, \ i = 1, \ldots, M. \quad (1)$$

Here n denotes the number of features, $x = [x_1, x_2, \ldots, x_n]^T$ is the input vector, g_i is the output of the ith rule and $A_{i1}, \ldots, A_{in}$ are the antecedent fuzzy sets. The **and** connective is modeled by the product operator, allowing for interaction between the propositions in the antecedent. The degree of activation of the ith rule is calculated as:

$$\beta_i(x) = \prod_{j=1}^{n} A_{ij}(x_j), \ i = 1, 2, \ldots, M. \quad (2)$$

The output of the classifier is determined by the rule that has the highest degree of activation:

$$y = g_{i^*}, \ i^* = \arg\max_{1 \le i \le M} \beta_i. \quad (3)$$

In the following we assume that the number of rules corresponds to the number of classes, i.e., $M = N_c$. The certainty degree of the decision is given by the normalized degree of firing of the rule:

$$CF = \beta_{i^*} / \sum_{i}^{M} \beta_i. \quad (4)$$

2.2 Data Driven Initialization

From the K available input-output data pairs $\{x_k, y_k\}$ we construct the n-dimensional pattern matrix $X^T = [x_1, \ldots, x_K]$ and the corresponding label vector $y^T = [y_1, \ldots, y_K]$. The fuzzy antecedents $A_{ij}(x_j)$ in the initial rule base are now determined in by a three-step algorithm. In the first step, M multivariable membership functions are defined in the product space of the features. Each describes a region where the system can be approximated by a single fuzzy rule. This partitioning is often realized by iterative methods such as clustering [7]. Here, given the labeled data, a one-step approach is proposed. This assumes that each class is described by a single, compact construct in the feature space. If this is not the case, other methods such as, e.g, relational classification [9], can be applied. Similar to the Gustafson and Kessel's clustering algorithm [4], the approach proposed here assumes that the shape of the fuzzy sets can be approximated by ellipsoids. Hence, each class prototype is represented by a center v and its covariance matrix Q:

$$v_i = \frac{1}{K_i} \sum_{k|y_k=i} x_k , \tag{5}$$

$$Q_i = \frac{1}{K_i} \sum_{k|y_k=i} (x_k - v_i)(x_k - v_i)^T . \tag{6}$$

where i denotes the index of the classes, $i = 1, \ldots, N_c$, and K_i represents the number of samples that belong to the ith class. In the second step, the algorithm computes the fuzzy partition matrix U whose ikth element $u_{ik} \in [0, 1]$ is the membership degree of the data object x_k in class i. This membership is based on the distance between the observation and the class center:

$$D_{ik}^2 = (x_k - v_i)Q_i^{-1}(x_k - v_i)^T . \tag{7}$$

Using this distance, the membership becomes:

$$u_{ik} = 1 \left/ \sum_{j=1}^{K} \left(\frac{D_{ik}}{D_{jk}} \right)^{2/(m-1)} \right. , \tag{8}$$

where m denotes a weighting exponent that determines the fuzziness of the obtained partition ($m = 1.8$ is applied in the example).

The rows of U now contain pointwise representations of the multidimensional fuzzy sets describing the classes in the feature space. In the third step, the univariate fuzzy sets A_{ij} in the classification rules (1) are obtained by projecting the rows of U onto the input variables x_j and subsequently approximate the projections by parametric functions [1]. In the example we apply triangular fuzzy sets.

2.3 Ensuring Transparency and Accuracy

Fixed membership functions are often used to partition the feature space [5]. Membership functions derived from the data, however, explain the data-patterns in a better way. Typically less sets and fewer rules result than in a fixed partition approach. Hence, the initial rule base constructed by the proposed method fulfills many criteria for transparency and good semantic properties [11,13]: moderate number of rules, distinguishability, normality and coverage. The transparency and compactness of the rule base can be further improved by model reduction methods. Two methods are presented here. The first method is an open-loop feature selection algorithm that is based on Fisher's interclass separability criterion [2] calculated from the covariances of the clusters. The other method is the similarity-driven simplification proposed by Setnes et al. [10].

2.4   Feature Selection Based on Interclass Separability

Using too many features results in difficulties in the prediction and interpretability capabilities of the model due to redundancy, non-informative features and noise. Hence, feature selection is usually necessary. We apply the
Fischer interclass separability method which is based on statistical properties of the labeled data. This criterion is based on the *between-class* (12)
and *within-class* (13) scatter or covariance matrices that sum up to the *total
scatter matrix* (11) which is the covariance of the whole training data:

$$Q_t = \frac{1}{K} \sum_{i=1}^{K} (x_k - v)(x_k - v)^T , \tag{9}$$

$$v = \frac{1}{K} \sum_{i=1}^{K} x_k = \frac{1}{K} \sum_{i=1}^{N_c} K_i v_i \tag{10}$$

The total scatter matrix can be decomposed as:

$$Q_t = Q_b + Q_w , \tag{11}$$

$$Q_b = \sum_{i=1}^{N_c} K_i (v_i - v)(v_i - v)^T , \tag{12}$$

$$Q_w = \sum_{i=1}^{N_c} Q_i . \tag{13}$$

The feature interclass seperatibility selection criterion is a trade-off between
Q_b and Q_w. A feature ranking is made iteratively by leaving out the worst
feature in each step and is exploited for the open-loop feature selection:

$$J_j = det(Q_b) / det(Q_w) , \tag{14}$$

where *det* is the determinant and J_j is the criterion value including j features.

2.5   Similarity-driven rule base simplification

The similarity-driven rule base simplification method [10] uses a similarity
measure to quantify the redundancy among the fuzzy sets in the rule base. A
similarity measure based on the set-theoretic operations of intersection and
union is applied:

$$S(A, B) = \frac{|A \cap B|}{|A \cup B|} \tag{15}$$

where $|.|$ denotes the cardinality of a set, and the $\cap$ and $\cup$ operators repre-
sent the intersection and union, respectively. If $S(A, B) = 1$, then the two
membership functions A and B are equal. $S(A, B)$ becomes 0 when the membership functions are non-overlapping.

Similar fuzzy sets are merged when their similarity exceeds a user defined threshold $\theta \in [0,1]$ ($\theta = 0.5$ is applied). Merging reduces the number of different fuzzy sets (linguistic terms) used in the model and thereby increases the transparency. If all the fuzzy sets for a feature are similar to the universal set, or if merging led to only one membership function for a feature, then this feature is eliminated from the model. The method is illustrated in Fig. 1

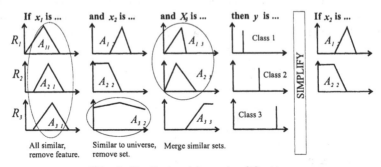

Fig. 1. Similarity-driven simplification.

2.6 Genetic Multi-Objective Optimization

To improve the classification capability of the rule base, we apply a genetic algorithm (GA) optimization method [11]. Also other model properties can be optimized by applying multi-objective functions, like, e.g., search for redundancy [7]. When an initial fuzzy model has been obtained from data, it is simplified and optimized in an iterative fashion. Combinations of the GA with the model reduction tools described above can lead to various modeling schemes. Three different approaches are shown in Fig. 2.

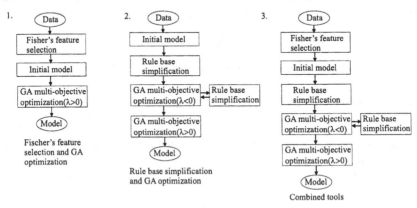

Fig. 2. Modeling schemes resulting from a combination of tools.

The model accuracy is measured in terms of the number of misclassifications. To further reduce the model complexity, the misclassification rate is combined with a similarity measure in the GA objective function. Similarity is rewarded during the iterative process, that is, the GA tries to emphasize the redundancy in the model. This redundancy is then used to remove unnecessary fuzzy sets in the next iteration. In the final step, fine tuning is combined with a penalized similarity among fuzzy sets to obtain a distinguishable term set for linguistic interpretation.

The GAs is subject to minimize the following multi-objective function:

$$J = (1 + \lambda S^*) \cdot MSE, \tag{16}$$

where $S^* \in [0, 1]$ is the average of the maximum pairwise similarity that is present in each input, i.e., S^* is an aggregated similarity measure for the total model. The weighting function $\lambda \in [-1, 1]$ determines whether similarity is rewarded ($\lambda < 0$) or penalized ($\lambda > 0$).

3 Example: Wine Data

The Wine data contains the chemical analysis of 178 wines produced in the same region in Italy but derived from three different cultivars. The problem is to distinguish the three different types based on 13 continuous attributes derived from chemical analysis. (Fig. 3). Corcoran and Sen [3] applied all

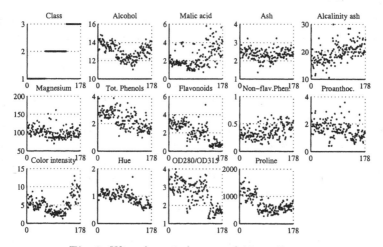

Fig. 3. Wine data: 3 classes and 13 attributes.

the data for learning 60 non-fuzzy if-then rules in a real-coded genetic based machine learning approach and Ishibuchi et al. [5] applied all the data for designing a fuzzy classifier with 60 fuzzy rules by means of an integer-coded genetic algorithm and grid partitioning (Table 2).

An initial classifier with three rules was constructed with the proposed covariance–based model initialization by using all samples resulting in 90.5% correct, 1.7% undecided and 7.9% misclassifications with the following average certainty factors (CF) [3] [82.0, 99.6, 80.5] for the three wine classes. Improved classifiers are developed based on the three schemes given in Fig. 2:

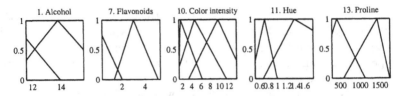

Fig. 4. The fuzzy sets of the optimized three rule classifier for the Wine data.

Scheme 1: The Fisher interclass separability criterion gives the following feature ranking $\{13, 12, 1, 4, 7, 6, 10, 9, 3, 2, 11, 5, 8\}$. Classifiers were made by adding features *one by one* and 400 iterations with the GA-optimization. The two best classifiers were obtained by using the first 5 or 7 features (15 or 21 fuzzy sets). This gave 98.9% and 99.4% correct classification with CF for the three classes $[0.95, 0.94, 0.84]$ and $[0.94, 0.99, 0.97]$, respectively.

Scheme 2: The similarity-driven simplification removed the following eight inputs in 3 steps: (i) $\{3, 5\}$, (ii) $\{2, 4, 8, 9\}$, (iii) $\{6, 12\}$. After each reduction, 200 GA-iterations were done and 400 after the last reduction. The final three-rule classifier (Table 1) contains only 11 fuzzy sets (Fig. 4). The classification result was 99.4% correct and CF for the three wine classes was $[0.96, 0.94, 0.94]$.

Scheme 3: Five features were selected based on the feature ranking initially resulting in 5% misclassification. Successively, 3 fuzzy sets and 1 feature were removed by iterative similarity-driven simplification and GA optimization (200 iterations). After the final GA tuning (400 iterations) the classification rate was 98.3% with CFs $[0.93, 0.91, 0.91]$. The final model contains features $\{1, 7, 12, 13\}$. The fuzzy sets obtained for $\{1, 7, 13\}$ are similar to those obtained in Scheme 2 (Fig. 4).

In this example, feature reduction is obtained by all three schemes. Differences in the reduction methods are: (i) Similarity analysis results in a closed-loop feature selection because it depends on the actual model while the applied open-loop feature selection can be used beforehand as it is independent from the model. (ii) In similarity analysis, a feature can be removed from individual rules. In the interclass separability method the feature is omitted in all the rules.

The obtained result is comparable to those in [3] and [5], but our classifiers use far less rules (3 compared to 60) and less features. Comparing the fuzzy sets in Fig. 4 with the data in Fig. 3 shows that the obtained rules are highly interpretable.

Table 1. Three rule fuzzy classifier (L=low, M=medium , H=high).

	1	2	3	4	5	6	7	8	9	10	11	12	13	
	Alc	Mal	Ash	aAsh	Mag	Tot	Fla	nFlav	Pro	Col	Hue	OD2	Pro	Class
R_1	H	-	-	-	-	-	H	-	-	M	L	-	L	1
R_2	L	-	-	-	-	-	-	-	-	L	L	-	H	2
R_3	H	-	-	-	-	-	L	-	-	H	H	-	H	3

Table 2. Classification rates on the Wine data for ten independent runs.

Method	Best result	Aver result	Worst result	Rules	Model eval
Corcoran and Sen [3]	100%	99.5%	98.3%	60	150000
Ishibuchi et al. [5]	99.4%	98.5%	97.8%	60	6000
This paper	99.4 %	various schemes	98.3%	3	4000-8000

4 Conclusion

The design of fuzzy rule-based classifiers is approached by combining separate tools for feature selection, model initialization, model reduction and model tuning. It is shown that these can be applied in an iterative way. A covariance-based model initialization method is applied to obtain an initial fuzzy classifier. Successive application of feature selection, rule base simplification and GA-based tuning resulted in compact and accurate classifiers. The proposed approach was successfully applied to the Wine data.

References

1. Babuška R. (1998) Fuzzy Modeling for Control. Kluwer Academic Publishers, Boston.
2. Cios K.J., Pedrycz W., Swiniarski R.W. (1998) Data Mining Methods for Knowledge Discovery. Kluwer Academic Press, Boston.
3. Corcoran A.L., Sen S. (1994) Using real-valued genetic algorithms to evolve rule sets for classification. In IEEE-CEC, June 27-29, 120–124, Orlando, USA.
4. Gustafson, D.E., Kessel, W.C. (1979) Fuzzy clustering with a fuzzy covariance matrix, In Proc. IEEE CDC, 761-766, San Diego, USA.
5. Ishibuchi H., Nakashima T., Murata T. (1999) Performance evaluation of fuzzy classifier systems for multidimensional pattern classification problems. IEEE Trans. SMC–B **29**, 601–618.
6. Nauck D., Kruse R. (1999) Obtaining interpretable fuzzy classification rules from medical data. Artificial Intelligence in Medicine **16**, 149–169.
7. Roubos J.A., Setnes M. (2000) Compact fuzzy models through complexity reduction and evolutionary optimization. In FUZZ-IEEE, 762-767, May 7-10, San Antonio, USA.
8. Setiono R. (2000) Generating concise and accurate classification rules for breast cancer diagnosis. Artificial Intelligence in Medicine **18**, 205-219.
9. Setnes M., Babuška R. (1999) Fuzzy relational classifier trained by fuzzy clustering, IEEE Trans. SMC–B **29**, 619–625
10. Setnes M., Babuška R., Kaymak U., van Nauta Lemke H.R. (1998) Similarity measures in fuzzy rule base simplification. IEEE Trans. SMC–B **28**, 376–386.
11. Setnes M., Roubos J.A. (1999) Transparent fuzzy modeling using fuzzy clustering and GA's. In NAFIPS, June 10-12, 198–202, New York, USA.
12. Setnes M., Roubos J.A. (in press, 2000) GA-fuzzy modeling and classification: complexity and performance. IEEE Trans. FS.
13. Valente de Oliveira J. (1999) Semantic constraints for membership function optimization. IEEE Trans. FS **19**, 128–138.

Increasing Diversity in Genetic Algorithms

Tim Watson and Peter Messer

Department of Computer Science,
De Montfort University, Leicester, UK

Abstract. Providing a genetic algorithm (GA) with the ability to control population diversity has been shown to be advantageous in both static and dynamic environments. Previous work has demonstrated that if the mutation rate of individuals is under genetic control then the optimal mutation rate rises in proportion to the speed of environmental change. This paper attempts to show that such an 'automute' GA outperforms a standard GA at keeping track of the fitness optimum in a simple, fast-changing environment. The paper also introduces an apparently equally effective method of controlling population diversity, based on the Hamming distance between pairs of individuals. It is argued that this 'autoham' GA is more suited to co-operative evolutionary systems since it does not rely on an increase in mutational 'noise' to provide an increase in diversity.

1 Introduction

In a stable environment, where the most successful replicators in generation k are likely to be the most successful in generation $k+1$, it would appear that a high degree of conformity both within and between generations is desirable in evolving populations. In this way, the best (fittest) phenotype yet found is maximally exploited. This can be seen in GA populations where the increase in conformity is so rapid that it often results in premature convergence. Consequently, since the best yet found is not necessarily the global optimum, if one exists, some diversity is usually provided by mutation to allow the population to explore the fitness landscape further (the crossover operator can also help with exploring the fitness landscape when a population is itself diverse but not when it has converged). Getting the balance right between exploring and exploiting is thus a matter of setting the correct level of mutation within the population.

When the environment changes over time, previous work by us [8] has shown that the optimal level of mutation increases as the rate of environmental change increases. It was also shown that by including an 'automute' bit in every individual within a GA population, which boosts an individual's own mutation rate when set, the population maintained a low, mean mutation rate when the environment was stable and automatically raised the mean mutation rate when the environment changed. It was argued that this behaviour would enable an automute GA to outperform a standard GA at keeping track of fitness optima within a fast-changing environment, thus improving overall performance without any significant increase in algorithm complexity and without the need for any extra external control of the population. The work presented here develops this self-adapting, mutation-based diversity approach by comparing the performance of both a standard GA and an automute GA within a simple model of a fast-changing environment. This paper also introduces an apparently equally effective method of controlling population diversity, based on the Hamming distance between pairs of individuals. It is argued that this 'autoham' GA is more suited to co-operative evolutionary systems since it does not rely on an increase in mutational 'noise' to provide an increase in diversity.

2 Mutation-Based Diversity

Controlling diversity within an evolving population by altering the mutation rate has been studied previously, most notably by Bäck [1] and Grefenstette [3]. While Bäck's work differs from previous attempts in its use of bits within the individual's chromosome to encode the mutation rate, thus allowing it to adapt by selective advantage and consequently removing the need for the rate of mutation to be controlled externally, the work only considered static fitness landscapes and was designed to help with the application of GAs by removing the complication of determining the best mutation rate for a given problem. Grefenstette's work is the most similar to the research outlined in this paper but his focus is on 'hypermutation,' i.e. randomly resetting an individual's genotype. However, like Bäck, he also prefers the self-adaptation of mutation rates to externally imposed heuristics. While Grefenstette correctly points out that GAs are expected to be well-suited to dynamic fitness landscapes, his fitness function is far more complicated than the one used in this paper, consisting of hundreds of sub-optimal fitness peaks and one globally optimal peak all moving randomly over time. Grefenstette also highlights two different interpretations of mutation: that a mutated bit is either flipped – the most common interpretation within the GA literature; or that a mutated bit is reset at random – Holland's [5] original interpretation. In his work, Grefenstette uses the latter form of mutation. However, since a probability of one that a bit is reset has the same effect as a probability of a half that it is flipped, the distinction, while important, is only one of magnitude. In this paper, a mutated bit is flipped rather than reset.

Before describing the experiment to compare the performance of a standard GA and an automute GA, a few definitions are needed. The 'standard' GA used in this paper consists of a fixed-size population of 300 individuals per generation, each individual represented by a fixed-length bitstring (13 bits). The next generation was produced using roulette-wheel selection followed by one-point crossover of 70% of the paired individuals and then each bit was mutated with a probability of either 0.001 or 0.002, depending on the experimental run. In the standard GA, the rightmost 12 bits were interpreted as representing a binary integer phenotype, the value of the first bit being ignored. An automute GA is identical to the standard GA except for the interpretation of the first bit: in an automute GA, when the first bit is set for an individual it will undergo mutation at a boosted rate. In the experiment the 'muteboost' factor was 5, 10, 20 or 50 times the base mutation rate, depending on the experimental run.

To compare the performance of a standard GA and an automute GA, the simplest possible dynamic environment was chosen, consisting of a single optimum fitness of 20, all other phenotypes producing a fitness of one. At the start of an experimental run, the inital population was allowed to evolve until 95% of the individuals had converged to the optimum. Then the optimum was moved to a distant phenotype and the number of generations taken until 95% of the population had converged on the new optimum was recorded. The optimum was then swapped back to its original position and the experiment continued, recording the number of generations taken until convergence. The optimum was swapped 500 times in each experimental run and the mean number of generations taken to find the new optimum, together with the associated standard deviation, was calculated. The experimental design is summarised in Fig. 1. To cater for populations that failed to find the new optimum, an upper limit of 4000 generations was used: if a population failed to find the new optimum after 4000 generations then the optimum was swapped and the number of generations taken to find the optimum was recorded as 4000.

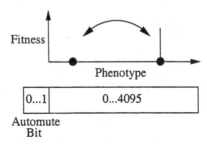

Fig. 1. Chromosome format and fitness function for an automute GA in a simple, dynamic environment

The design of the experimental fitness function was influenced by the work of van Nimwegen and Crutchfield [7] who have shown that a metastable population, i.e. one that is temporarily 'stuck' at a suboptimal fitness, will most likely reach a higher fitness by crossing an entropy barrier (a plateau in the fitness landscape) rather than a fitness barrier (a valley in the fitness landscape). Consequently, the experimental fitness landscape was designed so that the population has to cross a base fitness plateau to find the new optimum (cf. Grefenstette's fitness landscape [3]).

The two positions for the optimum were chosen so as not to favour the automute GA. Mutation acts on a population as a spring-like force, dragging each bit position away from the extrema of all ones or all zeros towards a state of half ones and half zeros. Crossover combines individuals from one generation into the next, resulting in a mutational bias towards individuals containing half ones and half zeros. Thus, the two positions for the optimum were chosen as follows:

Optimum position A: 0100 0000 1001
Optimum position B: 1101 0110 1111

where the number of ones in position A is one quarter of the length of the phenotype and the number of ones in position B is three-quarters of the phenotype length (i.e. 3 and 9 out of 12 respectively).

The experimental results are shown in Table 1. These results show that an automute GA outperforms a standard GA at keeping track of the fitness optimum – the automute GA needing approximately half the number of generations than the standard GA before the new optimum is found. It would appear that by adding a single bit to each individual and by modifying the mutation operation slightly, a standard GA's ability to track dynamic environments can be improved dramatically.

Table 1. Number of generations needed to find new optimum fitness in a simple, dynamic environment for both a standard GA and an automute GA

Muterate	Muteboost	Standard GA		Automute GA	
		Mean	Std. Dev.	Mean	Std. Dev.
0.001	5	1163	1050	563	501
	10			528	512
	20			502	448
	50			544	473
0.002	5	468	353	288	181
	10			266	168
	20			253	165
	50			266	189

2.1   Is the Automute Bit a New Type of Gene?

Traditional 'selfish gene' descriptions of evolutionary adaptation [2] concentrate on the selective advantage conferred on exons (genes that affect the phenotype) by the environment. Introns are not subject to selective pressure as they do not (it is assumed) affect the phenotype, hence they are classed as 'junk DNA.'

In what way does a gene for replication accuracy, an automute gene, affect the phenotype? It certainly doesn't affect the current generation's phenotype, and its only effect on the next generation is to alter the distribution of phenotypes[1] – a phenotypic meta-effect. Exons appear to thrive by solving problems that exist at an instant (in one particular generation). Genes such as automute genes appear to thrive by solving problems that only exist over an interval (a number of generations). Genes that regulate mutation rate can be thought of as not associated to the phenotype of the individual, but rather to the relatedness between the individual and its offspring. This suggests that a different form of selective pressure exists within the chromosomes of individuals in fast-changing environments.

2.2 Mutation-Based Diversity and Co-operative Systems

A consequence of increasing the mutation rate of an individual is that its offspring will become less like itself. If the individual is part of a co-operating population then increasing the mutation rate will tend to make the environment more hostile towards co-operation. This is because the two main mechanisms that produce co-operating populations – kin selection and reciprocal altruism [4,6] – are both detrimentally affected by an increase in mutational 'noise.'

Since GAs seem to be one of the few research areas in computer science that are suitable for developing co-operative systems in dynamic environments it would be helpful if a method for controlling diversity could be found that does not rely on increasing mutation rates. The next section outlines just such a method.

3 Frequency-Based Diversity

Although controlling diversity by altering the rate of mutation is effective, it is not the only method. It is well known that diversity is maintained in populations in which an individual's rarity confers a selective advantage. While it would be possible to keep statistics on the number of individuals with identical genotypes in any given population it would be too much of a computational burden. So a method of controlling diversity based on the frequency of occurrence of genes within a population, which does not require the maintenance of any global statistics, would offer a possible alternative to the mutation-based control of diversity within an automute GA. Such a method

---

[1] For a unimodal fitness function and Gaussian mutation the effect of an increased mutation rate is to flatten the distribution.

would also be preferable within co-operative systems as the population diversity would not be controlled by increasing the mutation rate. It is proposed that a modification of the fitness function to include a measure of the Hamming distance between two individuals will provide such a frequency-based control of diversity.

3.1 Controlling Diversity with an Autoham GA

Consider a change to an automute GA so that the setting of the first bit in an individual (now called the 'autoham' bit), rather than increasing the mutation rate, forces its fitness to be based on the Hamming distance between it and another randomly chosen individual from the population. As long as the maximum Hamming-based fitness is less than the environmental fitness function's optimum fitness, when the environment is stable the population would be expected to converge on the environmental optimum. Now, if the environment changes and the optimum moves, a mutated (rare) individual can gain a higher fitness if it is based on Hamming distance than if the autoham bit is not set and the environmental base fitness of one is assigned to it (assuming that it is not at the new optimum). Thus, it would be expected that the population would become dominated by autoham-on individuals until the new optimum is reached. However, the initial experimental results for this 'autoham' GA, using the same experimental design as before, were not promising.

When the optimum had been found the population did indeed converge to almost all autoham-off individuals (mutation creating a few autoham-on individuals at random). And when the optimum was moved the population became dominated by autoham-on individuals. But they failed to find the new optimum within 4000 generations. It was conjectured that this was because the population quickly evolved to a very stable state in which each individual was as far away (in terms of Hamming distance) from the others as possible. To reduce this effect it was decided to modify the interpretation of the autoham bit to mean that if it was set then there was a non-zero probability (Hprob.) that the individual's fitness would be based on Hamming distance rather than environmental fitness. Experimental runs were performed using this autoham GA with different values for the Hprob. value – the results are presented in Table 2 along with the best results for both the standard and automute GAs.

The experimental results suggest that an autoham GA not only outperforms a standard GA at tracking the optimum in a fast-changing environment but that it also significantly outperforms an automute GA. Since the autoham GA does not suffer from the disadvantages associated with systems that increase the mutation rate, and since it only requires one extra bit per individual and a slight change to the calculation of fitnesses, it would seem to be preferable to both standard and automute GAs for dynamic systems.

Table 2. Number of generations needed to find new optimum fitness in a simple, dynamic environment for a standard, an automute and an autoham GA

Muterate	Hprob.	Standard GA Mean	Std. Dev.	Automute GA Mean	Std. Dev.	Autoham GA Mean	Std. Dev.
0.001	0.05	1163	1050	502	448	369	224
	0.1					346	172
	0.2					253	112
	0.5					232	136
0.002	0.05	468	353	253	165	260	147
	0.1					240	108
	0.2					192	76
	0.5					212	139

4 Conclusion

It has been shown that both an automute and an autoham GA can significantly outperform a standard GA at keeping track of the fitnes optimum in a fast-changing environment. The autoham GA also benefits from not relying on an increase of the mutation rate to control population diversity, thereby making it more suitable for co-operative systems. Since neither technique requires the maintenance of any global statistics and since the extra computational load is minimal both techniques should be an improvement over standard GAs in dynamic environments.

Although the emphasis in this paper has been on introducing a single automute or autoham bit into each individual there is no reason why such a bit could not be attached to each gene in the chromosome. This bit would automatically raise the mutation rate or the Hamming fitness probability when the selective pressure drops for that gene, and would lower it again when a new selective pressure emerges, thus producing gene-level control of the diversity within the population.

References

1. T. Bäck. Self-adaptation in genetic algorithms. In F. J. Varela and P. Bourgine, editors, *Proc. First European Conference on Artificial Life*, pages 263–271, Cambridge MA, 1992. MIT Press.
2. Richard Dawkins. *The Selfish Gene*. Oxford, 1976. New edition, 1989.
3. John J. Grefenstette. Evolvability in dynamic fitness landscapes: A genetic algorithm approach. In *Proc. 1999 Congress on Evolutionary Computation (CEC99)*, pages 2031–2038, Washington, DC, 1999. IEEE Press.

4. W. D. Hamilton. The genetical evolution of social behaviour (I and II). *Journal of Theoretical Biology*, 7:1–16; 17–52, 1964.

5. John H. Holland. *Adaptation in Natural and Artificial Systems*. University of Michigan Press, 1975. MIT Press edition, 1992.

6. J. Maynard Smith. The evolution of social behaviour—a classification of models. In King's College Sociobiology Group, editor, *Current Problems in Sociobiology*, pages 29–44. Cambridge University Press, 1982.

7. Erik van Nimwegen and James P. Crutchfield. Metastable evolutionary dynamics: Crossing fitness barriers or escaping via neutral paths? Technical Report 99-06-041, Santa Fe Institute, 1999. Santa Fe Institute Working Paper, submitted to *Bull. Math. Biol.*

8. Tim Watson and Peter Messer. Mutation genes in dynamic environments. In Robert John and Ralph Birkenhead, editors, *Soft Computing Techniques and Applications*, Advances in Soft Computing, pages 152–157, Heidelberg, 1999. Physica-Verlag.

Modelling Non-Numeric Linguistic Variables

Jon Williams, Nigel Steele, and Helen Robinson

Computational Intelligence Group, School of Mathematical and Information Sciences, Coventry University, Priory Street, Coventry CV1 5FB UK

Abstract. We consider how non-numeric linguistic variables may take their values from a pre-ordered set of vaguely defined linguistic terms. The mathematical structures that arise from the assumption that linguistic terms are pair-wise tolerant are considered. A homomorphism between tolerance spaces, filter bases and fuzzy numbers is shown. A proposal for modelling non-numeric linguistic variables with an ordered set of fuzzy numbers is introduced.

1 Introduction

In some application domains there is a need to work with both imprecise numeric data and linguistic variables which have no underlying numeric scale. A very simple example is deciding whether a student should pass or fail a course based on their mark and performance in seminars. The mark is imprecise because of marker variation and performance in a seminar takes a linguistic value such as **competent**.

There is a substantial body of work dealing with linguistic variables and their modelling with fuzzy sets. It is Zadeh's contention that Fuzzy logic = Computing with words [10]. However in applications fuzzy sets and fuzzy logic are most often applied to variables which have an underlying numeric scale. Modelling non-numeric linguistic variables is acknowledged to be less well developed. [1] The usual definition of a linguistic variables is given in definition 1.

Definition 1 [Fuzzy Linguistic Variable [9]] A linguistic variable is characterized by a quintuple $\langle v, L, X, g, m \rangle$; in which v is the name of the variable, L is a finite set of linguistic terms $\{l_0, \dots, l_n\}$ which describe v whose values range over a universal set X of values of v; g is a grammar for generating linguistic terms, and m is a semantic rule which assigns to each term $l \in L$ its meaning $m(l)$ which is a fuzzy set on X; (i.e. $m(l) : T \to \mathcal{F}(X)$).

In this paper we define a vague non-numeric linguistic variable, make a set of assumptions about the structure of linguistic terms and indicate how the alternative mathematical structures of *filter bases* and *tolerance spaces* justify the use of fuzzy sets to model non-numeric linguistic variables.

---

[1] For example by Cox on who wrote in the comp.ai.fuzzy newsgroup on 28 March 1999 *"The application of fuzzy logic and fuzzy metrics to non-numeric objects (and events) has long been a difficult task"*

Definition 2 [Non-Numeric Linguistic Variable] A non-numeric linguistic variable is characterised by a quintuple $\langle v, L, X, g, m \rangle$; in which v is the name of the variable, L is a finite set of linguistic terms $\{l_0, \ldots, l_n\}$ which describe v whose states range over a universal set X of states of v; g is a grammar for generating linguistic terms, and m is a semantic rule which assigns to each term $l \in L$ its meaning $m(l)$ on X; that is $m(l) : L \to A \subseteq X$).

Example 1 Consider the performance of a student in a seminar. Then $v =$ **seminar**. The set X_{seminar} of possible states of a student's performance ranges from **never attended** to **superb** and might also include **attended but did not contribute**, **answered questions well** and so on. These states are described by a pre-ordered set L_{seminar} with a grammar (g) of at least three terms, for example {**poor,competent, good**}. The grammar (g), might also specify how many additional terms may be added. So for example the terms **very poor** and **very good** might be added. Then $m(\textbf{poor})$ maps to the lower portion of the seminar performance range so that $m(\textbf{poor}) \precsim m(\textbf{competent})$.

2 Sets of Linguistic Terms - Mathematical Structures

In this section assumptions will be made about the mathematical structure of sets of linguistic terms. The following definitions are required.

2.1 Orderings

Definition 3 [Preorders] A preorder is a set equipped with a reflexive transitive operation $\precsim$ such that if $a, b, c \in A$ then $a \precsim a$, and also where $a \precsim b$ and $b \precsim c \Rightarrow a \precsim c$.

Definition 4 [Partial Orders and Chains] A partial order is a preorder equipped with an antisymmetric relation such that for $a, b \in A$ then $a \precsim b$ and $b \precsim a \implies a = b$. A partial order relation is *totally ordered or a chain* if for all $a, b \in A$ either $a \precsim b$ or $b \precsim a$.

2.2 Vague Linguistic Terms

The remainder of his paper is based on the following assumptions about the sets of vague linguistic terms which are used to valuate variables. Let $V := v_1, \ldots, v_p$ be a finite set of linguistic variables.

Preorder Each v_k takes a value or range of values from a finite pre-ordered set of linguistic terms value : $V \to L$ to give value$(v_k) = l_i$ $i \in I$ (I an indexing set) and the pair $\langle l_i, v_k \rangle$ which we will denote l_{i,v_k}.

Kernels For each l_{i,v_k} let there be at least one state of v_k to which only that term applies, the *kernel* $\ker(l_{i,v_k})$ of the term so that $m(\ker(l_i)) : L \to X$ is injective for each $l_i \in L$.

Pairwise tolerance Let vague linguistic terms be pairwise tolerant so that

$$l_{i,v_k} \sim l_{i+1,v_k} \Rightarrow l_{i,v_k} \cap l_{i+1,v_k} = \tau_R(l_{i,v_k}) = \tau_L(l_{i+1,v_k}) \neq \emptyset$$

so that the meaning $m : L_{v_k} \to X$ gives $m(\tau_R(l_i)) = m(\tau_L(l_{i+1}))$. Here τ_R is the *right tolerance* and τ_L the *left tolerance*. The least element of L_{v_k} is assumed to have no left tolerance and the greatest element no right tolerance. Note that $\tau_L(l_i) \prec \ker(l_i) \prec \tau_R(l_i)$.

Pairwise concatenation The operation of concatenation $\oplus$ of the linguistic terms $l_i, l_m \in L_{v_k}$ is defined pairwise. So that

$$l_{i \oplus m} = l_i \oplus \ldots \oplus l_m = \bigcup_i^m l_j \ \ (i \leq j \leq m).$$

This is equivalent to the logical *OR* '$\bigvee$' operation.

Note that $\ker(l_{i \oplus m}) = \{\ker(l_i), \tau_R(l_i), \ldots, \tau_L(l_m), \ker(l_m)\}$

Products The product $\prod$ of two sets of linguistic terms is defined on the product space of their respective variables $v_k \times v_j$ to give the pair l_{i,v_k}, l_{i,v_j} and naturally extended to $\prod_1^p v_k$ to give $(l_{i,v_k}, \cdots, l_{i,v_p})$.

3 Mathematical Structures and Linguistic Variables

Albrecht [1] draws attention to the fact that many elements of knowledge based systems and uncertain reasoning can be captured by traditional mathematics and in particular by topology. Hovesepian [4] has shows that a tolerance space is sufficient to model the sorites paradox using a three valued logic and Stout [7] uses tolerance spaces as a basis for fuzzy sets.

Definition 5 [Topological Space] Let X be a non-empty set. A Class $\mathcal{T}$ of open subsets of X is a *topology* on X iff $\mathcal{T}$ satisfies the following axioms.

O1 $X \in \mathcal{T}$ and $\emptyset \in \mathcal{T}$
O2 The union of any number of sets in $\mathcal{T}$ belongs to $\mathcal{T}$
O3 The intersection of any two sets in $\mathcal{T}$ belongs to $\mathcal{T}$

In a topological space the members of $\mathcal{T}$ are referred to as open sets. The complement of any open set is in is a closed set. This gives another definition of a topological space using closed sets [2].

Definition 6 [Bases] Let $(X, \mathcal{T})$ be a topological space. A class $\mathcal{B}$ of open subsets of X i.e $\mathcal{B} \subset \mathcal{T}$, is a base for the topology $\mathcal{T}$ on X iff every open set $\mathcal{O} \in \mathcal{T}$ is the union of members of $\mathcal{B}$.

Definition 7 [Sub-bases] Let $(X, \mathfrak{T})$ be a topological space. A class $\mathfrak{S}$ of open subsets of X i.e $\mathfrak{S} \subset \mathfrak{T}$, is a sub-base for the topology $\mathfrak{T}$ on X iff the finite intersections of members of $\mathfrak{S}$ form a base for $\mathfrak{T}$.

Definition 8 [Tolerance Space - [11]] A *tolerance space*, $\langle X, \xi \rangle$ is a set X with a symmetric reflexive relation $\xi \in X \times X$, the tolerance on X. If $\langle x, y \rangle \in \xi$ denoted $x\xi y$, then x is said to be within ξ tolerance of y. A space may be equipped with more than one tolerance. A bi-tolerant space is a space $\langle X, \langle \xi, \zeta \rangle \rangle$ with $\xi \supseteq \zeta \supseteq \delta$, where δ is the discrete tolerance. In a tolerance space $\langle X, \xi \rangle$ the set $N(x)\{y : y\xi x\}$, is called a *t-neighborhood* of $x \in X$.

A topological space $(X, \mathfrak{T})$ is *tolerable*[4] if there exists a ξ on X such that the set $\{N(x) : x \in X\}$ of t-neighborhoods serves as a sub-basis for the set $\mathfrak{T}$ of all open subsets of X. So if we take X to be the set $\{\ker(l_i), \tau_L(l_i), \tau_R(l_i)\}$ and with $i \in I$ an indexing set and for $a, b \in X$ we have a tolerance relation such that $a\xi b \Leftrightarrow m(a) \& m(b) \in m(l_i)$ where m is defined as in definition 2 then $\{N(\ker(l_i))\} = l_i$ is a set of t-neighborhoods.

3.1 Topologies of Linguistic Terms

Following on from this we show that the supports sets of the linguistic terms give an open sub-base for a tolerable topology.

Theorem 1 *Let S_{v_k} be the set of elements of the kth linguistic variable then L_{v_k}, is a sub-base for an open topology $(S_{v_k}, \mathcal{L}_{v_k})$ on S_{v_k}.*

Proof. Let $S_{v_k} = \{\{\tau_L(l_i)\}, \{\ker(l_i)\}, \{\tau_R(l_i)\}\} : 0 \leq i \leq |L_{v_k}| - 1\}$ be the set of all elements of a base set of linguistic terms.
The set of base terms $L_{v_k} = \{l_i\}$ is a class of subsets of S_{v_k}; and the finite intersections of L_{v_k} give the class

$$\mathcal{B} = \{\{l_i\}, \{\tau_L(l_i)\}, \{\tau_R(l_i)\}, \emptyset, S\}.$$

Taking unions of members of $\mathcal{B}$ gives the class $\mathcal{L}$, which is the Topology $(S_{v_k}, \mathcal{L}_{v_k})$ on S_{v_k} generated by the set of base terms $L_{v_k} = \{l_i\}$.

A topology on $(X, \mathfrak{T})$ is T_2 or Hausdorff if and only if, given a pair of distinct points x, y of X there exist an open sets $x \in \mathcal{M}$ and $y \in \mathcal{N}$ such that $\mathcal{M} \cap \mathcal{N} = \emptyset$. It can be shown that the topology $(S_{v_k}, \mathcal{L}_{v_k})$ is not Hausdorff.

3.2 Filter Bases

It is convenient to introduce here the concepts of a *Filter Base* .

Definition 9 [Filter Base] A non empty system $\mathcal{B}$ of subsets of the set X is called a *filter basis* on X if the following conditions are satisfied.

FB1 the intersection of any two sets from $\mathcal{B}$ contains a set from $\mathcal{B}$
FB2 the empty set does not belong to $\mathcal{B}$

Example 2 For any $a, x \in \mathbb{R}$ the set $\mathcal{B} = \{x, [x - a, x + a]\}$ is a filter base.

Given this definition we prove the following theorem

Theorem 2 *Let $l = \{l_i, \ker(l_i)\}$ with $l_i = \{\tau_L(l_i), \ker(l_i), \tau_L(l_{i+1})\}$ then l is a filter-base.*

Proof. Both FB1 and FB2 are satisfied since: $l_i \cap \ker(l_i) = \ker(l_i) \in l$ and $\emptyset \notin l$

4 Filter Bases and Fuzzy Sets

Definition 10 [Fuzzy Set] Zadeh defines [8] a *fuzzy subset* A of a set X as a nonempty subset

$$A = \{(x, \mu_A(x)) : x \in X\} \text{ of } X \times [0, 1] \text{ for some function } \mu_A : X \to [0, 1].$$

the common practice of referring to fuzzy subsets as fuzzy sets will be adopted from now on. The *alpha-level* set of a fuzzy set A_α on X is defined as $A_\alpha = \{x \in X : \mu_A(x) \geq \alpha \text{ for each } \alpha \in (0, 1]\}$. The *support* of a fuzzy set is given by $A_{0+} = \{x \in X : \mu_A(x) > 0\}$ and the *kernel* of a fuzzy set by $A_1 = \{x \in X : \mu_A(x) = 1\}$

Fuzzy subsets of $\mathbb{R}$ are often referred to as fuzzy numbers or fuzzy intervals and are defined as follows:

Definition 11 [[3]] A *fuzzy number or fuzzy interval* is a fuzzy set with membership function $\mu : \mathbb{R} \to I = [0, 1]$ such that μ is upper semi-continuous, $\mu(x) = 0$ outside some interval $(a, d) \in \mathbb{R}$ and there are b and $c \in \mathbb{R}$ with $a \leq b \leq c \leq d$ such that μ is increasing on $(a, b]$; decreasing on $[c, d)$ and $\mu(x) = 1 \; \forall x \in [b, c]$

Two representations which are particularly computationally efficient are triangular fuzzy numbers and trapezoidal fuzzy intervals. A *Triangular Fuzzy Number* $\tilde{n}$ is characterized by an ordered triple $< a_1, a_2, a_3 >$ with $a_1 \leq a_2 \leq a_3$ such that $\tilde{n}_{0+} = (a_1, a_3)$ and $\tilde{n}_1 = \{a_2\}$, and a *Trapezoidal Fuzzy Interval* $\tilde{I}$ by an ordered quadruple $< a_1, a_2, a_3, a_4 >$ with $a_1 \leq a_2 \leq a_3 \leq a_4$ such that $\tilde{I}_{0+} = (a_1, a_4)$ and $\tilde{I}_1 = [a_2, a_3]$.

Having introduced the concept of fuzzy sets we can now show how they are related to filter bases and tolerance spaces.

Theorem 3 (Albrecht) *A fuzzy set, fuzzy interval or fuzzy number is a valuated filter base*

Proof. Take $B = [a, b] \subset \mathbb{R}$, with $a < b$, and $C = (0, 1] \subset \mathbb{R}$ and a function $\mu : B \to C$ with the requirement that $\exists x \in B : \mu(x) = 1$. Define a filter base $\mathcal{C} = \{[\alpha, 1] : \alpha \in (0, 1]\}$ and $B_\alpha := \mu^{-1}([\alpha, 1])$ as an alpha-cut. Then the filter base $\mathcal{B} = \{B_\alpha : \alpha \in (0, 1]\}$ describes a fuzzy set, B with membership function μ.

Remark 1. Since fuzzy intervals and fuzzy numbers are fuzzy sets this result applies to them equally. It is easy to see that the support and kernel of a trapezoidal fuzzy interval form a filter base since $A_1 \cap A_{0+} = A_1$ and neither A_1 nor A_{0+} is empty.

Theorem 4 *A fuzzy set is a valuated neighborhood in a tolerance space*

Proof. Let $\langle X, \xi \rangle$ be a tolerance space then a tolerance ζ is said to be finer than ξ if $\xi \supset \zeta$, the finest tolerance is the discrete tolerance δ and the space $\langle X, \delta \rangle$ is the discrete tolerance space where every point is only in tolerance of itself. A neighborhood of $a \in X$, $N(a) \supset N'(a)$ if $N(a) \in \langle X, \xi \rangle$ and $N'(a) \in \langle X, \xi' \rangle$ with $\xi \supset \xi'$. So $\{N_i(a)\} := \{N_i(a) \in \langle X, \xi_i \rangle : \xi_i \supset \cdots \supset \xi_n \supset \delta\}$ is a filter base and the result follows from theorem 3.

Taking these two results together gives the following theorem.

Theorem 5 *If $l = \{l_j, \ker(l_j)\}$ with $l_j = \{\{\eta_i(l_j)\}, \ker(l_j), \{\tau_{r_i}(l_j)\}\}$ then l can be represented by a fuzzy set.*

Proof. Apply theorems 3 and 4

In this section we have demonstrated that a non-numeric linguistic variable can be represented by a fuzzy set. In section 5 the problem of representing a non-numeric linguistic term with a fuzzy number or fuzzy interval is discussed in detail.

5 Numeric Representations of Non-Numeric Linguistic Variables

We have shown that non-numeric linguistic variables may be modeled with fuzzy sets. In applications we need to represent non-numeric linguistic terms for which there is no underlying numeric scale other than an ordinal one. This section looks at a principled way of arriving at that representation.

Shepard [6] and Nofosky [5] suggest that the similarity η of two non-identical point stimuli x and y is given by a Universal Law of Generalization $\eta(x, y) = e^{-\alpha d(x, y)}$; where $d(x, y)$ is a the Hamming or Euclidean metric and α is a constant.

If we fix a finite set $P = \{p \in \mathbb{N}\}$ of points in the state space of a non-numeric linguistic variable and assume they are distributed evenly in the state space of the variable the probability that a state $y \in [0, |P|]$, will be generalized to $a \in P$ can be found as follows.

The similarity $\eta(a, y)$ of any point y to a fixed point $a \in P$ is given by $\eta(a, y) = e^{-\alpha d(a, y)}$. The probability that a point $y \in [0, p]$ is generalized to $a \in p$ is given by

$$P(a|y) = \frac{\eta(a, y)}{\sum_{n=1}^{p} \eta(n, y)} \tag{1}$$

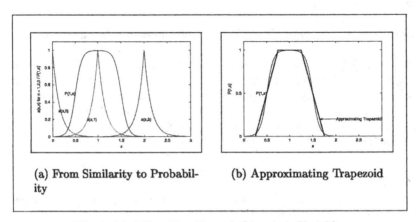

(a) From Similarity to Probability

(b) Approximating Trapezoid

Fig. 1. Modelling Non Numeric Linguistic Variables

If $d(x, y) = 1$ and $\alpha = 7$ then $\eta(x, y) = e^{-\alpha d(x, y)} \approx 0$.
Define

$$\eta'(x, y) = \begin{cases} e^{-7d(x, y)} & d(x, y) < 1 \\ 0 & d(x, y) \geq 1. \end{cases} \tag{2}$$

then by (1) the probability P that a point $y \in \mathbb{R}$ generalizes to the ordinal 1 is approximated by:

$$P(1|y) = \frac{\eta'(1, y)}{\eta'(0, y) + \eta'(1, y) + \eta'(2, y)} \text{ for } y \in [0, 2]$$

By defining tolerances ξ and ζ such that $1\xi a$ if $P(1|a) \leq 0.95$ and $1\zeta b$ if $P(1|b) \geq 0.05$ then $1\xi a$ if $|a - 1| \lesssim 0.25$ and $1\zeta b$ if $|b - 1| \lesssim 0.75$. The set of neighborhoods $\{N(1), N'(1)\}$ with $N(1) \in \xi$ and $N'(1) \in \zeta$ is a filter base and the distribution can be approximated by a fuzzy interval with $\mu_1(a) = 1$ for $a \in 1 \pm 0.25$ and $\mu_1(a) = 0$ for $a \notin 1 \pm 0.75$ to give the trapezoidal fuzzy interval $\langle 0.25, 0.75, 1.25, 1.75 \rangle$ as illustrated in figure(1). This process can be generalized to any $i \in \mathbb{N}$, $0 \leq i \leq |L_{v_k}|$ so that l_i is represented by the fuzzy interval $\langle i - 0.75, i - 0.25, i + 0.25, i + 0.75 \rangle$. A non-numeric linguistic variable valuated by n linguistic terms can be modeled by $\langle(i - 0.75)/n, (i - 0.25)/n, (i + 0.25)/n, (i + 0.75)/n\rangle$ given the assumption that the terms are evenly distributed. We are currently investigating the use of this representation in decision aids which use similarity based reasoning.

References

1. R.F. Albrecht (1998): On Mathematical Systems Theory. In R.F. Albrecht, (Ed.): Systems: Theory and Practice, Springer, 33–86.
2. Kelley, J. L. (1955): General Topology, Van Nostrand, New York.
3. R. Goetschel, W. Voxman (1983): Topological Properties of Fuzzy Sets,Fuzzy Sets and Systems 10, 87 - 99.
4. Hovesepian. F. (1992): A Metalogical Anaysis of Vagueness: An Exploratory Study into the Geometry of Logic, Ph.D. Thesis, University of Warwick.
5. Nofosky, R.M.(1984): Choice, Similarity, and the Context Theory of Classification. Journal of Experimental Psychology: Learning, Memory, and Cognition 10, 104 -114.
6. Shepard, R.N.(1987): Towards a Universal Law of Generalisation for Psychological Science. Science 237, 1317-1323.
7. Stout,L.N. (1992): The Logic of Unbalanced Subobjects in a Category with Two Closed Structures, In E. Rodabaugh, et al (Eds.): Applications of Category Theory to Fuzzy Subsets, Kluwer Academic Publishers, 73-106,
8. Zadeh, L.A.(1965): Fuzzy Sets. Information and Control 8, 856-865.
9. Zadeh, L. A.(1973): The concept of a linguistic variable and its application to approximate reasoning. Memorandum ERL-M 411, Berkley.
10. Zadeh, L. A.(1996): Fuzzy Logic = Computing with Words, IEEE Transactions on Fuzzy Systems 4,103–111.
11. Zeeman, E.C.(1962): The topology of the brain and visual perception. In Fort,M.K. (Ed.): The Topology of 3-Manifolds, Prentice Hall, 240-256.

Part 2

Application Exemplars

A Preliminary Fuzzy Model to Identify Abnormal Cervical Smears Using Fourier Transform Infrared Spectroscopy

Robert Adama-Acquah[1], Jonathan Garibaldi[1], Ian Symonds[2]

[1]Centre for Computational Intelligence
Faculty of Computing Sciences and Engineering
De Montfort University
Leicester LE1 9BH
United Kingdom

[2]School of Human Development
Academic Division of Obstetrics & Gynaecology
Derby City General Hospital
Derby DE22 3NE
United Kingdom

Abstract: Cervical cancer accounts for 6% of female malignancies with an estimated 4,000 new cases and 1,200 deaths per year in England and Wales. Current methods of screening are difficult to perform, error prone and subjective. A technique known as Fourier transform infrared spectroscopy (FT-IR) can be used to observe differences in vibrational modes of molecules in tissue proteins, and has been shown to hold promise for the early diagnosis of malignant changes. Accurate prediction of potential malignancy is thought to involve analysis of key parameters such as peak ratios and / or peak location at certain known important frequencies. A small database of cases with confirmed clinical diagnosis was used to investigate an initial fuzzy model of expertise capable of assessing the likely presence of malignancy. Two established, conventional rule-induction techniques (C4.5 and CN2) were used to induce a provisional set of rules which were then translated into fuzzy rule equivalents. The principles of FT-IR and its application to cervical cancer diagnosis, the development process of the initial fuzzy model of expertise, and provisional evaluation results are presented. Early results indicate that this model will need to be refined through knowledge elicitation with clinical experts and by fuzzy model tuning on more cases with known diagnosis.

Keywords: fuzzy logic, medical diagnosis, fourier-transform infrared spectroscopy

1 Medical Background

Cervical Cancer accounts for 6% of female malignancies with estimated 4,000 new cases and 1,200 deaths per year in England and Wales. Current methods of screening are difficult to perform, error and subjective. For example, Papanicolaou smears which are the current means for initial screening of cervical cancer, involves microscopic search, by eye, for the small percentage of abnormal cells from hundreds of thousands of cells on a smear. Clearly this is fatiguing, time consuming and reliant on human judgement [2].

With the inconsistencies occuring from current screening misdiagnosis, a more reliable means of cancer screening is desirable. Since FT-IR spectroscopy directly detects molecular changes rather than morphological changes, it makes it a powerful technique for earlier detection of abnormalities.

The use of the FT-IR techinque for accurately predicting potential malignancy is thought to involve analysis of key parameters such as peak height and/or peak position of the spectrum at certain known frequencies. Now, there is a need to develop an automated technique for the analysis of FT-IR spectra of cervical tissue to accurately diagnose the presence and degree of potential malignancy.

1.1 General Principles of Fourier Transform Infrared Spectroscopy

The diagram below (Fig. 1) shows the basic components of a FT-IR spectrometer. The radiation emerging from the source is passed through an interferometer where the "spectral encoding" takes place. The resulting interferogram signal exits the interferometer. The beam then enters the sample compartment where it is conditioned by the absorption of specific frequencies of energy which are uniquely characteristic of the sample. Finally the beam is passed to the detector to measure the special interferogram signal.

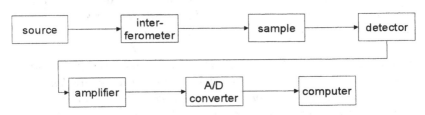

Fig. 1. Block diagram of basic components of a FT-IR spectrometer

Upon amplification of the signal, in which high-frequency contribution have been eliminated by filter, the measured signal is converted to a digital form by an A/D converter and transferred to the computer where Fourier Transform takes place.

1.2 Application to Cervical Tissues

FT-IR spectroscopy involves the measurement of absorption of electromagnetic radiation by matter as a function of wavelength covering 0.8 μm to 300 μm region of the elctromagnetic spectrum. Absorption by tissue is in the mid-infrared portion of the spectrum (2 - 20 μm) and is mainly associated with the vibrational modes of the functional groups of biomolecules in the cells [4].

The FT-IR spectra from a cell or tissue represents an average of the effects of its constituents cell components and varies according to their relative proportions and conformation within that tissue. However, by relating these spectra to those known for different molecules, it is possible to identify key biochemical and structural component of intact cells. It is on this basis that detection of abnormalities in cervical tissues is carried out using FT-IR spectroscopy

1.2.1 Spectral Analysis

The FT-IR spectrum consists of absorption peaks at different frequencies. The peaks are as a result of absorption by certain biochemical functional groups constituting the cell components of the tissue. These form the underlying key features for differentiating normal tissues from abnormal ones.

1.2.2 Spectroscopic Data Presentation

The digitised spectrum is passed through an established software package to extract the peak heights and their locations. As absolute peak heights depend on the strength of infrared radiation and sample thickness, relative peak heights, or 'peak ratios', with clinical significance are derived. Forty one cases consisting of six peak ratios were supplied by the clinicians along with confirmed clinical diagnosis for each case. These diagnoses had been based on examination of the cervix and confirmed by biopsy

2   The Preliminary Fuzzy Model

A preliminary model of fuzzy analysis was constructed using the MATLAB fuzzy logic toolbox. No explicit rules were available from the clinical experts and so a data-driven approach to induce the fuzzy model was used. A basic Mamdani style inference was used, with classical Zadeh Min-Max operators. In all cases conventional centre-of-gravity defuzzification was utilised to produce a single crisp output value.

2.1   Input Variables

The input peak ratios data were broken down by diagnosis and the mean and standard deviation (s.d.) for each input variable for *normal* diagnosis were calculated. A fuzzy input variable was created for each of the six peak ratios with universe of discourse (U.o.D.) given by the maximum range of values found in each variable. Initially, three membership functions corresponding to meanings of *low*, *mid* and *high* were assigned to each variable. These membership functions (m.f.s) were formed by generating a triangular function for *mid* that was centered around the *normal* diagnosis mean with a width of the *normal* diagnosis standard deviation. The *low* m.f. was drawn as a straight line from the 1 at the left edge of the U.o.D., down to 0 at the mean value, and the *high* m.f. was drawn as a straight line from 0 at the mean to 1 at the right hand edge of the U.o.D.

However, it was found that this gave insufficient resolution to the input variables as examination of the raw data showed that very similar input values could give rise to totally different diagnoses. Thus it was necessary to increase the number of input functions to improve discrimination of such close values. After an iterative process described in section 2.3 below it was found that 5 m.f.s, each with a width of 1 s.d., were required for input variables PR1 and PR2, and that 7 m.f.s, each with a width of ½ s.d., were required for input variables PR3, PR4, PR5 and PR6. Examples of the resultant membership functions are shown in Fig. 2 and 3.

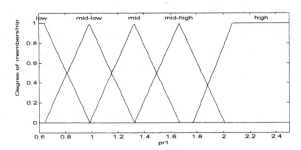

Fig. 2. Diagram of PR1 with 5 membership functions.

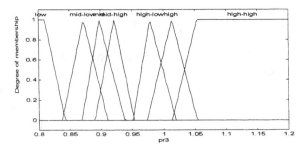

Fig. 3. Diagram of PR3 with 7 membership functions.

2.2 Output Variable

A single output variable was used with an arbitrary universe of discourse of 0 to 100, consisting of four membership functions, one for each of the diagnoses: *normal*, *inflammation*, *CIN-I*, and *CIN-II/III*. Initially symmetrical membership functions of equal width and spacing were used, but these were found to be inadequate. Consequently, a non-symmetrical set were developed manually by trial and error to ensure full discrimination. The non-symmetric output sets reflect the proportions of diagnoses found in the data set — i.e. the *normal* m.f. covers roughly half the output U.o.D. (20 / 41 cases), the *inflammation* m.f. covers a narrow range (3 / 41 cases), and the *CIN-I* and *CIN-II/III* m.f.s cover roughly a quarter of the U.o.D. each (10 / 41 cases and 8 / 41 cases respectively). The resultant m.f.s are shown in Fig. 4.

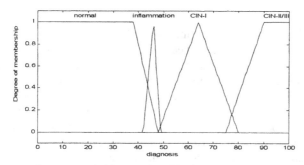

Fig. 4. Diagram of output variable membership functions.

2.3 Preliminary Rule Set

A preliminary rule set that was capable of discriminating the 41 cases in the data set was developed as follows. For each case the value for each of the six input peak ratios was plotted on its respective U.o.D. of the fuzzy variable and the membership function with the greatest membership value, μ, at that point was noted. This is equivalent to partitioning the U.o.D. into crisp membership sets with the interval of each set being given by the crossover points of the fuzzy m.f.s. This process resulted in the forty one cases with crisp input variables.

These crisp inputs were then examined with their associated diagnoses to discover whether any cases with the same inputs had different (conflicting) diagnoses. For example, when three m.f.s were used for each input the results shown in Table 1 were obtained. Clearly such conflicting data could not result in an accurately discriminating rule-set — hence, the number of m.f.s were increased and the process was repeated in an iterative manner until sufficient discrimination was achieved.

Case ID	PR1	PR2	PR3	PR4	PR5	PR6	Diagnosis
60	L	L	H	H	H	M	NORM
45	L	L	H	H	H	M	INFLAMM
24	L	L	H	H	H	M	CIN-I
37	L	L	H	H	H	M	CIN-II/III

Table 1. Illustration of cases with identical 'crisp' inputs but conflicting diagnoses generated by crisp partitioning with three membership functions in each input variable

When the number of m.f.s. had been increased to give sufficient discrimination to the data, the associations between 'crisp' input values and their corresponding diagnosis were encoded into a set of fuzzy rules.

2.4 Results

When the number of membership functions had been increased to 5 for PR1 and PR2 and 7 for PR3 to PR6, as described in section 2.1, there was one pair of cases with duplicated 'crisp' inputs and the same diagnosis and one pair of cases with duplicated 'crisp' inputs and differential diagnosis, shown in Table 2. Obviously, only one rule was required to describe the duplicate cases with same diagnosis. For the duplicate cases with differential diagnoses, the rule was decoupled by introducing a *not* operator to the input clause with greatest discrimination. A summary of results is shown in Table 3. The cases can be diagnosed with 100% accuracy by using crisp intervals also shown in Table 3.

Case ID	PR1	PR2	PR3	PR4	PR5	PR6	Diagnosis
6	MH	MH	L	ML	L	L	NORMAL
55	MH	MH	L	ML	L	L	CIN1

Table 2. Illustration of the two cases with identical 'crisp' inputs but conflicting diagnoses generated by crisp partitioning with 5-5-7-7-7-7 membership functions

Diagnosis	Mean	St. Dev.	Crisp Interval
NORMAL	24.1	3.1	0 - 40
INFLAMM	48.7	5.4	40 - 50
CIN-I	64.0	0.0	50 - 75
CIN-II/III	87.7	2.8	75 - 100

Table 3. Mean and standard deviation of fuzzy centroid output grouped by actual diagnosis

3   Rule Induction

Although the forty rule set described above classifies the input cases with 100% accuracy, it is clearly tailored specifically to the input data and so is unlikely to generalise to new data. The next course of action was to investigate whether the rule set could be generalised by passing the 'crisp' data set through classical rule induction algorithms.

3.1   Methodology

The 'crisp' data set was converted into the appropriate data format for two popular rule induction algorithms, C4.5 [3] and CN2 [1]. The data was passed through the induction algorithms and the rule set and classification matrix produced from 'crisp' inputs was examined. If the resultant rule set was deemed plausible (see below) the rules were encoded into their fuzzy equivalent and the fuzzy system re-run with the newly induced rules. The classification performance of this new fuzzy system was then examined.

3.2   C4.5

The C4.5 algorithm is a good example of a decision tree induction algorithm that uses an entropy based measure to determine the best attribute test to be made at each node of the tree. C4.5 starts with a general tree and grows a more and more specific tree until maximal classification is attained. It then prunes the tree as much as possible up to pre-defined acceptable misclassification rates. Having built a decision tree, C4.5 includes a mechanism for translating the decision tree into a set of 'IF ... THEN ...' production rules.

3.2.1   C4.5 Results

When run on the FT-IR data set, C4.5 initially generated a reasonable decision tree (~ 10 misclassifications) which it then, unfortunately, proceeded to prune back to the original default classifier tree consisting of the constant prediction of class *normal* for all cases! Alteration of C4.5 algorithm parameters to improve this situation resulted in, at best, a set of rules that predicted only two of the four possible diagnoses. Consequently, these rules were deemed implausible.

3.3   CN2

The CN2 algorithm is an example of a general-to-specific rule induction algorithm which starts, for example, with a single rule of the form 'IF *true* THEN *normal*' and adds new conjunctive terms until the improvement in classification is not considered significant. Once CN2 has determined a single such rule, all the cases that are correctly classified by the rule are removed from the training set and the process is repeated. CN2 uses a Laplacian based measure to assess the significance of classification performance.

3.3.1 CN2 Results

When run on the FT-IR data set, CN2 generated a rule set consisting of 19 rules with 6 / 41 misclassifications (87.8% accuracy). This rule set appeared promising and so was encoded into fuzzy equivalents and tested in the fuzzy system. It was found that a significant number of misclassifications were obtained. The process was however, tried on a fuzzy system with 5 m.f.s on all the input variables and a misclassification rate of 10 out of 41 was obtained. As this is a clinical screening process 'over-classification' is regarded as not being too serious, whereas 'under classification' is. It was found that 5 of the cases were under classified.

4 Conclusion

A preliminary fuzzy model of analysis has been developed. However, more work is needed to clarify the plausibility of the use of either 5 m.f.s or combination of 5 & 7 m.f.s on the input variables.

To further refine the model:

1. more data is required to test its generality and

2. expert clinical input is required to establish whether the rules are plausible and to assess whether the supplied peak ratios are adequate for determining pre-malignancy.

References

1. Clark P., Niblett T., (1989). The CN2 Induction Algorithm, *Machine Learning Journal*, **3(4)**, 261-283.

2. Gay D.J., Donaldson L.D., Goellner J.R., (1985). False Negative Results in Cervical Cytologic Studies, Acta Cytol., **29**, 1043-1046.

3. Quinlan R., (1993). *C4.5: Programs for Machine Learning*, Morgan Kaufmann, San Mateo, CA, USA.

4. Wong P.T. et al. (1991). Infrared Spectroscopy of Exfoliated Human Cervical Cells, *Proc. Natl. Acad. Sci. USA*, **88(24)**, 10988-10992.

Application of Soft-Computing Techniques in Modelling of Buildings

D Azzi, A E Gegov, G S Virk, B P Haynes and K Alkadhimi

University of Portsmouth, Department of EEE, Anglesea Building, Portsmouth
PO1 3DJ, UK, Tel: +44-(0)23-92842763, Fax: +44-(0)23-92842766,
alexander.gegov@port.ac.uk

Summary:
The paper presents recent results on the application of soft computing techniques for predictive modelling in the built sector. More specifically, an air-conditioned zone (Anglesea Building, University of Portsmouth), a naturally ventilated room (Portland Building, University of Portsmouth), and an endothermic building (St Catherine's Lighthouse, Isle of Wight) are considered. The zones are subjected to occupancy effects and external disturbances which are difficult to predict in a quantitative way and hence the soft computing approach seems to be a better alternative. In fact, the overall complexity of the problem domain makes the modelling of the internal climate in buildings a difficult task which is not always carried out in a satisfactory way by traditional deterministic and stochastic methods. The approach adopted uses fuzzy logic for modelling, as well as neural networks for adaptation and genetic algorithms for optimisation of the fuzzy model. The latter is of the Takagi-Sugeno type and it is built by subtractive clustering as a result of which the initial values of the antecedent non-linear membership functions and the consequent linear algebraic equations parameters are determined. A method of a combinatorial search over all possible fuzzy model structures for a specified plant order is presented. The model parameters are further adjusted by a back-propagation neural network and a real-valued genetic algorithm in order to obtain a better fit to the measured data. Modelling results with actual data from the three buildings are presented where the initial (fuzzy) and the final (fuzzy-neuro and fuzzy-genetic) models are shown.

Keywords: Soft-computing, intelligent modelling, building management systems.

1 Introduction

Soft Computing (SC) is a heuristic methodology which has attracted significant interest in recent years and has shown to be successful in many areas such as modelling, control, fault diagnosis and pattern recognition. It is based on the implementation of different approaches such as Fuzzy Logic (FL), Neural

Networks (NN), Genetic Algorithms (GA), and some others [5], [6]. Each of these techniques is suited for solving specific types of problems. In this respect, FL is powerful for approximate modelling and reasoning, NN are well suited for learning-based adaptation while GA are efficient for evolutionary-based optimisation. The underlying idea of SC is to use these heuristic approaches in combination with each other as well as with some conventional approaches, rather than using them separately.

Recent research in the field has shown a steady trend to hybrid solutions incorporating different SC approaches together as well as other classical approaches. A typical example is the so-called Takagi-Sugeno fuzzy models exploiting the idea of conventional dynamic modelling from numerical data embedded into a fuzzy logic inference framework. These models can be further improved by NN or GA to obtain a better fit to the measured data.

However, Takagi-Sugeno models usually assume a structure of the plant which is given *a priori* rather than trying to find it by some search procedures. In this respect, the paper presents a method of a combinatorial search over all possible model structures for a specified plant order. The method is demonstrated for a fuzzy model which predicts internal temperature and relative humidity values in three different buildings but can be applied to other types of plants as well.

2 Predictive Modelling Based Control

The work proposed here is concerned with the efficient control of the internal climate in office buildings. The authors' aim is to develop good predictive models which will allow a proactive control policy to be adopted rather than the traditional reactive ones in current use. In other words, instead of applying a control action only on the basis of the current sensor readings, it is also necessary to predict the values over a certain time interval. The main advantage of this proactive philosophy lies in the possibility to apply heating and cooling control efforts more efficiently as a result of which the control becomes smoother, together with smaller overshoots and shorter settling times. This, in turn, leads to decreased energy consumption and reduced pollution of the environment. However, to obtain predictive models for these buildings is not an easy task because their performance is affected by climatic and occupancy effects which are characterised by significant complexity and uncertainty.

The notion of a proactive control philosophy is the following. The control action at the current time instant k is computed not only on the basis of the measured output at the same time instant and the previous ones $(k-1)$, $(k-2)$, etc, but also by taking into account the predicted values of the output at the future time instants $(k+1)$, $(k+2)$, etc.

It would be interesting to see, if the SC methodology can provide good models for Building Management Systems (BMS). Some investigations have recently been carried out in this domain but most of them are too narrow and are thus leading to limited conclusions. In most cases, they are focused on one modelled parameter in one building during one season, and make use of separate SC techniques, rather than adopt a coordinated SC methodology. In other words, the potential of SC methodology for BMS has still not been explored in any detail.

This paper presents recent results from a research project aimed at investigating in a systematic way the capabilities of the SC methodology for predictive modelling of internal parameters in buildings, namely temperature and relative humidity [1], [2], [3], [4]. In this respect, air conditioned, naturally ventilated and endothermic types of buildings are considered. The three specific buildings under investigation are: Anglesea Building (University of Portsmouth), Portland Building (University of Porsmouth) and St Catherine's Lighthouse (Isle of Wight). These types of buildings are widely used nowadays and it must be pointed out that they differ substantially in their mode of functioning. Therefore, it is intended to find how the SC methodology is suited to each type of building.

3 Data Based Fuzzy Modelling

The approach adopted is based on a Takagi-Sugeno (TS) fuzzy model which has received considerable attention recently because of its suitability for processing information from input-output measurements. This is the case in BMS where the main information source is numerical data from sensor readings rather than expert knowledge which is difficult to obtain because of the multivariable and coupled nature of the process [2], [5]. Another advantage of the TS fuzzy model is its capability to approximate non-linear input-output mappings by a number of locally linearised models.

The TS fuzzy model consists of linguistic if-then rules in the antecedent part and linear algebraic equations in the consequent part. There are two types of parameters in this model: non-linear (in the membership functions in the antecedent part) and linear (in the algebraic equations in the consequent part). The task of the fuzzy model is to determine the initial values of both types of parameters on the basis of the input-output data. The method used in the paper is based on the idea of subtractive clustering, i.e. by assuming that each data point is a potential cluster centre and gradually finding the final clustering.

The Takagi-Sugeno fuzzy model for a system with two rules, two inputs (u_1, u_2) and one output (y) is presented by Equation (1). The linguistic labels (membership functions) of the inputs are denoted by A_i, B_i, $i=1,2$ and their parameters are the non-linear antecedent parameters. The coefficients a_i, b_i, $i=1,2,3$ are the linear consequent parameters used for the computation of the output.

If u_1 is A_1 and u_2 is A_2 then $y = a_1.u_1 + a_2.u_2 + a_3$ (1)
if u_1 is B_1 and u_2 is B_2 then $y = b_1.u_1 + b_2.u_2 + b_3$

Equation *(1)* represents a static Takagi-Sugeno fuzzy model which does not contain the time argument in the input and the output variables. However, in order to predict future temperatures, the time argument needs to be included in the equation, i.e. the model must be a dynamic one. In this respect, two types of dynamic models are introduced and investigated in the paper, namely Regression Delay (RD) and Proportional Difference (PD). Examples of such models are represented by Equations *(2)* and *(3)*, respectively.

$$\text{If } y_{k-1} \text{ is } A_1 \text{ and } y_{k-2} \text{ is } A_2 \text{ and } u_{1,k-1} \text{ is } A_3 \text{ and } u_{1,k-2} \text{ is } A_4 \text{ and } u_{2,k-2} \text{ is } A_5 \qquad (2)$$
$$\text{then } y_k = a_1.y_{k-1} + a_2.y_{k-2} + a_3.u_{1,k-1} + a_4.u_{1,k-2} + a_5.u_{2,k-2} + a_6$$

$$\text{If } y_{k-1} \text{ is } A_1 \text{ and } Dy_{k-1} \text{ is } A_2 \text{ and } u_{1,k-1} \text{ is } A_3 \text{ and } Du_{2,k-1} \text{ is } A_4 \qquad (3)$$
$$\text{then } y_k = a_1.y_{k-1} + a_2.Dy_{k-2} + a_3.u_{1,k-1} + a_4.Du_{2,k-1} + a_5$$

where $Dy_{k-1} = y_{k-1} - y_{k-2}$, $Du_{2,k-1} = u_{2,k-1} - u_{2,k-2}$

It can be seen that Equation *(2)* contains two auto-regressive terms of the output y, two regressive terms of the input u_1 and one delay term of the input u_2. As opposed to this, Equation *(3)* contains one proportional and one derivative term of the output y, one proportional term of the input u_1 and one derivative term of the input u_2. For simplicity, each of the equations includes only one rule, but in general the number of rules is higher. More specifically, it is equal to the number of the linearised submodels applicable to the respective local regions of the whole operating range.

Equations *(2)-(3)* represent examples of fuzzy model structures. Usually, these structures are obtained on the basis of evaluation of a number of structures in accordance with a performance criterion that is usually the Root Mean Squared Error (RMSE). The latter is a measure of the closeness of the model to the plant.

However, the majority of identification techniques apply partial rather than extensive model structural searching. They tend to represent the plant dynamics by either regression or delayed terms. As far as proportional or difference terms are concerned, they are usually considered up to the most recent data point in the past. This might be a serious disadvantage as the dynamics of the plant are not fully explored and some important terms in the model structure might be missed.

This paper presents a method of extensive searching of the model structures to explore the possible dynamics of the plant for a specified order. This method is demonstrated here for Takagi-Sugeno fuzzy models but can be also applied to any other types of models, including traditional ones. In this case, for a plant with m input variables and backward horizon equal to b, the whole number of investigated models is given by the equation:

$$C = (2.b)^m - 1 \qquad (4)$$

It is evident from Equation *(4)* that the number of investigated models is an exponential function of the number of inputs and the backward horizon which leads to a considerable increase of the computational complexity as the order grows. This is the price to pay for the extensive searching.

4 Neural Adaptation and Genetic Optimisation

The task of neural adaptation is to adjust the model parameters in order to obtain a better fit to the measured data. The method used in the paper is based on the idea of back-propagation, i.e. by iterative propagating of the model error (the difference between the real and the modelled plant output) from the consequent to the antecedent part of the fuzzy rules until a specified number of iterations is reached.

The neural adaptation algorithm involves the following steps:
1. Fix the antecedent parameters A_i in the non-linear membership functions.
2. Estimate the consequent parameters a_i by a least squares procedure.
3. Compute the model output y_k.
4. Keep the consequent parameters a_i in the linear equations fixed.
5. Estimate the antecedent parameters A_i by a gradient descent procedure.
6. Compute the RMSE of the model.
7. Go to step 1 if the specified number of iterations has not been reached.
8. Stop.

The purpose of genetic optimisation is also to adjust the model parameters as an alternative to the neural adaptation. The method used in the paper is based on the idea of real-valued coding, i.e. by representing the individuals with real valued genes and sequential evaluation of the model error until a pre-specified number of generations is reached.

The genetic optimisation algorithm involves the following steps:
1. Define the variation ranges for the antecedent and the consequent parameters A_i and a_i.
2. Create initial generation of individuals containing the parameters A_i and a_i as genes.
3. Evaluate the fitness function of all individuals by the RMSE of the model.
4. Select the fitter half of individuals for crossover.
5. Apply crossover on these individuals and create new ones.
6. Replace the less fit half of individuals with the new ones.
7. Apply mutations on some individuals
8. Evaluate the fitness function of all individuals by the RMSE.
9. Go to step 4 if the specified number of generations has not been reached.
10. Stop.

5 Experimental Results

This section presents modelling results from the three buildings under study. The results show that the outputs (temperature and relative humidity) can be predicted to a high level of accuracy on the basis of measurements. The most important variables used in the modelling are chosen by carrying out a cross-correlation analysis involving temperatures and relative humidities in the same and neighbouring zones, as well as external (weather) variables, e.g. solar radiance, wind speed and direction, etc. To ensure systematic modelling, both regression-delay and proportional-difference types of fuzzy model structures have been considered. The best model structure corresponding to the smallest training (identification) error was chosen by evaluating all possible structures of models up to some specified order, i.e. involving all combinations of input terms. Afterwards, the quality of the models was evaluated with new data and the validation errors obtained to give a measure of the prediction accuracy of these models. The validation errors are the difference between the model predictions and the actual outputs. The membership functions of the inputs in the fuzzy model were chosen to be of the Gaussian type while the selected options for the neural network and the genetic algorithm were 500 iterations and 50 generations with 10 individuals each, respectively. These options seem to give a good comparison between the two model improvement techniques used in our work.

Each one of the above model structures was chosen from a set of 1023 possible models, representing all the combinations of (auto)regression and (auto)delay terms. The backward (dynamic memory) horizon was chosen equal to 2, i.e., the model predictions at time k are obtained on the basis of measurements at times $k-1$ and $k-2$. The plant and model outputs for each of these models and for each building are shown in Figures 1-3.

6 Conclusions

Both the neural adaptation and the genetic optimisation schemes lead to a substantial improvement of the prediction capabilities of fuzzy model that have been formulated using traditional TS methods. These methods can be improved by incorporating a model structure selection capacity. The improvement can be considerable, especially in the cases where the model is not very good. The quality of the temperature prediction is better than the humidity prediction for all three buildings because of the smaller variational range and smoother profile.

The proportional-difference fuzzy model performs better than the regression-delay model in most cases for all the buildings indicating that it can capture the dynamics of the buildings more precisely. Concerning the model improvement, using genetic algorithms is in most cases superior to using neural networks for both temperature and relative humidity, for both types of regression-delay and proportional-difference fuzzy models, as well as for all three buildings. It has to be

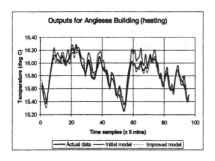
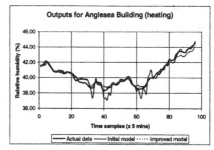

Figure 1. Temperature and relative humidity for Anglesea Building.

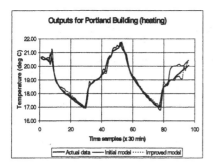
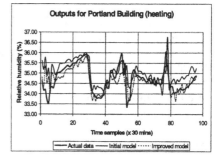

Figure 2. Temperature and relative humidity for Portland Building.

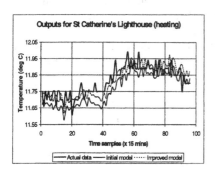
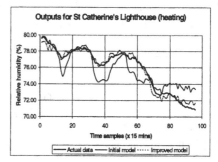

Figure 3. Temperature and relative humidity for St Catherine's Lighthouse.

noted that the best prediction results have been obtained for the naturally ventilated room, while the results for the air-conditioned zone and the ambient energy building are not as good but are comparable to each other.

With respect to the comparison between the two model improvement techniques, genetic algorithms seem to be superior. They show considerably better convergence properties and the best model parameters are usually obtained from the last genetic generations. In contrast, when using neural networks, the best model parameters are in most cases found from the first neural iterations. Taking also into account the parallel search capabilities of genetic algorithms, it is possible to conclude that they offer a far more reliable approach for improving fuzzy models than neural networks.

Acknowledgement

This work was carried out within an EPSRC funded project 'Soft Computing Models for Building Applications – a Feasibility Study' (Ref: GR/L84513). This funding is gratefully acknowledged. In addition, the project involves collaboration with Satchwell Control Systems, Caradon Trend Ltd, Ambient Energy Systems Ltd, Hampshire County Council, the Building Research Establishment and Trinity House Lighthouse Service. The technical and financial support provided by these partners is also greatly appreciated.

References

[1] Gegov, A, Virk, G, Azzi, D, Haynes, B and Alkadhimi, K, "Soft-computing based predictive modelling of building management systems", International Workshop on Recent Advances in Soft Computing, Leicester, UK, 69-77, 1999.
[2] Gegov, A, Virk, G, Azzi, D, Haynes, B and Alkadhimi, K, "Soft-computing based modelling of the internal climate in office buildings", UK Workshop on Fuzzy Systems, Uxbridge, UK, 145-152, 1999.
[3] Gegov, A, Virk, G, Azzi, D, Haynes, B, Alkadhimi, K and Matthews, I, "Neuro-fuzzy adaptive modelling of air-conditioning systems", European Congress on Intelligent Techniques and Soft Computing, Aachen, Germany, 267-268, 1999.
[4] Gegov, A, Virk, G, Azzi, D, Haynes, B, Alkadhimi, K, "Soft computing models of naturally ventilated buildings", CIBSE National Conference, London, UK, 421-428, 1999.
[5] Haupt, R and Haupt, S, "Practical Genetic Algorithms", John Wiley & Sons, New York, 1998.
[6] Jang, J, Sun, C and Mizutani, E, "Neuro-Fuzzy and Soft Computing", Prentice Hall, Upper Saddle River, 1997.

Neuro-Fuzzy Adaptive Strategies Applied to Power System Stabilization

Walter Barra Junior (1),   **José Augusto Lima Barreiros (2)**

(1) Federal Center of Technological Education of Pará–CEFET-PA, Brazil,
e-mail: barra@etfpa.br

(2) Federal University of Pará –UFPA-PA, Brazil, e-mail: barreiro@ufpa.br,

Address: Programa de Pós-Graduação em Engenharia Elétrica- Centro
Tecnológico, Campus Universitário do Guamá, UFPA, Belém, PA,Brasil,
CEP 66075-900 , fax: +55 021 211-1634;

Summary: This work presents a Local Model Network (LMN) neuro-fuzzy control strategy for stability and voltage regulation improvements in electric power systems. At each sample time, the control output is calcutated from a smooth (fuzzy) switching among a set of pre-designed linear local controllers. The local controllers are designed from ARX local models identified from field tests, for several plant operating conditions. The proposed strategy was assessed, by simulation studies, using a high order nonlinear power system dynamic model. The results show that a remarkable voltage regulation as well as dynamic stability improvements can be obtained when applying the proposed neuro-fuzzy strategy.

Keywords: Neuro-fuzzy Modelling and Control, Power System Stability and Control

1 Introduction

Electric Power Systems are time-variable nonlinear dynamic systems which often are operated near their instability boundary. Automatic controllers based on classical linear control strategies are the most applied for stability improvements. However, they cannot, in general, to cope with time-variable and nonlinear characteristics of the electric power system. In order to avoid these limitations, several advanced soft-computing based strategies, such as neural networks, fuzzy systems, and genetic algorithms, are emerging in power systems research and applications fields (Flynn *et alli*, 1997). Neuro-fuzzy systems allow the merging of quantitative and qualitative knowledge. The ultimate objective is to obtain improved plant performance. Local Model Networks (LMN) (Wang *et alli* ,1995; Hunt & Johansen,1997) is a recent neuro-fuzzy approach which has very interesting properties for modelling and control of nonlinear systems with unknown physical parameters. LMN applications are emerging from several different fields, including electric power systems (Irwin *et alli* , 1998).

This paper proposes a neuro-fuzzy LMN control strategy for dynamic stability and terminal voltage regulation in large electric power systems. The strategy works in an adaptive way, performing a smooth (fuzzy) switching among set of pre-designed local controllers. The paper is organized as follow: section 2 presents a brief introduction to LMN based modelling and control design; section 3 describes the proposed LMN based neuro-fuzzy strategy for power systems; section 4 presents simulation results; and the conclusions are presented in section 5.

2 Neuro-Fuzzy LMN Based Controller Design

Let S be a nonlinear dynamic system. Assume that exists a set of measurable operating variables, $o_1,...,o_{N_o}$, $\in R$. Let $O = [o_1,...,o_{No}]^T$, $\in R^{No}$, be the operating point vector. Assume that the operating space of the nonlinear system S can be partitioned in M local fuzzy operating regions and, for each local fuzzy operating region, the parameters of an ARX local model, in the form

$$A^{(l)}(q^{-1})y(t) = q^{-d}B^{(l)}(q^{-1})u(t) + c_0^{(l)} + e(t) \quad , l=1,..,M \tag{2.1}$$

can be estimated from field tests. For each local model (2.1), a corresponding local controller

$$u^{(l)}(t) = \frac{1}{S^{(l)}(q^{-1})}\left[T^{(l)}(q^{-1})r(t) - R^{(l)}(q^{-1})y(t)\right], l=1,..,M \tag{2.2}$$

is designed, where $y(t)$ is the output signal, $r(t)$ is the reference signal, and $R^{(l)}(q^{-1})$, $S^{(l)}(q^{-1})$, and $T^{(l)}(q^{-1})$, are polynomial whose coefficients can be calculated from coefficients of the local ARX model as well as from the desired local control performance. After the design of the local controllers, a global neuro-fuzzy controller can be defined using the following set of fuzzy rules

$$R^{(l)}: \text{IF } O(t) \text{ is } O^{(l)} \text{ THEN} u^{(l)}(t) = -S^{*(l)}(q^{-1})u(t) + T^{(l)}(q^{-1})r(t) - R^{(l)}(q^{-1})y(t)$$
$$l=1,2,...M \tag{2.3}$$

where $O(t)$ is the operating point vector and $S^{*(l)}(q^{-1}) = S^{(l)}(q^{-1}) - 1$. It is possible to show (Wang *et alli*, 1995) that the neuro-fuzzy controller output, for the operating point , $O(t)$, can be expressed as the following weighted mean of the M local linear controllers outputs

$$u(t) = \frac{\sum_{l=1}^{M} \rho^{(l)}(O(t))u^{(l)}(t)}{\sum_{l=1}^{M} \rho^{(l)}(O(t))} \qquad (2.4)$$

where $\rho^{(l)}(O(t))$ are the validation functions of the local controllers. The value of each validation function represents the intensity of contribution of each local controller, $u^{(l)}$, to the controller net output, at the current operating condition. The values of the validation functions are calculated from knowledge of the membership functions, which are specified by the designer, and from measurements of the operating variables, using the following relationship (obtained from application of product inference)

$$\rho^{(l)}(O(t)) = \mu_{o_1}^{(l)}(o_1(t))\mu_{o_2}^{(l)}(o_2(t))..\mu_{o_{no}}^{(l)}(o_{no}(t)) \qquad (2.5)$$

After some algebraic steps, the output of the neuro-fuzzy controller (equation (2.4)) can be expressed by the following polynomial form that is dependent on the operating point

$$u(t) = -S^*(q^{-1},O(t))u(t) + T(q^{-1},O(t))r(t) - R(q^{-1},O(t))y(t) \qquad (2.6)$$

where the coefficients of the global polynomials S^*, R e T, in (2.6), can be calculated from knowledge of the coefficients of the local controllers and the values of the validation functions, for the current operating condition $O(t)$.

3   Neuro-Fuzzy Power System Control

The power system consists of a synchronous generator interconnected to a large power system (infinite busbar), through a double transmission line. The power system, together with the conventional automatic voltage regulator (AVR), is the plant to be controlled by the neuro-fuzzy controller (see dashed block in figure 3.1). The control objectives are to improve the dynamic stability, damping the rotor angular speed oscillations, and also to improve the voltage regulation performance. The neuro-fuzzy controller is designed to actuate in a supplementary way, through the modulation of the signal reference of the fixed AVR .

In order to simulate the nonlinear dynamic of the power system, a 5th order state-space nonlinear continuos model for the generator-infinite bus bar system (model IV in Arrilaga et alli , 1983) was used. This nonlinear high order model has a set of well defined physical electric and mechanic parameters which were supposed completely unknown to the proposed neuro-fuzzy control strategy. The excitation system dynamic was simulated using a 1st order model. The fixed AVR was simulated by using a digital PID controller, designed to provide a damping relative factor of $\xi = 0.7$ (a max overshoot of 5 percent) and natural angular frequency $\omega_n = 4\pi$ rad/s (about two times the angular frequency of the rotor oscillations), with the generator at no load condition. The sample interval used for identification and control was $T_s = 0.020$ s.

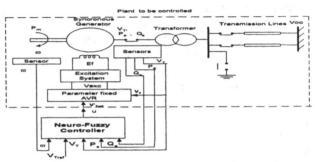

Fig. 3.1 Power plant to be controlled and the proposed neuro-fuzzy controller.

Using qualitative knowledge, obtained from visual analysis of many terminal voltage step responses, for different operating conditions, the universe of discourse for the operating variable active power, $P_e(t)$, was partitioned in seven fuzzy sets (see figure 3.2), while the universe of discourse for the operating variable reactive power, $Q_e(t)$, was partitioned in ten fuzzy sets (see figure 3.3). In order to efficiently capture the plant nonlinearities effects, a more refined partitioning was adopted for $P_e(t)=$ "HIGH" and $Q_e(t)=$ "NEGATIVE" or "ALMOST ZERO" fuzzy regions. It has been qualitatively observed that, in these regions the dynamic oscillations effects are more intensive. Triangular as well as trapezoidal membership functions were chosen to allow a more fast on-line calculation.

The fuzzy partitioning of the operating space as well as the membership functions choice are very important design consideration. It was shown for some authors (Hunt and Johansen, 1997) that a very coarse operating space fuzzy partitioning as well as a very high overlapping between validation functions, mainly for those that are not very close in the operating space, can lead to instability of the control system. On the other hand, it is not practical to perform a very refined fuzzy partitioning of the operating space because the number of local controllers and, as a consequence, the time requested to perform the on-line calculations will increase exponentially. It is also not practical to use a very low degree of overlapping between validations function because this imply to a poor capability to generalize. Taken into consideration the trading between stability, generalization capability, and on-line fast calculations, a 50 percent degree of membership function overlapping, only for the neighbors membership functions, was chosen in the present study. With these choices, the operating PxQ plane was partitioned in 60 local fuzzy operating regions which implies that 60 local controllers need to be designed.

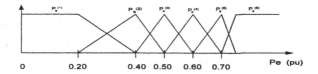

Fig. 3.2. Fuzzy partitioning of the operating variable P_e .

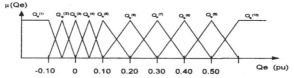

Fig. 3.3. Fuzzy partitioning of the operating variable Q_e

For each fuzzy operating region, the corresponding local models (in the form (2.1)) were identified. The coefficients of the local models for the terminal voltage channel were used to design a set of corresponding local supplementary voltage regulators. These supplementary local regulators (in the form (2.2)) were designed to obtain an uniform terminal voltage performance, for the allowed operating region (a desired relative damping factor $\xi = 0.7$, and natural angular frequency $\omega_n = 4\pi$ rad/s, for all selected operating points). A global neuro-fuzzy supplementary voltage regulator was then obtained applying equations (2.3) to (2.6). In order to damp the rotor dynamic oscillations, instead of using the terminal voltage, V_T , as the input to the neuro-fuzzy supplementary voltage regulator, a modified plant output in the form

$$y(t) = V_T(t) + \gamma\Delta\omega(t), \qquad -1 < \gamma < 0 \qquad (3.2)$$

was used, where γ is a scalar that governs the degree of feedback of the stabilizing variable speed deviation , $\Delta\omega = \omega - \omega_o$, in order to provides more damping for rotor oscillations. The scalar γ can be chosen by performing a trial and error adjustment. However, it is not easy to choose a single value for γ which implies good performance for all operating condition.

To cope with this tuning difficulty, an automatic tuning procedure for γ was developed in the present work. It consists in the following steps : (i) visualize γ as an unknown nonlinear function of the operating condition, i.e. $\gamma = \gamma(P_e, Q_e)$, and approximate the unknown relationship $\gamma = \gamma(P_e, Q_e)$ by using a fuzzy system in the form

$$\gamma(P_e(t), Q_e(t)) = \frac{\sum_{l=1}^{M} \rho^{(l)}(P_e(t), Q_e(t))\gamma^{(l)}}{\sum_{l=1}^{M} \rho^{(l)}(P_e(t), Q_e(t))} \tag{3.3}$$

where the parameters $\gamma^{(l)}, l = 1, ..., M$, are to be estimated by automatic learning;

(ii) derive a learning law to estimate the parameters $\gamma^{(l)}, l = 1, ..., M$, in such way that the following cost function is minimized

$$J = \tfrac{1}{2}\lambda_V [V_{TRef}(t) - V_T(t)]^2 + \tfrac{1}{2}\lambda_\omega [\Delta\omega(t)]^2 \tag{3.3}$$

where the weighting factors $\lambda_V, \lambda_\omega$ are non-negative scalars to be chosen by the designer. It is known (Wang, 1994) that a learning law in the form $\gamma_{k+1}^{(l)} = \gamma_k^{(l)} - \alpha\partial J / \partial\gamma^{(l)}$, with $0 < \alpha < 1$, can minimize the cost function (3.3).

Therefore, by using the identified coefficients for the ARX local models for the voltage and speed channels as the predictors for values of $V(t)$ and $\Delta\omega(t)$, in the function cost (3.3), and calculating the partial derivative $\partial J / \partial\gamma^{(l)}$, the following learning law to automatic tuning of the stabilizing parameters $\gamma^{(l)}, l = 1, ..., M$, was obtained

$$\gamma^{(l)}(t) = \gamma^{(l)}(t-1) + \alpha \frac{\rho^{(l)}(P_e, Q_e)}{\sum_{l=1}^{M} \rho^{(l)}(P_e, Q_e)} x(t), \qquad \gamma_{min} < \gamma^{(l)}(t) \le 0 \tag{3.4}$$

where $x(t) = \left(\lambda_\omega b_{\omega 0}^{(l)} \Delta\omega(t) - \lambda_V b_{V0}^{(l)}(V_{Tref}(t) - V_T(t))\right)R(q^{-1}, P_e, Q_e)\Delta\omega(t-1)$, the parameters $b_{V0}^{(l)}, b_{\omega 0}^{(l)}$ are the b_0 coefficient for the local ARX models for the voltage and speed channels, λ_{min} $(-1 < \lambda_{min} < 0)$ is the lowest value allowed for the parameters $\gamma^{(l)}, l = 1, ..., M$, and α $(0 \le \alpha < 1)$ is the learning rate. In order to apply the learning law (3.4), the learning parameters α, $\lambda_{min}, \lambda_V, \lambda_\omega$, must be chosen by the designer by trial and error. For this present study the used values were $\alpha = 0.005$, $\lambda_{min} = -0.3$, $\lambda_V = 0.001$, and $\lambda_\omega = 1$.

4 Simulation Results

The results of tests performed to assess the terminal voltage regulation improvements are presented in figure 4.1.a and 4.1.b. For these tests, the initial operating condition was $P_e = 0.90$ and $Q_e = 0.10$ (pu). At time t = 1 seconds, a 0.010 pu step variation was applied to the reference of the fixed AVR.

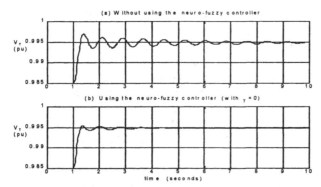

Fig. 4.1. Responses for a 0.010 pu V_{Tref} step variation.

As can be observed , in figure 4.1.a, when only the fixed AVR is used the terminal voltage output has approximately a 15 percent overshoot as well as a settling time of approximately 10 seconds. This poor performance is because the fixed AVR is not able to provide a satisfactory performance for all operating conditions. The terminal voltage response, under action of the neuro-fuzzy controller, is shown in figure 4.1.b, to the same step variation as before. It can be observed that the terminal voltage regulation is very superior than when using only the fixed AVR. The neuro-fuzzy supplementary regulation has reduced the overshoot to less than 5 percent (as desired) and has also reduced the settling time to less than 2 seconds, as can be seen from figure 4.1.b.

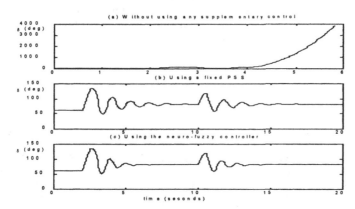

Fig 4.2. Rotor angle variations (in degree).

In order to evaluates the stability improvements, the neuro-fuzzy controller performance was compared with the performance of a fixed power system stabilizer (PSS) which was designed, according to the recommendations of (Larsen & Swann,1981), to provide a relative damping $\xi = 0.3$, for the operating condition (Pe=0.90, Qe=0.10). The system was submitted to a sequence of two severe faults. The first one, at time t=2 seconds, was a short circuit, with 50 ms of duration, followed by the loss of one transmission line. The second fault , at time t= 10 seconds, was a short circuit with 50 ms duration, but without line loss. Figure 4.2.a shows that without using supplementary stabilizing control, the system becomes unstable after the first fault. This is a situation where it is necessary to use power system stabilizer supplementary control. In figure 4.2.c., it can be observed that the supplementary neuro-fuzzy controller was able to maintain the stability of the power plant, after the occurrence of both severe faults, damping the oscillations of the rotor very quickly. The curves show that the performance of the neuro-fuzzy controller (figure 4.2.c) is better than that of the fixed PSS (figure 4.2.b). This superior performance was obtained even taking into consideration that the fixed PSS was projected exactly for the point of operation initial operation of the experiment, while, for the neuro-fuzzy controller, any local controller was designed for this the particular operating point ($P_e = 0.90$, $Q_e = 0.10$). In this way, the neuro-fuzzy controller has obtained a very satisfactory performance by means of its generalization capability.

5 Conclusions

In this article a neuro-fuzzy LMN strategy for power system control was presented. The proposed controller carries out a double function: supplementary terminal voltage regulation as well as power system stabilization. It was presented a learning method that allows to adjust, automatically, the feedback intensity of the stabilizing signal, according to the current operating point, avoiding using adjustment based on trial and error. Simulation results have shown a remarkable regulation and stability improvements.

6 References

Arrilaga, J., Arnold, C. P., Harker, B. J. (1983). *Computer Modelling of Electrical Power Systems.* John Wiley & Sons.

Flynn, M. S., Irwin , G. W. , Brown, M. D. , Swidenbank, E., Hogg, B. W. (1997). *Neural Control of Turbogenerators Systems.* Automatica , Vol. 33, No. 11, pp. 1961-1973.

Hunt , K. J.; Johansen, T. A. (1997). *Design and Analysis of Gain Scheduled Control Using Local Controller Network.* Int. Journal of Control, Vol 66, No. 5, pp. 619-651.

Irwin, G. W. , Brown , M., Lightbody , G. (1998). *Nonlinear Identification of a Turbogenerator By Local Model Networks.* IEE Proceedings of UKACC International Conference on Control' 98 , Swansea, Wales, September, pp. 1462-1467.

Larsen, E. V.; Swann, D. A. (1981). Applying Power Systems Stabilizers. Parts I ,II,III. IEEE Trans. Power Appar. Syst, pp. 3017-3024, pp. 3025-3033, pp. 3034-3046.

Wang , L. (1994). *Adaptive Fuzzy Systems and Control –Design and Stability Analysis.* Prentice Hall.

Wang, H., Liu, G. P., Harris, C. J., Brown , M. (1995). *Advanced Adaptive Control.* Pergamon Press.

Using Genetic Algorithms to Incorporate Taste into Diets

S.Berry and V.Lowndes

School of Mathematics and Computing, University of Derby, Kedleston Road, Derby.

1 Introduction

The objective in solving a Diet Problem is to select the best set of foods, from a given list, so that the resultant diet will both satisfy a set of nutrient restrictions and minimise the total cost of the diet. Where, for example, cost could be expressed in monetary terms or as the fat content of the diet. An early formulation of such a problem was due to Stigler, see Gass (1985).

Optimal solutions to Diet problems have been obtained through the use of Linear Programming techniques, see Fletcher (1994) or Smith (1959).

However, although this approach produces the optimal solution to the problem (the cheapest diet), the resultant diet tends to be unpalatable, typically implying the consumption of the same foods every day. The results from Stiglers work, quoted in Gass (1985), provide an extreme example of this type of solution.

Therefore research has concentrated on reformulating the problem to incorporate a consideration of 'taste' into the problem solution. Where 'taste' could be considered to have been incorporated either through the provision of a range of diets close to the optimal solution, or by the production of a diet which is close to a 'patients' chosen diet, Fletcher (1994).

Both approaches employ Post Optimality analysis on the optimal solution generated from the Linear Programming formulation to generate these new solutions.

The intention here is show how Genetic Algorithms allied to the traditional Linear Programming approach, can provide an alternative to the use of Post Optimality analysis, producing both a range of acceptable diets and a range of acceptable diets close to the patient chosen diet. Thus enabling the incorporation of taste into the generated diets.

This approach is proved through its application on the basic cost minimising formulation, and then applied to the 'taste formulation' developed by Fletcher (1994).

2 Traditional Formulation of the Diet Problem

This section aims to show how Genetic Algorithms can be employed to obtain a set of near optimal solutions to a "diet type" problem, thus incorporating taste through the provision of many diets.

This section assumes the traditional cost minimising formulation of the diet problem.

The objective of this formulation of the diet problem is the selection of a set of quantities of foods, x, which satisfy the dietary restrictions

$$Ax \geq b$$

and at the same time minimise the value of a cost function where

$$cost = c\,x$$

Note:

1. Matrix A defines the nutrient content of each food; a_{ij} indicating the quantity of nutrient i in one unit of food j;

2. b_i defines the restriction on the quantity of nutrient i in the chosen diet, here assumed to be the minimum intake per day,

3. c_j gives the cost of a unit of food j, and

4. x_j gives the quantity of food j in the diet.

The formulated problem will have m variables (foods) and n constraints (nutrient restrictions), where in general m will be much greater than n, consequently the optimal solution will consist of at most n non zero variables (foods). This factor implying the lack of 'taste' in the diet defined by this optimal solution, assuming that taste can be related to the number of different foods in the diet,

Stigler solved a 77 food problem in 1939 obtaining a five food diet costing $39.93 per year the Linear Programming solution was obtained later, nine foods yearly cost $39.67, thus suggesting that there are nine nutrient restrictions. A dietician working with the same data at the same time produced a more palatable diet costing $115 a year.

These results indicating the monotony of diet implied by this approach and the cost increase needed to produce a palatable diet.

2.1 Genetic Algorithm Approach

The structure within the problem, many variables few constraints, and the consequent limited number of foods in the optimal solution suggested that the use of a Genetic Algorithm approach to the problem might prove to be a viable alternative to the normal Linear Programming approach.

This (GA) approach starts with the selection of a set of s 'n variable' sub problems, the set of solution strings for the Genetic Algorithm, each of these sub problems defining one of the s "n constraint" Linear Programming formulation.

The GA string

$$3,5,.............,78$$

contains n values. Each value corresponds to a food to be considered for inclusion in the diet.

A set of 'n variable' sub problems are chosen because it is known that the optimal solution will consist of no more than n non-zero values, and $sn \geq m$.

The ith sub problem at the first iteration can be represented by

Minimise cost $C_i = c_i x_{i1}$

subject to

$$A_i x_{i1} \geq b$$

Where x_{i1} indicates the quantity of each food in diet i at iteration 1.

The optimal solutions to each of these sub problems can be obtained using Linear Programming techniques, giving

an optimal set of foods and quantities, S_{i1}

and a cost for the diet, C_{i1} .

These costs are used to define the fitness function within the genetic algorithm and are used to generate the next set of sub problems x_{i2} employing crossover and mutations. Tournament selection being used to select the GA strings from the first iteration and mutation replacing a food from the string with a randomly chosen other food.

This process is repeated, using the x_{in} (iteration i results) to generate the $x_{i(n+1)}$, (the strings for iteration $i+1$) continuing until the solution set converges onto a solution or until a set number of iterations have been completed.

This approach was employed to analyse a 280 food 5 nutrient constraint problem. The results showing that this (GA) process converges to a solution close to the optimal solution (see Table 1). A set of near-optimal solutions has been obtained, producing a set of alternative near-optimal diets thus incorporating taste through the provision of a set of alternative diets.

2.2 Results

The sample set of data, 280 foods and 5 nutrient constraints, was used to evaluate this approach. The nutrient requirements to provide an acceptable diet were obtained from Paul & Southgate (1978) and the food costs/unit were generated randomly to produce a large set of trial problems.

In each case the genetic algorithm procedure performed 10 iterations and every diet with a cost less than twice that of the optimal cost was recorded, the number of such diets is given in Table 1.

On average 48 alternative diets were generated using this approach, thus validating the use of Genetic Algorithms to introduce taste into the diet problem through the provision of a variety of solutions close to the optimal solution.

Test Problem	Optimal Solution (Ocost)	Number of Solutions within 2*Ocost
A	116	49
B	90	41
C	108	57
D	109	46

Table 1: Results using the Basic Model.

3 Taste Formulation

This section investigates the application of the Genetic Algorithm approach to the alternative 'taste formulation' for a diet problem.

This more satisfactory approach to the incorporation of taste into diets has been provided by Fletcher, who started with an existing diet, many foods, and investigated the necessary changes, to this diet, so that a feasible diet, obeying the nutrient restrictions, could be generated. The original diet can be considered to represent the taste of the 'patient' and the result of the analysis produces a set of diets as close as possible to this original diet.

Fletcher obtained a range of solutions from this formulation using post optimality analysis. Here the Genetic Algorithm approach outlined above is applied to this alternative formulation producing a range of solutions to the diet problem comparable with those generated by Fletcher.

3.1 GA Problem Formulation and Notation

In addition to the defined set of nutrient constraints

$$A\,x \geq b$$

and cost function

$$cost = c\,x,$$

there now exists a patient chosen diet, given by the vector of foods x_c where x_{ci} indicates the quantity of food i in the chosen diet.

This diet can be assumed to be infeasible, its nutrient content does not satisfy all of the constraints.

Let t be the vector defining the quantity of nutrients in this diet, then

$$t = A\,x_c$$

The problem is now reformulated in terms of y, where y is the vector containing additional foods (extra to those specified by the patient).

$$A\,y \geq b\text{-}t$$

Minimise $cost = c\,y.$

The final diet will be given by:

$$x_c + y$$

with a cost given by

$$c(x_c + y)$$

The Genetic Algorithm approach described above (see Section 2.1) was applied to this problem producing a range of diets close to the chosen diet.

3.2 Results

The same data set was used to evaluate each approach and to simulate the effect of allowing the customer or patient to choose desirable foods, 4 foods were randomly chosen to be included in the diet.

The Genetic Algorithm procedure employed in Section 2 was then used to determine second sets of foods so that these together with the pre-chosen foods would produce a diet that would satisfy the nutrient requirements as cheaply as possible. Because of the higher cost of the resultant diet (compared with those obtained in Section 2) only those diets with a cost less than 1.5*optimal cost were recorded.

Table 2 displays a typical set of results, it must be noted however that the initial customer selection could lead to an unsolvable problem, for example the total fat content from the chosen foods may be greater than the maximum allowed quantity.

Test Problem	Optimal Solution (Ocost)	Number of Solutions within 1.5*Ocost
E	222	45
F	212	37
G	184	24
H	195	49

Table 2: Results using the Model incorporating taste.

These results show that this approach, using Genetic Algorithms but allowing the customer to choose a number of foods, produces more varied but more expensive diets than those produced in Section 2. Here a diet will contain 4 preferred foods and 5 others whereas in Section 2 a solution contained a maximum of 5 foods (not necessarily favoured by the customer).

4 Conclusion

It can be seen, from the results given in Section 2, that the use of Genetic Algorithms does allow the production of a range of nearly optimal diets. Thus this approach can therefore be considered to provide a viable way to the problem of constructing a set of alternative diets given a single set of constraints.

However because each diet can only contain a set number of foods, the consequence of the formulation of the problem and Linear Programming approach, effectively the limited number of nutrient constraints in the problem, there is no guarantee that all, or even, any of these diets will be palatable. Thus the basic model has been adapted by allowing the customer to select a number of desirable foods before employing a Genetic Algorithm approach, results given in Section 3.

These results have been obtained because of the implicit parallelism within the genetic algorithm approach that allows an efficient search through the feasible solution space. Thus this approach has the effect of investigating many solution paths simultaneously, for example consider a problem where there are only two strings each of length n and the crossover interchanges just one piece of information:-

(a)   the original strings each represent a vertex of the feasible region;

(b)   changing one variable in a string effectively moves the process to an adjacent vertex, the Simplex Method;

(c)   changing more than one variable enables the investigation of a 'distant', not adjacent part of the feasible space;

(d)   there are N strings therefore N independent paths are explored simultaneously;

(e)   unlike the Simplex Method the result from a 'move' could increase the cost, move further away from the optimal solution and hence investigate other parts of the feasible region.

Thus this approach considers more 'good' vertices within the feasible region and will therefore produce a range of answers.

An important factor to consider is the length of the genetic string, the ideal length is such that the variety of solutions will be generated.

Here it will be between n the number of nutrients, and m the number of foods. To generate many alternative diets it seems that the string length should be greater than n.

This approach has generated the required set of near-optimal solutions and has thus demonstrated its ability to produce a range of acceptable near-optimal solutions and hence incorporate taste into diet problems.

Bibliography

Fletcher L.R, *LP Techniques for the Construction of Palatable Human Diets*, Journal of the Operational Research Society; 1994, Vol. 68, pp489-496.

Gass, S.I, *Decision Making Models and Algorithms*, pp67-73; John Wiley; 1985

Goldberg, D.E, *Genetic Algorithms*; Addison Wesley, 1989

Holland, J.H, *Adaptation in Natural and Artificial Systems*; MIT, 1994.

Paul, A. A., Southgate, D.A.T., *McCanse and Widdowson's The Composition of Foods*; HMSO 1978.

Smith, V.E., *Linear programming models for determination of palatable diet*, Journal of Farm Economics, May 1959, vol. 41, No. 2, pp. 272-283.

Stigler, G., *The Cost of Subsistence*, Journal of Farm Economy, 1945, Vol 27; p303-314.

Appendix 1

The foods used to construct both the Stigler and the optimum diet using the 1939 data were:-

Stigler Diet	Optimal Diet
Wheat Flour	Wheat flour
Evaporated milk	Corn meal
Cabbage	Evaporated milk
Spinach	Peanut butter
Dried navy beans	Lard
	Beef Liver
	Cabbage
	Spinach
	Potatoes

Source: Gass (1985)

Appendix 2

Diet generated by the customer selection procedure

Customer selected foods	GA generated extra foods
Salmon	Gammon
Red lentils	Avacodo pear
Tomatoes	Brussel sprouts
Spring greens	Blackberries

Suggesting the daily diet

Avacado Pear and Blackberries

Gammon, Red Lentils, and Brussel Sprouts

Salmon, Tomato, and Spring Greens

The Application of Fuzzy Logic and Genetic Algorithms to Oil Exploration

S.J.Cuddy* and P.W.J. Glover[√]

[√]Department of Geology and Petroleum Geology, University of Aberdeen.

*Petro-Innovations, An Caisteal, 378 North Deeside Road, Cults, Aberdeen. UK.

1 Introduction

Oil exploration has benefitted from the application of fuzzy logic and genetic algorithms[1]. The oil industry now uses these new interpretation techniques to predict permeability, litho-facies (specific rock type) and shear velocities in uncored wells. Oil explorers are forced to live with error, uncertainty and fragile correlations between data sets. These conditions are inherent to oil exploration, because of the challenge of designing and building well logging tools to measure complex formations in hostile environments. Even in the laboratory it is difficult to relate a logging tool response to a physical parameter. Several perturbing effects such as mineralogy, in-situ fluids and drilling fluid invasion can influence a simple measurement. Litho-facies and permeability prediction have presented a challenge to formation evaluation due to the lack of logging tools that measure them directly. The new methods can be used as a simple means for confirming known correlations or as a powerful predictor in uncored wells.

One clear application is to litho-facies determination. Litho-facies typing is used in well correlation and is important for building a 3D model of an oil or gas field. The technique makes no assumptions and retains the possibility that a particular litho-facies type can give any well log reading although some are more likely than others. This error or fuzziness has been measured and used to improve the litho-facies prediction in several North Sea fields. In one study, descriptions from 10 cored wells were used to derive litho-facies descriptions in 30 uncored wells. This technique gave near perfect differentiation between aeolian, fluvial and sabkha rock types.

A second application is permeability calculation. Knowledge of permeability is important in determining the well completion strategy and the resulting productivity. The problem with permeability prediction is derived from the fact that permeability is related more to the aperture of pore throats rather than pore size, which well logging tools find difficult to measure. Determining permeability from well logs is further complicated by the problem of scale, well logs having a vertical resolution of typically 2 feet compared to the 2 inches of core plugs. The new techniques quantify these errors and use them, together with the measurement, to improve the prediction.

A third application is shear velocity estimation. The measurement of shear velocities is essential for understanding reservoir rock behaviour such as sand production and fracturing. It is also becoming important for enhanced seismic interpretation. Because the value of shear velocity data is only now being realised and acquisition costs are high, there is limited amount of shear data available in the North Sea. Genetic algorithms have been used to determine the shear velocities in oil wells based on calibrations elsewhere in the oil field. Genetic algorithms determine the parameters and evolve the equations of these calibrations.

2 Litho-Facies Prediction Using Fuzzy Logic

Litho-facies typing is useful in well correlation and can be important for building a 3D model of the field by stochastic techniques. These models can be used for volumetrics, well placing and reservoir engineering. Using fuzzy logic for litho-facies prediction makes no assumptions and retains the possibility that a particular facies type can give any log reading although some are more likely than others.

2.1 The Fuzzy Mathematics of Litho-Facies Prediction

The normal distribution is given by:

$$P(x) = \frac{e^{-(x-\mu)^2/2\sigma^2}}{\sigma\sqrt{2\pi}} \qquad\qquad ....(1)$$

P(x) is the probability density that an observation x is measured in the data-set described by mean μ and standard deviation σ. Where there are several litho-facies types in a well, the porosity value x may belong to any of these litho-facies but some are more likely than others. Each of these litho-facies types has its own mean and standard deviation such that for f litho-facies types there are f pairs of μ and σ. If the porosity measurement is assumed to belong to litho-facies f, the fuzzy possibility that porosity x is measured (logged) can be calculated using the Gaussian equation by substituting μ_f and σ_f. Similarly the fuzzy possibilities can be computed for all f litho-facies. These fuzzy possibilities refer only to particular litho-facies and cannot be compared directly as they are not additive and do not add up to one. It is necessary to devise a means of comparing these possibilities.

We would like to know the ratio of the fuzzy possibility for each litho-facies with the fuzzy possibility of the mean or most likely observation. This is achieved by de-normalising the Gaussian equation. The fuzzy possibility of the mean observation μ being measured is:

$$P(\mu) = \frac{e^{-(\mu-\mu)^2/2\sigma^2}}{\sigma\sqrt{2\pi}} = \frac{1}{\sigma\sqrt{2\pi}} \dotfill (2)$$

The relative fuzzy possibility $R(x_f)$ of a porosity x belonging to litho-facies type f compared to the fuzzy possibility of measuring the mean value μ_f is the Gaussian equation divided by Equation 2:

$$R(x_f) = e^{-(x-\mu_f)^2/2\sigma_f^2} \dotfill (3)$$

Each fuzzy possibility is now self-referenced to possible litho-facies types. To compare these fuzzy possibilities between litho-facies, the relative occurrence of each litho-facies type in the well must be taken into account. This is achieved by multiplying Equation 3 by the square root of the expected occurrence of litho-facies f. If this is denoted by n_f, the fuzzy possibility of measured porosity x belonging to litho-facies type f is:

$$F(x_f) = \sqrt{n_f}\, e^{-(x-\mu_f)^2/2\sigma_f^2} \dotfill (4)$$

The fuzzy possibility $F(x_f)$ is based on the porosity log (x) alone. This process is repeated for a second log such as the volume of shale, y. This will give $F(y_f)$, the fuzzy possibility of the measured volume of shale y belonging to litho-facies type f. This process can be repeated for another log, say z, to give $F(z_f)$. At this point we have several fuzzy possibilities ($F(x_f)$, $F(y_f)$, $F(z_f)$ ....) based on the fuzzy possibilities from different log measurements (x, y, z ....) predicting that litho-facies type f is most probable. These fuzzy possibilities are combined harmonically to give a combined fuzzy possibility:

$$\frac{1}{C_f} = \frac{1}{F(x_f)} + \frac{1}{F(y_f)} + \frac{1}{F(z_f)} + \dotfill (5)$$

This process is repeated for each of the f litho-facies types. The litho-facies that is associated with the highest combined fuzzy possibility is taken as the most likely litho-facies for that set of logs. The associated fuzzy possibility $C_f(\text{max})$ provides the confidence factor to the litho-facies prediction.

One recent well in the Southern North Sea with substantial core coverage was used to calibrate litho-facies and as a permeability predictor for the older wells. Figure 1 shows the results of this analysis. The left track of Figure 1 shows the several core described facies from this well. The result of the fuzzy predicted litho-facies is shown in the middle track. There is near perfect differentiation between aeolian, fluvial and sabkha rock types. In addition, the technique goes some way towards differentiating between sandy, mixed and muddy sabkhas.

2.2 The Application of Fuzzy Logic to Permeability Prediction

Knowledge of permeability, the ability of rocks to flow hydrocarbons, is important for understanding oil and gas reservoirs. Permeability is best measured in the laboratory on cored rock taken from the reservoir. However coring is expensive and time-consuming in comparison to the electronic survey techniques most commonly used to gain information about permeability. In a typical oil or gas field all boreholes are "logged" using electrical tools to measure geophysical parameters such as porosity and density. Samples of these are cored, with the cored material used to measure permeability directly. The challenge is to predict permeability in all boreholes by calibration with more limited core information.

In principle, determining permeability from electrical measurements is a matter of solving equations in rock physics. In practice, there are numerous complicating factors that make a direct functional relationship difficult or impossible to determine. One problem is that permeability is related to the aperture of pore throats between rock grains which logging tools find difficult to measure. Several perturbing effects such as mineralogy, reservoir fluids and drilling fluid invasion can influence the permeability measurement.

Litho-facies determination is a clear application of fuzzy logic as the litho-facies types are described in clear "bin" types such as aeolian or fluvial. These predicted litho-facies, in wells without core, have several uses from inter-well correlation to geostatistical modelling. One of the main drivers behind litho-typing is to predict permeability as the different litho-facies exhibit different permeabilities. It was soon realised that fuzzy logic could be used to predict permeability directly, by-passing the litho-facies step.

Fuzzy logic is used for litho-facies prediction by assigning a data bin to each litho-type. The challenge for litho-typing is how to combine the fuzzy possibilities between the litho-types, as the litho-facies are not equally frequent in the cored section of the well. Predicting permeability using fuzzy logic avoids this problem by ensuring, at the outset, that the bins are of equal size. First the core permeability values are scanned by the program and divided into ten equal bin sizes on a logarithmic scale. Each of these bins is then compared to the electrical logs. The electrical log data associated with levels in the well corresponding to each bin are analysed and their mean and standard deviation calculated. Fuzzy logic asserts that a particular log porosity can be associated with any permeability but some are more likely than others.

The program uses any number of permeability bins with any number of input curves. The distribution of bin boundaries depends on the range of expected permeabilities, as described above. The number of bins depends on the statistical sample size, the number of core permeabilities available for calibration. A reasonable sample size is around 30. Consequently the number of bins is determined so that there are at least 30 sample points per bin. For a well with 300 core permeabilities it would be appropriate to use 10 permeability bins. The right track of Figure 1 shows the excellent comparison of core derived and fuzzy predicted permeabilities. Permeability prediction has also been attempted using genetic algorithms[2].

3 Shear Velocity Prediction Using Genetic Algorithms

The measurement of shear velocities is important for understanding reservoir rock properties. Shear sonic data (Vs) is required for rock strength analysis to determine fracture propagation and formation breakdown characteristics and to improved porosity prediction as Vs is largely unaffected by fluid type. It is also becoming important for enhanced seismic interpretation. Because the value of shear velocity data is only now being realised and acquisition costs are high, there is limited amount of information available in the North Sea. Vs can be acquired by dipole logging tools. If Vs data have not been acquired by logging, it can be estimated from other curve responses using genetic algorithms. Genetic algorithms have been used to determine the shear velocities in oil wells based on calibrations elsewhere in the oil field. Genetic algorithms determine the parameters of these calibrations as well as evolving the equations. In a recent study, calibration data from 4 wells with shear velocity data were used to populate all the wells in a large field. This gave the oil company a cost effective method of building a 3D reservoir model that enabled the better location of oil wells.

Shear velocities are related to porosity (ϕ), formation resistivity (Rt) and the volume of shale (Vsh). Our objective is to empirically construct a function $f(\phi, Rt, Vsh)$ which predicts shear velocities at each depth, i given ϕ, Rt, Vsh and at each depth. We are therefore searching for an appropriate function of the form:

$$Vs = f(\phi, Rt, Vsh) = a\, \phi^b \bullet_1 c\, Rt^d \bullet_2 e\, Vsh^g \bullet_3 h \quad \dots\dots\dots\dots\dots\dots\dots$$
(6)

where $\bullet_1 \bullet_2 \bullet_3$ etc represent algebraic operators addition and multiplication.

The next step is to provide a method for determining how good a given $f(\phi, Rt, Vsh)$ is as a predictor of Vs. The approach we adopt is to sum absolute errors in prediction over all depth levels for a given borehole. We seek a function of the form (5), which minimises this sum. A more standard way to do this might be to use least squares rather than absolute values of residuals. The reason is that the borehole data are noisy and include many "outliers". These can only be removed by extensive manual editing of the data sets and rechecking of measurements. By using the absolute value of residuals, one diminishes the effect of these and produces more appropriate predictor functions. Mathematically, the problem can be stated as:

$$Minimise_f : \sum_i \left| Vs_i - f(Phi_i, Rt_i, Vsh_i) \right| \quad \dots \dots \dots \dots \dots \dots \dots \dots (7)$$

The genetic algorithms were constructed as follows. An initial population of individuals is picked randomly in the solution space. The fitness criterion of each of these individuals is determined by equation 7. The best existing algorithm for minimising 7 starts with a randomly generated f and uses local search by mutating the coefficients one at a time or flipping the operator. The mutation range is initially set very high in order that the individuals search all of the solution space. After a number of generations a pool of individuals are selected, by linear ranking, for mating and cloning. Mating is achieved by coefficient merging. Some of the best individuals are cloned to add more individuals to where solutions are most promising. After a number of generations the operator is fixed and the percentage change in mutated coefficients is gradually reduced. The algorithm stops when the percentage improvement in evaluation reaches a predefined lower limit or a maximum number of iterations has been reached.

Each chromosome is a vector of length 10. Three alleles are binary values that represent $\bullet_1, \bullet_2, \bullet_3$. The rest of the alleles are float values that represent the coefficients a, b, c, d, e, g, h. The initial population is generated by creating chromosomes with random binary numbers for $\bullet_1, \bullet_2, \bullet_3$ and random float numbers for the coefficients a, b, c, d, e, g, h. If the allele represents the operator $\bullet$, its value is binary and it will be switched. If the allele represents one of the real variables, it will be modified by multiplying a value between randomly picked from a range 0.8 to 1.2. This range decreases in value as the number of generations increases. This provides a method to concentrate on local search towards the end of the algorithm as better solutions emerge.

4   Conclusions

Fuzzy logic and genetic algorithms have found several applications throughout the North Sea including the prediction of litho-facies, permeability and shear velocities. These are simple tools for confirming known correlations or as powerful predictors in uncored wells. Litho-facies typing is used for well correlation and as input for building a 3D model of the field. Permeability prediction is useful to complement current technology and to gain insight to older wells without core and extensive logging programmes. The measurement of shear velocities is important for understanding reservoir rock properties.

The methods described here use basic log data sets such as porosity and density, which are cheap and easy to obtain, rather than depending on new and expensive logging technology. Over recent years, oil exploration has suffered due to erratic and often low oil prices. Oil producing countries are now struggling to meet demand and there is an urgent need to find new reservoirs and make efficient use of existing resources. Fuzzy logic and genetic algorithms make an important contribution to this endeavour.

5   Nomenclature

x	= log variable
μ	= mean
σ	= standard deviation.
nf	= expected occurrence of x in litho-facies f
μf	= mean value of x in litho-facies f
σf	= standard deviation of x in litho-facies f
$P(x)$	= fuzzy possibility density of an observation x
$R(x\,f)$	= relative fuzzy possibility of x
$F(x\,f)$	= fuzzy possibility of x belonging to litho-facies f
C_f	= combined fuzzy possibility
V_s	= shear velocity
ϕ	= porosity
R_t	= resistivity
V_{sh}	= volume of shale
a,b,c,d,e,g,h	= numerical coefficients to be determined
$\bullet_1, \bullet_2, \bullet_3$	= operators representing either addition or multiplication
f	= family of functions

6   References

1. Cuddy, S.J., "The Application of Fuzzy Logic to Petrophysics", The Thirty-Eighth Annual Logging Symposium of the Society of Professional Well Log Analysts, June 1997.

2. Brown, D.F, Cuddy S.J., Garmendia-Doval A.B. and McCall J.A.W., "The Prediction of Permeability in Oil-Bearing Strata using Genetic Algorithms" Third IASTED International Conference Artificial Intelligence and Soft Computing, July 2000, to appear.

Figure 1. Permeability & Facies Prediction

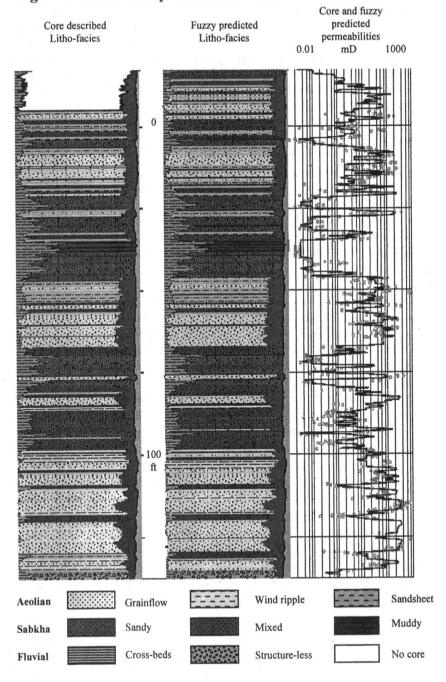

Symbolic and Numerical Regression: Experiments and Applications

J. W. Davidson, D. A. Savic and G. A. Walters

School of Engineering and Computer Science,

University of Exeter, Exeter EX4 4QF, UK

Summary: This paper describes a new method for creating polynomial regression models. The new method is compared with stepwise regression and symbolic regression using three example problems. The first example is a polynomial equation. The two examples that follow are real-world problems, approximating the Colebrook-White equation and rainfall-runoff modelling.

Keywords: genetic programming, least-squares, rule-based programming, stepwise regression, symbolic regression

1 Introduction

This paper describes a new regression method for creating polynomial models. The new technique, referred to as the hybrid method, is compared with two established regression methods, symbolic regression and stepwise regression using three example problems.

2 The Methods

2.1 The Hybrid Method

The hybrid method combines the parameter optimisation of numerical regression with the evolutionary search of symbolic regression. The new approach overcomes several potential problems with symbolic regression including sub-optimal parameters, code bloat and the creation of underdetermined functions. However, the new approach restricts the wide range of operators normally used in symbolic regression to a subset consisting only of addition, multiplication and non-negative integer powers. The expressions that result from the limited set of operators are forms of polynomials. A rule-based program consisting of 56 rules algebraically transforms all expressions produced through the evolutionary process to a form amenable to parameter optimisation by the method of least-squares.

The rule-based program eliminates all non-functional code (introns) produced by evolutionary operations. The rule base simplifies expressions by evaluating terms and coefficients that consist entirely of constants and replaces them with a single constant where possible. Once the rule base has transformed the expressions to the required polynomial form the program computes the optimal value for constants in the expressions by the method of least-squares. The rule base and method of least-squares optimise the constant values in every new solution before the algorithm evaluates the fitness of the solution.

Experience has shown that the methods for generating starting solutions normally used in genetic programming, such as "ramped half" occasionally produce expressions that have an extremely large number of terms when expanded algebraically. The hybrid method uses a new technique for generating starting solutions that creates short, two-term polynomial expressions. With successive generations the expressions grow to a maximum length specified by the user. The hybrid regression method uses modified operations of crossover and mutation rather than the conventional genetic programming operations. The new crossover operation divides expressions at locations between terms in the expression and cannot operate within individual terms. New mutation operations act to modify power values within terms and occasionally create entirely new terms at random. The new crossover operation produces child solutions that are a sum of terms found in either of the two parents. The crossover operator can impose limits on the number of terms that appear in child solutions and thereby restrict the maximum size of expressions, controlling the rate by which the length of expressions grows.

2.2 Stepwise Regression

Stepwise regression is a popular and highly effective method for building regression models. Draper and Smith (1998) regard stepwise regression as "one of the best variable selection procedures." There are two approaches to stepwise regression, (1) stepwise selection and (2) forward selection. Both methods begin by creating the best first-order linear regression equation consisting of two terms, a single transformed variable and a constant. With each step a term consisting of the product of a constant and a transformed variable is added to the model. The transformed variable selected is the one that produces the greatest reduction in mean square error (MSE). Forward selection is the simpler form of stepwise regression. This method continues to add terms to the model by iterations of a best-first search. Stepwise selection, the more complex procedure, can remove terms on the basis of partial F statistics provided for each term by the method of least-squares. Stepwise selection removes the least significant term from the regression model if one or more partial F statistic falls below a minimum level of significance specified by the user, usually set at 95% or 99%. The algorithm then calculates a new set of coefficients and partial F statistics and the elimination procedure repeats until all terms remaining in the model exceed the minimum significance level. Both the forward selection and stepwise selection methods make use of partial F statistics when examining the most recent term to enter a model. If the most recently added term falls below the minimum significance level both methods reject the newly added term. The procedures must terminate at this point to avoid cycling.

2.3 Symbolic Regression

The symbolic regression procedure is described in greater detail in Koza (1992). The method uses ephemeral random constants that have fixed values determined on initialisation. The method can make use of non-linear equation forms, a wide variety of function types and even programming constructs such as "if-then" statements. The commercial software package known as Discipulus Pro (Francone, 1998) was used to obtain the symbolic regression results for the first two examples in this paper. The third example used software developed by Poyhonen and Savic (1996). Discipulus Pro implements the standard symbolic regression algorithm with several enhancements including the ability to produce expressions directly in machine language.

3 Example 1: A Polynomial Problem

This section of the paper compares the three methods, stepwise regression, symbolic regression and the hybrid method using an example problem for which the solution equation is known in advance. The data set for the sample problem consists of three independent variables x_1, x_2, and x_3 with values selected randomly on an interval between 0 and 1. Equation 1 is the equation used to calculate the values of the dependent variable, y.

$$y = 3x_1^3x_2^2x_3 + 4x_1^2x_2^2x_3 + 2x_1x_2^3x_3^2 \tag{1}$$

The number of transformed variable terms available to stepwise regression and the hybrid regression method depends on a maximum power value specified by the user. For this demonstration a maximum power value of 6 is arbitrarily selected for both stepwise regression and the hybrid method.

Three different values of maximum length of expressions were used with the hybrid regression method. The values consisted of maximum lengths of 5, 7 and

14 terms. Table 1 shows the results of a total of 30 trials, ten with each maximum length value. The hybrid regression method was able to find the correct solution in every trial by generating relatively few solutions. The rows in Table 1 list the mean, maximum and minimum number of solutions generated for each of the three maximum lengths. The bottom row lists the ratio of possible expression forms (N) to optimal solutions (N_o), which represents the inverse of the probability of producing the solution by random generation. As the maximum length restriction increases the probability of generating the optimal solution at random improves greatly although the mean number of solutions required to find the optimal solution remains relatively unaffected. For a maximum length of 5 terms the probability of producing the optimal solution at random is 1 in 1,666,895 and the hybrid method required an average of 3,010 solutions to find the correct form.

Table 1: Number of solutions required by hybrid method for example 1 (30 trials)

	5 term maximum	7 term maximum	14 term maximum
mean	3010	3417.6	2793.5
maximum	6697	10262	9879
minimum	1717	931	1230
N/No	1,666,895	333,414	23,324

Both the forward selection and stepwise selection methods used 95% as the minimum significance for terms and both methods failed to find the optimal solution to the problem. For the data set used in this example stepwise selection terminated at a sub-optimal 11 term model with MSE equal to 0.000473. At that point the next term to enter fell below the 95% minimum significance level. Forward selection terminated with a 19 term expression (MSE = 1.68×10^{-8}) when it reached the limits imposed by 20 data points.

The symbolic regression method required two separate data sets, a training set and a validation set. The training set consisted of the same 20 data points used by the hybrid method and stepwise regression. The validation set consisted of an additional 20 points generated using Equation 1. For this problem the Discipulus Pro software was used with 6 different settings in 60 trials. In all 60 runs the population size was set at 500 and the search consisted of 100,000 tournaments (equivalent to 200 generations). The entries in Table 2 are the maximum, minimum and mean MSE values of the best of run solutions based on the training data for 10 trials. The columns referred to as 'poly' designate trials in which no transcendental functions were used and the 'non-poly' trials used transcendental functions. The use of transcendental functions had no significant impact on the results obtained for this problem. Symbolic regression did not find the target expression in any of the trials. All of the solutions with four or more terms produced by stepwise regression (MSE < 0.53) were better than the best results obtained by symbolic regression (MSE = 0.93).

Table 2: Mean square error of symbolic regression models (60 trials)

	3 constants		6 constants		12 constants	
	Poly	Non-poly	Poly	Non-poly	Poly	Non-poly
Maximum	13.2000	5.3142	5.7642	4.4838	19.8708	6.0032
Minimum	2.6170	1.5281	1.4198	0.9313	1.3570	1.5604
Mean	6.5474	3.0950	3.0883	2.6609	5.6587	3.0419

4 Example 2: The Colebrook-White Formula

This section of the paper compares the effectiveness of the three methods on a non-polynomial problem. The Colebrook-White formula, Equation 2, calculates f, the friction factor for turbulent fluid flowing through a pipe:

$$\frac{1}{\sqrt{f}} = -2\log\left(\frac{2.51}{Re\sqrt{f}} + \frac{k}{3.7D}\right) \tag{2}$$

where Re is the Reynolds number; k is the wall roughness; and D is the diameter of the pipe. The formula is often used in pipe network simulation software. It has an implicit form in which the value of f appears on both sides of the equation. Obtaining an accurate solution for f can be very time consuming, requiring many iterations. An approximate equation for f that does not require iteration can be used to improve the speed of simulation software.

The three methods were used to derive explicit approximators to the Colebrook-White formula for a range of Reynolds numbers and relative roughness values (k/D) where the surface of the response variable f is known to be highly non-linear. The data set consists of a two dimensional grid of 220 data points, created from twenty Reynolds values selected in equal increments of 100,000 on the interval of 100,000 to 2,000,000, and 11 relative roughness values selected in equal increments of 0.0005 on the interval of 0 to 0.005. The target friction values, f, for the 220 points are values obtained using the Colebook-White formula (Equation 2).

The set of transformed variables used by the stepwise regression method and the hybrid method consist of 48 terms resulting from a maximum power value of 6. The maximum length was 25 terms and the minimum significance was 95%.

Figure 1 summarises the results obtained from the three methods. The thin line in Figure 1 represents the solutions generated by stepwise selection. The dotted line in Figure 1 represents the path of solutions generated by forward selection after it diverges from stepwise selection. The bold line represents the best solutions obtained through the hybrid method. The dashed horizontal line at the bottom of the figure represents the best result obtained through symbolic regression. A horizontal line is used because the number of terms does not directly apply to symbolic regression solutions.

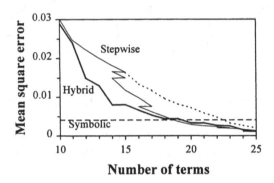

Figure 1: Accuracy and complexity of Colebrook-White approximations

As in the previous example symbolic regression solutions were obtained from 60 trials using the Discipulus Pro software with different parameter settings following the same pattern in Table 2. Unlike the previous example the average results of the expressions that used transcendental functions were approximately an order of magnitude more accurate. The best MSE obtained from trials with transcendental functions is 0.0041 compared with 0.1633 for non-transcendental forms. Mean MSE values were 0.0651 for transcendental trials and 0.4545 for non-transcendental.

The solutions produced by the hybrid method represent the best trade-off between accuracy and computational effort for expressions with 18 terms or fewer. Stepwise selection overtakes the hybrid method for expressions with 19 terms or more. The best solutions generated by symbolic regression were competitive in terms of accuracy, but were very complex and required much greater computational effort than the polynomial solutions.

5   Example 3: Rainfall-Runoff Modelling

In this example problem stepwise regression and the hybrid method are compared with a wider variety of modelling techniques. Savic et al. (1999) have reported the results of several modelling techniques to simulate rainfall-runoff in the Kirkton catchment in Scotland. The methods include the conceptual model HYRROM and a more complex variation of the same program (Eeles, 1994), an artificial neural network and symbolic regression using a variation of the method that incorporates two adjustable parameters. The data set consists of daily rainfall, daily stream flow and monthly evaporation from May 1984 to December 1988, a total of 1706 days. The objective of the model is to predict daily stream flow from the rainfall, evaporation and previous stream flow data.

The genetic programming model and the artificial neural network model use a set of 10 input variables to predict daily stream flow. The set of variables consists of rainfall, stream flow and evaporation for each of the three days prior to the current day as well as rainfall on the current day. The stepwise regression and hybrid methods use a subset of 6 of the 10 predictor variables consisting of rainfall for the current day and two previous days and stream flow from the three previous days. The conceptual models use rainfall and evaporation from the current day and create other lagged inputs through a complex arrangement of calibrated internal storages and delays.

Table 3: Rainfall-runoff models reported in Savic et al., 1999

Model	MSE
Symbolic regression	8.102
9 parameter conceptual model	9.859
35 parameter conceptual model	9.394
Artificial neural network	8.712

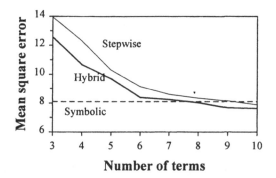

Figure 2: Accuracy and complexity of rainfall-runoff models

For the hybrid method the maximum length of expressions was set at 8 and the maximum power was set to 3. After the hybrid method generated 20,000 solutions the maximum length restriction was relaxed to 10 terms. Figure 2 shows the accuracy-complexity trade-off curve generated by the hybrid method after 60,000 solutions as a bold line. The thin line represents the best solutions generated by both stepwise regression methods up to the generation of the first 10 term model. Forward selection and stepwise selection produce identical results in this case. The dashed line represents symbolic regression, the best of the four methods reported in Savic et al. (1999) and Table 3 lists the MSE values for all the methods reported in Savic et al. (1999). The 9 and 10 term polynomials produced by the hybrid method are the most accurate.

6 Conclusions

It is not surprising that the hybrid and stepwise regression methods produce better solutions than symbolic regression in the first example. However, as Figures 2 and 3 indicate the hybrid and stepwise regression methods were able to produce better and more efficient solutions than symbolic regression in the other two non-linear examples. For all of the problems the new hybrid method outperformed stepwise regression except for the larger expressions in the second example. The computational effort required to generate good solutions appears to be unaffected by the maximum length of the expression for both stepwise regression methods while the performance of the hybrid method appears to be adversely affected by the length of expressions.

Acknowledgements

This work was supported by the U.K. Engineering and Physical Sciences Research Council, grant GR/L67189.

References

Draper, N. R., and H. Smith. 1998. *Applied regression analysis*. New York: John Wiley and Sons.

Eeles, C. W. O. 1994. "Parameter optimization of conceptual hydrological models," Ph.D. Thesis, Open University, Milton Keynes, UK.

Francone, F. D. 1998. *Discipulus Pro owner's manual*. Oakland: Register Machine Learning Technologies Inc.

Koza, J. R. 1992. *Genetic programming: on the programming of computers by means of natural selection*. Cambridge, Massachusetts: MIT Press.

Poyhonen, H. O., and D. A. Savic. 1996. *Symbolic regression using object-oriented genetic programming (in C++): report number 96/04*. Exeter: Centre for systems and control engineering, University of Exeter.

Savic, D. A., G. A. Walters and J. W. Davidson. 1999. "A genetic programming approach to rainfall-runoff modelling," *Water Resources Management*, 13, pp. 219-231.

G.A. Optimisation of PID Controllers - Optimal Fitness Functions

D. Drabble, P.V.S. Ponnapalli, M. Thomson

Control Systems Research Group, Department of Engineering & Technology,

Manchester Metropolitan University, John Dalton Building,

Chester St., Manchester M1 5GD, United Kingdom

Summary:
Genetic Algorithms (GAs) have been in many cases successfully applied to a wide variety of optimisation problems. The work described here focuses on the application of genetic algorithms to the optimisation of linear & non-linear PID controllers. The techniques used here are based around the formulation of a suitable objective function, which, as part of the GA evaluates the fitness of a given PID parameter set. The proposed objective function is based directly on performance criteria specified in terms of the rise time, settling time and peak overshoot of a physical system. The functions are evaluated via a set of trials on a range of systems with varying dynamics and the success rate determined by comparison with sets of target step response characteristics. The results show that the objective function is more robust than ISE based methods in the optimisation of multiple step response objectives, having a low deviation from the target across the range of parameters (rise time, settling time & peak overshoot).

1 Introduction

One of the most popular controellers in industrial applications is the proportional integral and derivative (PID) controllers because of its simplicity and well-proven reliability [8]. The tuning a PID controller still relies heavily on methods developed using heuristic rules and experience of the operators in individual applications. Various techniques have been proposed to improve and automate the process of tuning, and recently the use of Genetic Algorithms (GAs) to automatically select PID parameters has also received interest [1-5].

2 Genetic Algorithms for PID Tuning

2.1 Introduction

GAs are useful tools in search and optimisation tasks. There are various forms and implementations of GAs, but in this case the basic form will be considered, based on the GA devised by Goldberg [6]. This uses binary encoding of the parameters to be optimised, and the most common operators, selection, crossover and mutation. The key feature which separates one of these GAs from the rest is the fitness function which can be designed for a specific task. In this case the task is the optimisation of a set of PID parameters in closed loop systems.

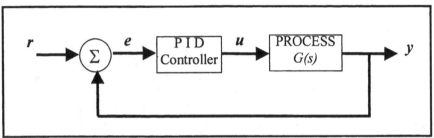

Figure 2.1 Closed loop control model.

The aim of a GA is to find the optimal solution for a problem by maximising the relative fitness of the population of candidate solutions. Often the problem is one of minimising an error, E(s), so the fitness is defined as:

$$f(s) = \frac{\alpha}{E(s)} \tag{1}$$

where α is a constant for scaling the fitness.

The major challenge is in the selection of a suitable objective function, which can provide a good measure of the effectiveness of a PID controller. Most traditional PID optimisation techniques aim to improve the process Rise Time (T_R), Settling Time (T_S), or reduce Peak Overshoot (M_P). Any or all of these are potential fitness function objectives. The most common objective functions are used based on Integral Square Error (ISE) and its time-weighted variant, Integral Time-weighted Squared Error (ITSE).

These functions utilise the closed loop error but do not explicitly consider all closed loop step response characteristics $(T_R, T_S$ and $M_P)$. In this work, a new form of fitness function based on step response characteristics is proposed for used in GA-based optimisation of PID controllers. This method, named Step Response Method (SRM), is evaluated against the more commonly used ISE-based fitness functions and is aimed at maintaining the overall robustness of the controller in stead of purely concentrating on the minimisation of closed-loop error.

2.2 GA Cost Functions

2.2.1 Integral Square Error (ISE) Cost Function [2], [7]

Kawabe et al [7] assume the performance measure is given by a generalised ISE:

$$J(q,\theta) = \int_0^\infty \left\{ e^2(t) + \rho \ddot{u}^2(t) \right\} dt \qquad (2)$$

$q = (Kc \; Ti \; Td) \in Q$

$\theta \in \Theta$ is the parameter of the plant.

ρ is a positive weighting constant.

The aim of the above function is to penalise loop errors and large controller effort. ρ can be selected to dictate the extent to which the controller effort is penalised. Using an I-PD controller, It has shown that this is an effective cost function for the control of a time-varying plant and ρ is used to control the transient response of the closed loop system [5]. Another commonly used variant is the time-weighted ISE function (ITSE), which by its nature is designed to penalise steady-state errors, thereby reducing the settling time of the closed loop system.

2.2.2 Step Response Method (SRM)

This method defines the fitness of a given PID controller by the quality of its corresponding closed loop step response characteristics. These are compared with a set of target parameters to obtain the relative deviation from the targets. The objective function is defined as:

$$f(s) = \frac{\alpha}{(1 + \Delta T_R)(1 + \Delta T_S)(1 + \Delta M_P)} \qquad (3)$$

where ΔT_R, ΔT_S and ΔM_P are the relative deviations from the target rise-time, settling time and peak overshoot, respectively.

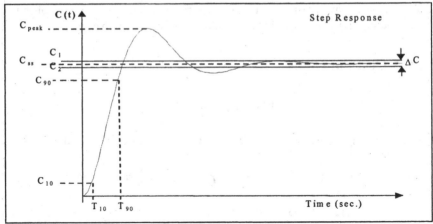

Figure 2.2 Step response characteristics

Based on the closed loop step response (Fig. 1), the corresponding step response parameters are calculated as follows:

Rise-time, $T_R = T_{90} - T_{10}$ (4)

Settling time, $T_S = max\{t: |C(t) - C_{SS}| \geq \Delta C / 2\}$ (5)

where $\Delta C = C_1 - C_2$

Peak overshoot, $M_P = \dfrac{(C_{peak} - C_{ss})}{C_{ss}} \times 100\%$ (6)

Given a good process model, the PID controller is tuned to achieve a desired set of T_R, T_S and M_P. The advantage of the SRM method is that it provides a robust overall control solution compared to methods using only error-based criteria.

3 Simulation Studies

3.1 Simulation Set-up

Ten sets of PID parameters are evolved for five closed loop system models ranging from second to fifth order with varying time-delays. The corresponding target step response characteristics for these systems are shown in Table 3.1. In all the simulation studies, a reasonably accurate plant model is assumed, as is done in all such studies, so that the PID parameters determined by the GA can be validated before applying to the actual process.

	Model	TARGETS		
System		T_R	T_S	M_P
1	$G(s) = \dfrac{1}{(1+s)(1+0.25s)(1+0.5s)(1+0.75s)}$	1.4416	6.35	1.0516
2	$G(s) = \dfrac{e^{-s}}{(s+1)(2s+1)}$	1.6447	14.4503	1.09
3	$G(s) = \dfrac{1}{(s+1)^5}$	3.2681	10.6	1.115
4	$G(s) = \dfrac{0.8}{s(0.5s+1)}$	2.151	3.85	1
5	$G(s) = \dfrac{10e^{-2s}}{100s^3 + 80s^2 + 17s + 5}$	6.339	92.99	1.3027

Table 3.1 Closed loop step response characteristics of the five system models

The SRM fitness function is employed with the standard genetic algorithm using the parameter set {population size = 20, probability of crossover = 0.8 and probability of mutation = 0.01, maximum number of generations = 60}.

The same tests are then repeated for comparative purposes with the ISE and ITSE fitness functions. The criteria for evaluation are:

Success rate, $\quad SR = \dfrac{N_s}{N_T} \times 100\%$ \hfill (7)

where N_S = number of GA trials producing PID parameters that met the target performance criteria, and N_T = total number of GA trials.

% Deviation from target, when the target is not met over 60 generations, i.e., closeness of performance to target.

3.2 Results and Discussion

The results, illustrated in figures 3.1, 3.2 and 3.3 show respectively, the overall success rate, individual parameter success rate and percentage deviation from the targets. The better overall success rate of the SRM method compared to the ISE-based methods (Fig. 3.1) over the entire test set indicates that the SRM method produces better tuning of PID controller parameters.

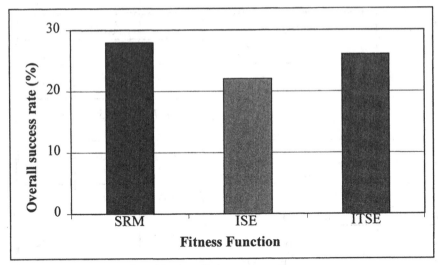

Figure 3.1 Success rate in achieving all three step response targets

The results (Fig. 3.2) show that the ISE method gives marginally better tuning in meeting closed loop rise time, while the ISTE method improves on peak overshoot and to a lesser extent, settling time, at the expense of an optimal rise time.

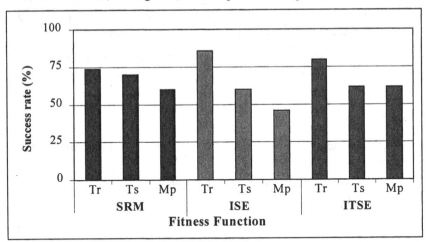

Figure 3.2 Success rates across all five system models

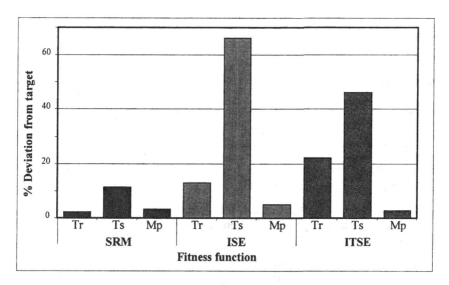

Figure 3.3 Percentage deviation from target parameters when GA did not meet the targets

The step response characteristic function has proven to be most proficient where a low settling time is most desirable. Although the SRM does not achieve good rise times as easily as the ISE and ITSE methods (Fig. 3.2) over the entire 60 generations, its low percentage deviation throughout (Fig. 3.3) indicates a more robust performance overall. This is further supported by the fact that it also had the highest success rate for simultaneous optimisation of all step response characteristics (Fig. 3.1).

4 Conclusion

The proposed SRM method is shown to be an effective alternative to more popular ISE methods. While the ISE methods tend to produce better rise time results, the performance of the SRM function is more robust in terms of overall performance across all three step response characteristics, and also in terms of failure, having low deviation from the targets across all three parameters. The similar characteristic values achieved by the step methods are due to the fact that there is no bias toward either parameter in the fitness function (eqn. 3).

It is expected that the final closed loop characteristics evolved from those simulations can be improved overall, by increasing the maximum number of generations. There are several ways in which the ISE functions may be improved. Simple constraints may be applied to reduce the peak overshoot. Possibilites for the step reponse method may include the biasing of the individual parameter objectives, but again this is also likely to have a knock on effect on the other parameters.

References

1. Vlachos, C., Williams, D., & Gomm, J.B.: Genetic approach to decentralised PI controller tuning for multivariable processes. IEE Proc. – Control Theory Appl., Vol. 146, No. 1 (1999), pp. 58-64.

2. Porter, B., Jones, A.H.: Genetic tuning of digital PID controllers. Electronics Letters, Vol. 28, No. 9 (1992), pp. 843-844.

3. Häußler, A., Li, Y., Ng, K.C., Murray-Smith, D.J., & Sharman, K.C.: Neurocontrollers designed by a genetic algorithm. GALESIA '95, IEE Conf. Pub. 414 (1995), pp. 536-542.

4. Krohling, R. – Design of PID Controller for Disturbance Rejection: A Genetic Optimization Approach. IEE Intl. Conf. GALESIA (1997), pp.498-503..

5. Chipperfield, A.J., Fleming, P.J. (Eds.) – MATLAB Toolboxes and applications for control. Peter Peregrinus Ltd. (1993), pp.139-144.

6. Goldberg, D.: Genetic Algorithms in Search, Optimisation and Machine Learning. (1989) Addison-Wesley Publishing, Inc.

7. Kawabe, T., Tagami, T., & Katayama, T.: A genetic algorithm based minimax optimal design of robust I-PD controller. UKACC Intnl. Conf. On Control (1996), IEE Pub. 427, pp. 436-441.

8. Åström, K.J.,Hägglund, T.: Automatic tuning of PID controllers. Research Triangle Park, N.C. : Instrument Society of America (1988).

Fuzzy Logic for Behaviour Co-ordination and Multi-Agent Formation in RoboCup

Hakan Duman and Huosheng Hu

Department of Computer Science
University of Essex
Wivenhoe Park, Colchester CO4 3SQ
United Kingdom
{hduman, hhu}@essex.ac.uk

Abstract. Robots participating in a soccer game need to determine the position of the ball, other robots, and the goal positions using real time visual tracking, along with being able to navigate safely, move the ball towards the opponents goal, and co-operate with teammates. Each soccer robot is equipped with basic behaviours such as chasing the ball and shoots it at the goal. Although the single-agent behaviours are very important, the issue of co-operation, or formation, among multiple agents in such a domain is essential. In this paper, we discuss the importance of robot formation in RoboCup and introduce new reactive behaviours and their co-ordination, based on Fuzzy Logic Control, to achieve co-operation among the soccer playing robots.

1 Introduction

The Robot World Cup, RoboCup, is an international competition designed to encourage artificial intelligence (AI) and intelligent robotics research by providing a standard problem, a soccer game, where a wide range of technologies can be integrated [Kitano *et al.*, 1997]. Designing a robot to play football is very challenging because the robot must incorporate the design principles of autonomous agents, multi-agent collaboration, strategy acquisition, real-time reasoning, strategic decision making, intelligent robot control, and machine learning. In the middle-sized RoboCup league, robots are playing in a 8.22m x 4.57m green-floor area surrounded by walls. The ball is an official FIFA size-4 soccer ball and the size of goal is 150x50cm[1]. In a game there are two competing teams. Each team can have up to four robot players with size less than 50cm in diameter.

For playing an aesthetic and effective game of robotic soccer each soccer agent must be equipped with a set of basic behaviours [Hu *et al.*, 1999].

---

[1] RoboCup Middle-Size League Regulations and Rules: http://www.robocup.org

Depending on whether the agent fills the role of the goal keeper or of a field player, there are different basic skills. The goalie is very simple minded and just tries to keep the ball from rolling into the own goal. The field players have a much more elaborate set of basic behaviours. These basic behaviours have been adopted from the CS Freiburg Team [Gutmann et al., 1999]. The first three skills below concern situations when the ball cannot be played directly, while the two last skills address ball handling:

Search-ball: Turn the robot in order to find the ball. If the ball is not found after one revolution go to home position and search again from there.

Observe-ball: Set the robots heading such that the ball is in the center of focus. Track the ball without approaching it.

Go-to-position: Plan and constantly re-plan a collision free path from the robot's current position to a target position and follow this path until the target position is reached.

Move-ball: Determine a straight line to the goal which has the largest distance to any object on the field. Follow line at increasing velocity and redetermine the line whenever appropriate.

Shoot-ball: To accelerate the ball either turn the robot rapidly with the ball between the flippers or use the kicker-mechanism. The decision on which mechanisms to use is made according to the current game situation.

Although the single-agent behaviours are very important, the issue of co-operation among multiple agents in such a domain is essential. It should be emphasised that "co-operation" in our approach is described as a formation-based attack or defence for the soccer playing robots. Formations allows individual team members to concentrate their sensors across a portion of the environment, while their partners cover the rest [Balch et al., 1998]. As in a real soccer match, formation-based attacks would increase the effectiveness and performance of tactical teamwork when combining with ball manipulation behaviours.

In this paper, we introduce reactive behaviours, based on Fuzzy Logic Control, to achieve observation-based formation among the soccer playing robots. Although many of the participating teams are designing their teams based on the multi-agent co-operation, most of them employ formation control using explicit communication. Other approaches to similar tasks include [Arkin, 1998], [Parker, 1999], [Pirjanian et al., 2000]. The introduced method has been inspired by [Balch et al., 1998], which achieves formation among multiple robots by using a referenced-based (e.g. leader, neighbor, center) type of cooperation. The co-ordination of behaviours consisting of a hierarchical behaviour-based fuzzy control architecture adapted from [Duman et al., 2000] is introduced in section 3. Section 4 presents experimental results based on the proposed method. Finally a brief conclusion is given in section 5.

2 Fuzzy Control and Multi-Agent Formation

2.1 Fuzzy Logic Control

Fuzzy control is one of the more active areas of application of fuzzy logic and the underlying fuzzy set theory introduced by [Zadeh, 1973]. A fuzzy logic controller works by encoding an experts knowledge into a set of rules which are smoothly interpolated and the resultant is defuzzified to give a crisp output.

Using fuzzy logic techniques provide control, which is less sensitive to sensor errors since information is always assumed to be imprecise. Consequently such fuzzy logic control techniques are used for several aspects of autonomous robot control such as wall following and targeting a specified goal position [Saffiotti, 1997]. The autonomous soccer robots, which consist of different simple fuzzy behaviours, should deal with very different control situations, e.g. follow a teammate by holding constant distance while avoiding an obstacle.

2.2 Multi-Agent Formation

Several formations exist for a team of four robots. In [Balch et al., 1998], the following are considered:

- *Line*, where the robots travel line-abreast.
- *Column*, where the robots travel on after the other.
- *Diamond*, where the robots travel in a diamond.
- *Wedge*, where the robots travel in a "V" or "Λ".

Despite of the fact, that only four players are playing in each team, and obviously one is the goalkeeper, there are only three robots, which can be used to employ the offensive and defensive formations. [Balch et al., 1998] also identifies three different techniques for formation position determination: *Unit-center-referenced*, *Leader-referenced*, and *Neighbor-referenced*. The most appropriate referenced-based type of cooperation for our soccer robots is the *Leader-referenced*. The robot which dribbles the ball towards the oppents' goal is being considered as the leader, while others stay on the side ready to recover the ball from any loses or pass the ball to the next closest teammate. The task of each robot is to simultaneously move to a goal location, avoid obstacles with other robots and maintain a formation position. In case of a defence, the robots organization choice can differ between the diamond and wedge formation. The diamond formation is used at game start and when all team robots are in the same side of the field. Whereby the wegde formation "V" has the advantage to prevent the opponent from dodging the defence and garanties a higher chance of stealing the ball from the opponents' player. Figure 1 (a) and (b) illustrates above configurations. The following section describes experimental results for group formation of multiple robots.

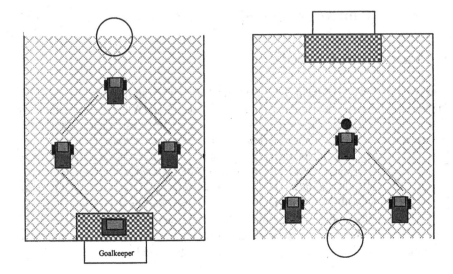

Figure 1: (a) Diamond formation at game start and defence.
(b) Wedge formation during attack to the opponents' goal.

3 The Methodological Approach

3.1 Robot Platform

The introduced system is implemented on a Pioneer 1 and Pioneer 2 mobile robot. The Pioneer 2 is equipped with an overhead vision system connected to a Ellips Rio frame grabber, 8 ultrasonic sensors, 2 position encoders. The Pioneer 1 basically consists of 7 ultrasonic sensors and 2 position encoders. The front sonars on both of the robots are used for obstacle avoidance and following a target.

3.2 Individual Behaviours

The autonomous soccer robots, which consist of different simple fuzzy behaviours, should deal with very different control situations such as follow a teammate or ball while avoiding an obstacle. In this section we describe these elementary behaviours that are essential for our approach. These behaviours consist of 1) obstacle avoidance 2) target following and 3) velocity control. Every behaviour is specified using a fuzzy rule-base and generate an output by fuzzy inferencing.

Obstacle Avoidance

In the robotic soccer field, there are often obstacles between the robot and its goal position. These can be in form of a wall or opponent player. Different possibilities can be taken to avoid obstacles. We have adopted this behaviour from [Duman *et al.*, 2000]. It controls the heading of the robots based on the sonar readings to avoid collisions with obstacles and maintain a safe trajectory.

Target Following

The target following behaviour consits of two main tasks. The leader of the group follows the ball whereby the rest of the robots are following the leader. This behaviour controls the heading of the robot based on the input from vision system. The difference between the target position and its origin generate the vector Δd. Depending on the role of the robot in the group, it either follows the ball or the team leader. Figure 2 shows the target following behaviour for a robot, following a leader, that tries to maintain its formation position.

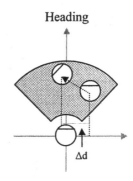

Figure 2: Target following

Velocity Control

Besides the target following behaviour, the formation approach requires multiple robots to form up and move in a specified distance to its neighbours. The velocity control behaviour controls the speed of the robot based on the sonar readings. Depending on how far out of position the robot is, the speed of the robot is being increased or decreased (Figure 3). Three designated areas a, b and c are considered for the robot.

a) the robot is too close to its neighbour; the desired velocity is set to be decreased

b) the robot is within the tolerance area; the velocity is kept constantly

c) the robot is far out of position; the desired velocity is set to be increased

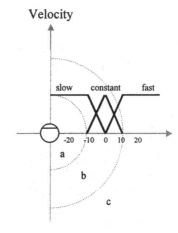

Figure 3: Velocity control

3.3 Hierarchical Behaviour Co-ordination

When a soccer playing mobile robot operates, several elementary behaviours of different type and goal can be active at the same time. This interaction can take the form of behavioural co-operation or competition. Each behaviour can be tuned independently to be more effective in its own context. In this way a complex behaviour can be obtained base on simpler behaviours. The fuzzy hierarchical controller, as shown in Figure 4, has been inspired by the technique proposed by Saffiotti [Saffiotti, 1997] for blending multiple behaviours with different tasks.

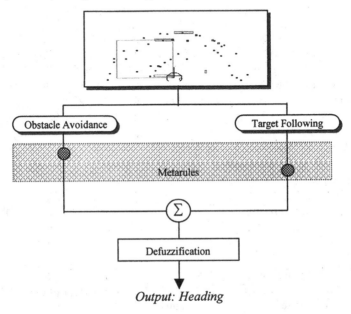

Figure 4: The hierarchical Behaviour Co-ordination

As described before, fuzzy logic was used to implement basic behaviours of the robot, e.g. obstacle avoidance and target following. Moreover the fuzzy meta-rules are implemented to describe strategies of behaviour arbitration. Depending on sensor readings the output control variable can be derived. The discounted values are then merged together according to a set of context rules of the form "if *condition/context* then *behaviour*", telling which behaviour should be active in each situation and to what degree. Finally, the resulting blended function is defuzzified to produce a crisp control.

For instance, in case an obstacle being detected, the obstacle avoidance behaviour weight needs to be increased respectively, at the expense of the other concurrent behaviours. When the obstacle is only partially close, both behaviours are partially activated.

4 Experimental Results

In the experimental setup we used two Pioneer robots (see section 4.1 for description) for achieving multi-agent formation and co-operation. In order to monitor the formation position and orientation of the robots, the experimental runs were conducted in a test area measuring approximately 6 by 4 metres with an overhead camera tracking system. The robots were directed to navigate to the opponents goal area while avoiding robots from the other team, here in form of a pillar. The robot that has the ball is assigned to be the team leader. The other robot's task is to maintain its position in the group formation. Figure 5 presents the formation and co-operative behaviour from the viewpoint of a lab camera as well as from a vision system mounted on top of the robot.

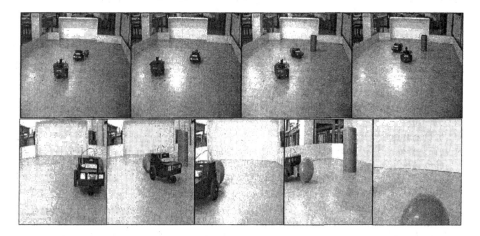

Figure 5: Formation and co-operative behaviour. Team formation and strategic attack to the opponents goal. Top row: Lab camera. Bottom row: An vision system mounted on top of the robot

The results show that the robot, which is on lead searches for both, ball and opponents goal. The leader approaches the ball and starts dribbling it to the opponents goal area. Since the view area of the overhead camera is narrow, it is easy to lose the target. Hence, the robot searches the leader constantly. The leading robot detects an obstacle and starts avoiding it. We are assuming that the obstacle here is an opponents player that tries to block our robots path. The leader starts turning away from the obstacle. The opponents player follows the leader of our team and tries to block again. Now, the formation is used for tactical attack. The robot that has the ball loose its position in the formation and start a co-operative behaviour by passing the ball to the other robot, which has an empty path to the opponents goal.

5 Conclusions

In this paper we have presented an approach to group formation for multiple autonomous mobile robots in general, soccer robots in particular. Elementary behaviours are implemented through fuzzy rules which provide robust and smooth navigation capabilities for a mobile robot. The generation of complex behaviours by combination of simpler behaviours has been proven to be effective and advantageous.

Currently, our approach has been implemented on two robots. The first robot, a Pioneer 1 robot, serves as a leader of the group and the second robot, a Pioneer 2 with an overhead camera, tries to maintain the formation. Experimental results confirm that the approach produces acceptable co-operation by organising the robots in formation. We intend to employ this approach to a team of four soccer playing robots.

References

[Arkin, 1998] Ronald C. Arkin. *Behavior-based Robotics.* Inteligent Robotics and Automous Agents series. MIT Press, May 1998.

[Balch *et al.*, 1998] Tucker Balch and Ronald C. Arkin. *Behavior-based Formation Control for Multi-Robot Teams.* IEEE Transactions on Robotics and Automation, Vol. 14, No. 6, December 1998.

[Duman *et al.*, 2000] Hakan Duman and Huosheng Hu. *Hierarchical Fuzzy Behaviour Coordination for Reactive Control of an Autonomous Mobile Robot in RoboCup.* EUREL Robotics 2000, Salford, 12-14 April 2000.

[Gutmann *et al.*, 1999] J.-S. Gutmann, W. Hatzack, I. Herrmann, B. Nebel, F. Rittinger, A. Topor, and T. Weigel, *The CS Freiburg Team: Playing Robotic Soccer Based on an Explicit World Model*, The AI Magazine, June 1999.

[Hu *et al.*, 1999] Huosheng Hu, Kostas Kostiadis and Zhenyu Liu. *Coordination and Learning in a team of Soccer Robots*, Proceedings of the IASTED Robotics and Automation Conference, Santa Barbara, CA, USA, 28-30 October 1999.

[Kitano *et al.*, 1997] Kitano H., Tambe M., Stone P., Veloso M., Coradeschi S., Osawa E., Matsubara H., Noda I., and Asada M. *The RoboCup Synthetic Agent Challenge*, International Joint Conference on Artificial Intelligence (IJCAI97), 1997.

[Parker, 1999] Lynne P. Parker. *Cooperative robotics for multi-target observation.* Intelligent Automation and Soft Computing, special issue on Robotics Research at Oak Ridge National Laboratory, 5(1):5-19, 1999.

[Pirjanian *et al.*, 2000] Paolo Pirjanian and Maja Mataric. *Multi-robot Target Aquisition using Multiple Objective Behavior Coordination.* IEEE International Conference on Robotics and Automation, San Francisco, April 2000.

[Saffiotti, 1997] Alessandro Saffiotti. The Uses of Fuzzy Logic in Autonomous Robot Navigation: a catalogue raisonné. Soft Computing 1(4):180-197, 1997.

[Zadeh, 1973] Lotfi Zadeh, *Outline of a new approach to the analysis of complex systems and decision processes.* IEEE Transactions on Systems, Man and Cybernetics, Vol. 3, No. 1, pp. 28 – 44, 1973.

A Hierarchical Fuzzy Genetic Multi-Agent Architecture for Intelligent Buildings Sensing and Control

Hani Hagras[†], Victor Callaghan[‡], Martin Colley[‡], Graham Clarke[‡]

[†]The Computer ScienceDepartment, The University of Hull, Hull, HU6 7RX, UK.

[‡] The Computer ScienceDepartment, Essex University, Colchester, CO43SQ, UK.

Email: h.hagras@dcs.hull.ac.uk

Abstract:

In this paper, we describe a new application domain for intelligent autonomous systems – Intelligent Buildings (IB). In doing so we present a novel approach to the implementation of IB based on a hierarchical fuzzy genetic multi embedded-agent architecture comprising a low-level behaviour based reactive layer whose outputs are co-ordinated in a fuzzy way according to deliberative plans. The fuzzy rules related to resident's comfort are learnt online in a short time interval using our patented Fuzzy-Genetic techniques (British Patent 99-10539.7) from the resident's actual behaviour in a learning phase. Our approach utilises an intelligent agent approach to autonomously governing the building environment. We discuss the role of learning in building control systems, and contrast this approach with existing IB solutions. We explain the importance of acquiring information from sensors, rather than relying on pre-programmed models, to determine user needs. We describe how our architecture, consisting of distributed embedded agents, utilises sensory information to learn to perform tasks related to user comfort, energy conservation, and safety. We show how these agents, employing a behaviour-based approach derived from robotics research, are able to continuously learn and adapt to individuals within a building, whilst always providing a fast, safe response to any situation. Such a system could be used to provide support for older people, or people with disabilities, allowing them greater independence and quality of life.

1. Introduction

We define an intelligent building as *"a building that utilises computer technology to autonomously govern the building environment so as to optimise user comfort, energy-consumption, safety and work efficiency"*. In simplified terms, an intelligent-building is one that utilises inputs from building sensors (light, temperature, passive infra-red, etc), and uses this information to control effectors (heaters, lights, electronically-operated windows, etc) throughout the building [Sharples99]. A essential feature of an intelligent system is an ability to learn from experience, and hence adapt appropriately. Thus the notion of "autonomous governing" is important, as it implies a system which can adapt and generate its own rules (rather than being restricted to simple automation). In controlling such a system one is faced with the imprecision of sensors, lack of adequate models of many of the processes and of course the non-deterministic and sometime idiosyncratic aspects of human behaviour. Such problems are well known and there have been various attempts to address them. The most significant of these approaches has been the pioneering work on behaviour-based systems from researchers such as Brooks [Brooks 91] & Steels [Steels 95] who have had considerable success in the field of mobile robots. It might not seem obvious that a building can be looked upon as a machine; indeed *"a robot that we live within"*, but, in other work we have justified this view that intelligent buildings, as computer-based systems are akin to robots, gathering information from a variety of sensors, and using behaviour-based techniques to determine appropriate control actions [Callaghan 2000]. This paper builds on these ideas and explains our use of a double hierarchical Fuzzy-Genetic system (similar to our previous work in mobile robotics [Hagras 99a, 99b]), to create *embedded-agents* for intelligent-buildings.

2. Distributed Architecture

The granularity of our distribution is room-based. Thus, each room contains an *embedded-agent*, which is then responsible, via sensors and effectors for the local control of that room as shown in Figure (1). This mirrors the architects vision of the functionality of the building. All embedded-agents are connected via a high level network (IP-ethernet in our case), thereby enabling collaboration or sharing of information to take place where appropriate. Within a room, devices such as sensors and effectors are connected together using a building services network (Lontalk in our case) and IP at the higher level. This DAI architecture is illustrated in Figure (1).

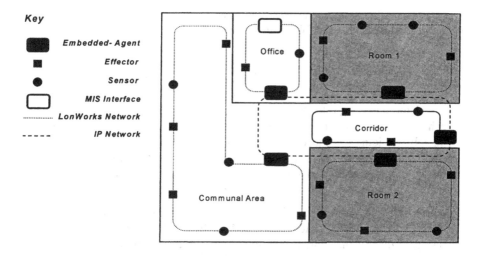

Figure (1): The DAI Building-Wide Architecture

3. The Embedded-Agents

Figure(2) shows the internal architecture of the embedded-agents which is based on the behaviour-based approach, pioneered by Brooks. Controlling a large integrated building system requires a complicated control function resulting from the large input and output space and the need to deal with many imprecise and unpredictable factors, including people. In our system we simplify this problem by breaking down the control space into multiple behaviours, each of which responds to specific types of situations, and then integrating their recommendations.

3.1 The Hierarchical Fuzzy Control Architecture

The behaviour based approach, pioneered by Brooks, consisting of many simple co-operating units, has produced very promising results when applied to the control of robotics (which we argue includes IB) [Brooks 91].

The problem of how to co-ordinate the simultaneous activity of several independent behaviour-producing units to obtain an overall coherent behaviour have been discussed by many authors. [Brooks 91] [Saffiotti, 1997]. The work described in this paper suggests a solution based on using fuzzy logic to both implement individual behaviour elements and the necessary arbitration (allowing both fixed and dynamic arbitration policies to be implemented). We achieve this by implementing each behaviour as a fuzzy process and then use fuzzy agents to co-ordinate them. In the resultant architecture, a hierarchical fuzzy logic controller

(HFLC) takes a hierarchical tree structure form and is shown in Figure (2). This hierarchical approach has the following advantages:

- It facilitates the design of the robotic controller and reduces the number of rules to be determined. It uses the benefits of fuzzy logic to deal with imprecision and uncertainty.

- Using fuzzy logic for the co-ordination between the different behaviours which allows more than one behaviour to be active to differing degrees thereby avoiding the drawbacks of on-off switching schema (i.e. dealing with situations where several criteria need to be taken into account). In addition, using fuzzy co-ordination provides a smooth transition between behaviours with a consequent smooth output response.

- It offers a flexible structure where new behaviours can be added or modified easily. The system is capable of performing very different tasks using identical behaviours by changing only the co-ordination parameters to satisfy a different high level objective without the need for re-planning.

Our room-based decomposition of behaviours consists of the following meta-functions. A *Safety behaviour* ensures that environmental conditions in the room are always at a safe level. In the case of an emergency this is the only active behaviour. Under normal circumstances each room has a fuzzy degree of safety (determined by fuzzy membership function) according to the needs of the room occupant. An *Economy behaviour* ensures that energy is not wasted. A *Comfort behaviour* ensures that conditions are maintained as the occupant would prefer (subject to being safe). This behaviour has an adaptable rule base, which learns from the room occupant's behaviour. This learning is done through reinforcement where the controller takes actions and monitors these actions to see if they satisfy the occupant or not, until a degree of satisfaction is achieved. Since this requires active responses from the user of the room this constitutes an unsupervised learning phase in the process. This process is clearly less appropriate where the occupants of the room are themselves in need of care or assistance as was the case in some of our earlier work [Sharples 99]. It would however be perfectly acceptable in other applications e.g. an hotel or apartment block: The complexities of training and negotiating satisfactory values for multiple use rooms depends upon having reliable means of identifying different users. The behaviours, resident inside the agent, take their input from a variety of sensors in the room (such as occupancy, light level, temperature, etc), and adjust device outputs (such as heating, lighting, blinds, etc) according to pre-determined, but settable, levels.

4. Overview of the Genetic Learning Architecture

For learning and adapting the dynamic comfort rule base according to the occupant behaviours we use an evolutionary computing approach based on a development of novel genetic algorithm (GA) technique. This mechanism operates directly on the fuzzy controller rule-sets. We refer to any learning conducted without user interaction, in isolation from the environment, using simulation as *offline* learning. In our case learning will be done *online* in real-time through interaction with the actual environment and user.

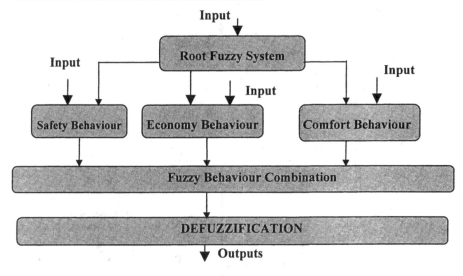

Figure (2): The Hierarchical Fuzzy Control System

4.1 The Associative Experience Engine

Figure (3) provides an architectural overview of what we term an *Associative Experience Engine* which forms the learning engine within the control architecture and is the subject of British patent application 99-10539.7. Behaviours are represented by parallel Fuzzy Logic Controllers (FLC). Each FLC has two parameters that can be modified which are the *Rule Base* (RB) of each behaviour and its *Membership Functions* (MF). The behaviours receive their inputs from sensors. The output of each FLC is then fed to the actuators via the *Co-ordinator* that weights its effect. When the system response fails to have a desired a response, the learning cycle begins.

The learning depends on the *Learning Focus* which is supplied by the *Co-ordinator* (the fuzzy engine which weights contributions to the outputs). When the *Learning Focus* is learning an individual rule base of a behaviour, then each rule base of each behaviour is learnt alone. When the *Learning Focus* is adapting the co-ordinated behaviours online, then the algorithm will adapt the rules in the comfort behaviour in response to the room occupant. The system recalls similar experiences by checking the stored experiences in the *Experience Bank*.

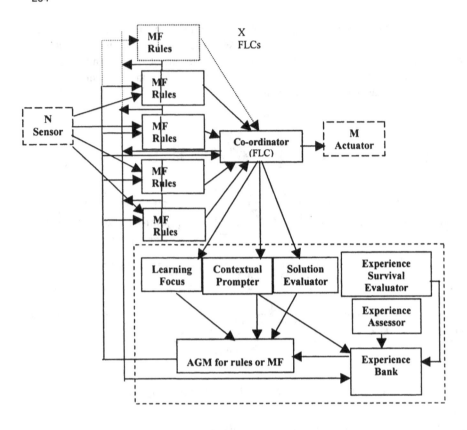

Figure (3): Architectural Overview of Associative Experience Learning Engine
(UK patent No 99-10539.7)

The controller tests different solutions from the *Experience Bank* by transferring the most recent experiences that are stored in a queue. If these experiences show success then they are stored in the FLC and thereby avoid generating new solution for our system. The Experience Assessor assigns each experience solution a fitness value. When the *Experience Bank* is full, we have to delete some experiences. To assist with this the *Experience Survival Evaluator* determines which rules are removed according to their importance (as set by the Experience Assessor). When past experiences did not solve the situation we use the best-fit experience to reduce the search space by pointing to a better starting point which is the experience solution with the largest fitness. We then fire an *Adaptive Genetic Mechanism (AGM)* using adaptive learning parameters (except when learning behaviour with immediate reinforcement, we use optimum mutation parameter) to speed the search for new solutions. The AGM is constrained to produce new solutions in certain range defined by the *Contextual Prompter* which is supplied by sensors and defined by co-ordinator according to the *learning focus* in order to avoid the AGM searching options where solutions are unlikely to be found. By using these mechanisms we narrow the AGM search space massively improving its efficiency. After generating new solutions (either rules or MFs) the system tests the new solution and gives it fitness through the *Solution Evaluator*. The AGM provides new options until a satisfactory solution is achieved. From a users viewpoint the system functions as follows. A user is asked to select his preference for any given programmable setting. The system then tries to adapt its rules to achieve this setting. The user is prompted to confirm or deny his satisfaction with the result. The system then either tries to re-adjust rules or , if the user is satisfied, the current rule set is accepted. Experiments to date show the *experience engine* achieves a satisfactory solution in a small number of iterations which most users find acceptable.

This same architecture was used in mobile robots learning and learnt rapidly (max 75s) complicated behaviours in a dynamic agricultural environment without simulation or human intervention [Hagras 99a, Hagras 99b].

5. Experimental Setting

In our preliminary experiments we had used an IB agent based on 68000 Motrolla processor, the agent is equipped with light and heat sensors and actutaors in the form of a heater and a light source, the IB agent is shown in Figure(4). This agent is used as a prototype simulator to simulate the control of light and temperature in a room with various condition such as multiple occupancy, different levels of natural light and temperature and different times of the day and different human desires. There is a built in economy behaviour that should switch the heat low and ventilation off after the room is vacated. It is arguable that there should also be a safety behaviour that prevents the heat going below a minimum safe level (e.g. zero degrees which would result in pipes freezing). Furthermore there is the comfort behaviour of the person himself which will be learnt using our patented fuzzy-genetic techniques.

The agent is dealing in a proactive way with the human occupier(s) and it just asks if the the action done is satisfactory or no, and if it is required to decrease or increase the heat or light levels. The agent have 5 input membership functions (which were found empirically to be the smallest number of membership functions that give a satisfactory response) to represent the input temperature and light sensors and 7 membership functions to repersent the heat and light. The agent using our patented techniques shown in Section (4.1) was able to find a satisfactory rule base for the different users in an average of 5 trials which is a small number of iterations. Also the agent is using the *Experience bank* of our patented technique so each time it identifies the room occupant it just retrieves his favourite rule base, if he changes his behaviour the agent can adapt by changing the necessary rules to adapt to the human desirse rather than changing the whole

206

rule base and repeating the learning from the beginning. If the agent locates a new room occupant it just tries to start learning his favourite rule base from a similar rule base that was stored the Experience Bank.

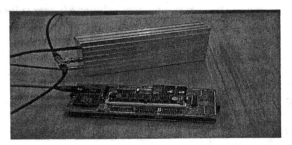

Figure (4): The IB agent

For our future work, we will construct intelligent rooms equipped with these agents and we will try to deal with more inputs and deal with different human desires in different rooms in a house.

References

[Brooks 91] R Brooks, "Intelligence Without Representation", Artificial Intelligence 47, pp139-159, 1991.

[Brooks 97] R. Brooks, "Intelligent Room Project", Proc 2nd Int'l Cognitive Technology Conference (CT'97), Japan 1997.

[Callaghan 2000] Callaghan V, Clarke G, Colley M, Hagras H "A Soft-Computing DAI Architecture for Intelligent Buildings" Journal of Studies in Fuzziness and Soft Computing on Soft Computing Agents, Physica-Verlag-Springer, July 2000

[Coen 97] M.H.Coen, "Building Brains for Rooms: Designing Distributed Software Agents", Proc. Ninth Innovative Applications of AI Conf., AAAI Press, 1997.

[Davidsson 98] P. Davisson "Energy Saving and Value Added Services; Controlling Intelligent-Buildings Using a Multi-Agent Sytem Approach" in DA/DSM Europe DistribuTECH, PennWell, 1998.

[Hagras 99a] H.Hagras, Victor Callaghan, M.Colley, "A Fuzzy-Genetic Based Embedded-Agent Approach to Learning and Control in Agricultural Autonomous Vehicles", 1999 IEEE International Conference on Robotics and Automation, pp. 1005-1010, Detroit- U.S.A, May 1999.

[Hagras 99b] H.Hagras, Victor Callaghan, M.Colley, "Online Learning of Fuzzy Behaviours using Genetic Algorithms & Real-Time Interaction with the Environment", 1999 IEEE International Conference on Fuzzy Systems, Seoul-Korea, pp. 668-672, August 1999.

[Mozer 98] M. Mozer "The Neural Network House: An Environment That Adapts To Its Inhabitants". In Proc of American Association for Artificial Intelligence Spring Symposium on Intelligent Environments, pp. 110-114, AAAI Press, 1998.

[Saffiotti 97] A. Saffiotti, " Fuzzy Logic in Autonomous Robotics: behaviour co-ordination", Proceedings of the 6th IEEE International Conference on Fuzzy Systems, Vol.1, pp. 573-578, Barcelona, Spain, 1997.

[Sharples 99] S. Sharples, V. Callaghan, G. Clarke, "A Multi-Agent Architecture for Intelligent Building Sensing and Control" International Sensor Review Journal, May 1999.

[Steels 95] L. Steels, "When are robots Intelligent autonomous agents", Journal of Robotics and Autonomous Systems, Vol. 15, pp.3-9, 1995.

The Use of Evolutionary and Fuzzy Models for Oncological Prognosis

A.A. Odusanya, M.O. Odetayo, D. Petrovic, and R.N.G. Naguib

Biomedical Computing Research Group (BIOCORE)
School of Mathematical and Information Sciences
Coventry University, Priory Street
Coventry, CV1 5FB, UK

Abstract. Evolutionary and fuzzy models have been used increasingly in many decision support, optimization, and control tasks. Oncological (cancer) data and are largely numerical in representation for analysis, however some are images or smears. The focus here is on the numerical nature of large samples. Lack of precise knowledge characterizes a lot of numerical samples for analysis in oncological decision making. The work here explores evolutionary and fuzzy models that are suitable for determining prognostic outcome.

1 Introduction

1.1 Evolutionary Algorithms

Evolutionary Algorithms (EAs) are nondeterministic algorithms that use key aspects of the evolution process as the basis for searching a solution space. EAs are classified into three main classes: evolutionary strategies (ESs), evolutionary programming (EP), and genetic algorithms (GAs) [1].

For each EA a fitness function is associated that determines the degree of feasibility of each individual in a given population. Individuals are recombined and mutated, on a generational basis, until the best fit individual representing the solution to the problem is found.

Genetic algorithms as the choice of evolutionary algorithm Bäck [1] discusses analytically differences between the various types of EAs, namely: ESs, EP, and GAs. While the probabilities of convergence of search solutions based on ESs and EP are not always one all of the time, if ever at all, the probability of convergence for genetic algorithms is one. This is due to the representation scheme. The first two (ESs and EP) rely on real-valued representations, and thus have an infinite search space, whereas GAs rely on discrete representation schemes, and have finite search spaces.

Given the certainty of convergence, i.e., given enough time, the optimum individual would be found. The research direction is in favour of GAs.

1.2 Fuzzy Logic systems

Fuzzy Logic (FL) systems are approximate systems utilised for modelling real life systems with focus on the imprecise nature (as opposed to precise in many computational mathematical models,) of real-life information. FL systems are premised on the notion of fuzzy sets [24].

A FL system has a series of rules comprising of an antecedent and a consequent, combined as if-then semantics.

An antecedent is a conjunction of input variables, each as an expressed and determinable degree of a fuzzy set (also known as a membership function). A consequent is a single output variable as an expressed and determinable degree of some fuzzy set.

A FL system comprises of four stages in its operation (with various methods establishing a specific system): fuzzification, inference ([2], [9], [21], and [23]), composition/aggregation ([2] often combined with the defuzzification process [23]), and defuzzification ([23], [9], [2], [21], and [14]).

Then a better model other than linguistic rule specifications is required that is non-linguistic (see Wang and Mendel [19] and [20]). Other methods include neural networks (so called neurofuzzy systems [13]), and evolutionary algorithms [10]. Indurkhya and Weiss [6] indicate that (genetic) classification does not perform as well as decision trees for rule generation. The experiments carried out by Lim et al [11], suggest that on average for a cross-section of domains, decision trees perform better than artificial neural networks. And thus rules can be constructed for a fuzzy system with decision trees, e.g. c4.5 (see Quinlan [15], [16], and [17]).

Fuzzy logic systems for numerical data Fuzzy logic systems are based on linguistic data, while artificial neural networks, for instance, are based on numerical data. The nature of many types of oncological data is numerical.

Thus while it is rather straightforward to apply artificial neural networks to cancer data that consists of variables, there is the extra step of consideration required to design an efficient fuzzy logic system with the necessary realistic rules associated with fuzzy systems. Wang and Mendel [19] and [20] had addressed a method of how to adapt fuzzy systems to handle numerical data.

The critical requirement is to build up a rule base that would be an acceptable description of the real life system to be modelled given certain variables. A number of methods present themselves, namely:

1. Wang and Mendel
2. Artificial Neural Network based rule generation [5]
3. Linguistic descriptions (traditional fuzzy systems, see Cox [2], and Kosko [9])
4. Decision tree method of rule generation
5. GA based rule generation [10].

With regards to Wang and Mendel, fuzzy rules lack generalization, whilst the measure of good data is suspect, negative examples are discouraged. Low degree of membership should not signify bad data, doing so invalidates relevant information. Bad data should be something that misses the target, low membership indicates weak encapsulation, but the membership function could be inaccurate, and it should accommodate low membership not rule it out. In any case the fuzzy requirement accommodates weak membership, and generalization should be favoured in lieu of exclusion.

Lim et al have presented a report that suggests after an exhaustive empirical survey, that decision trees are superior to artificial neural networks for classification tasks.

Indurkhya and Weiss suggest that classification models are not as optimal ("bias and variance") as decision trees which they point out are unbiased.

Thus this research effort has settled for decision trees to generate rules for fuzzy logic systems where linguistic rules would have played the part. c4.5 is the decision tree algorithm of choice. Janikow [7] discuss the rare instance of a synthesis of aspects of fuzzy logic and decision trees. However in their instance the fuzzy inferencing model is discarded, while fuzzy sets are incorporated into the decision tree. In this research, rules are extracted from a decision tree, and the fuzzy inferencing model is maintained , and built around these rules, thus retaining key essential properties of a fuzzy logic model, namely: fuzzification, inferencing, composition/aggregation, and defuzzification.

It is worthy of note that Wang and Mendel proved that fuzzy logic systems are universal approximators (can approximate to any desired arbitrary accuracy).

The TSK fuzzy model Takagi [21] discusses the TSK model, the fuzzy modelling method of choice. In this model the fuzzy output set for a rule is implied as the coefficients of the input variables. A rule is expressed as a linear equation. The defuzzified output is generated by a centroid-like method, that divides the sum of products of rule strengths (which are in turn products of membership values for each variable in a rule), and dependent value of the linear equation, by the sum of rule strengths.

For the TSK fuzzy model in this research, decision trees are used to generate the rules.

2   Evolutionary and fuzzy hybrids for oncological prognosis

Six models, four of them hybrids, have been designed to evaluate a prognostic score, namely:

1. A standalone FL system with linguistic rules (the crux of this model is a feasible description of the fuzzy sets for the variables and a keen essentially unaided appreciation of the linguistic rules applicable)
2. A standalone GA rule generator (this standalone GA is similar in function to Holland classifier systems (Holland [4]), but the focus is restricted to GAs (centralized to EAs))
3. A FL system with rules generated by a decision tree
4. A FL system with fuzzy sets optimized by a GA and rules generated by a decision tree
5. A GA rule generator with a decision tree rule based fitness function
6. A GA rule generator with a fuzzy logic influenced genetic operator (crossover), and a decision tree rule based fitness function.

2.1 A genetic algorithm that optimizes fuzzy sets

In this instance, Given m variables dispersed over n rules, and p_i variables per rule i, where $i \in N_n$, with q_{ij} fuzzy sets for each variable p_i, where $1 \leq j \leq p_i$, we have

$$m = \sum_i^n p_i$$

variables, and thus the total number of fuzzy sets, H, is given by:

$$H = m = \sum_i^n p_i$$

and we have a prototype function representing one class of fuzzy sets.

Now each fuzzy set would have a variable number of parameters. Each fuzzy set has a predefined prototype with unspecified parameters which would be determined optimally by the evolutionary system. Thus the evolutionary algorithm has individuals defined as fuzzy sets for each variable, parameters for each fuzzy set, and parameters for the TSK fuzzy logic model (the latter implicitly describe the output fuzzy set, for each rule/equation). There are H fuzzy sets, and g_k, where $k \in N_H$, parameters per fuzzy set, and z_i TSK parameters per fuzzy rule. Thus we have

$$\sum_k^H g_k + \sum_i^n z_i$$

parameters. And thus the length, L, of each individual in the evolutionary algorithm search would be

$$L = (H = \sum_i^n p_i) + \sum_k^H g_k + \sum_i^n z_i$$

Thus the GA determines an optimal permutation of fuzzy sets and the parameters for each fuzzy set.

The fitness function is the fuzzy system to be used for determining the prognostic score. Thus the key implementation variables required are n (determined by c4.5), the set of p (based on the rules), the set of q (based on the variables), and the set of g (based on each fuzzy set). If the number g varies based on the fuzzy set in question then the length of the chromosome varies, else it stays the same, it is suspected it should vary given the potpourri of fuzzy sets available and the varying requirements. One can easily fix the number of fuzzy sets for each variable if triangular fuzzy sets are the choice, make it a constant number, off the cuff, based on fuzzy design practice, and knowledge of the markers, usually $2N + 1$ symmetrical fuzzy sets per variable (see Woodard and Garg [22], Wang and Mendel, and Kosko [9]), one centre set, and N on either side. But it was opted to leave the choice of fuzzy sets to the GA (a similar design is reported by Kim and Zeigler, [8], and thus a variable number of fuzzy sets per variable is the resolution.

A summary of system specifications is given as follows:

1. Probability of mutation - between 0.001, and 0.1
2. Crossover - two point, or eight point
3. Selection - roulette wheel, tournament, or elitist
4. Termination criteria - error less than 0.1
5. Representation - arbritary choice
6. Size of population - arbritary choice

2.2 Evolving rules for evaluating oncological prognosis using genetic algorithms

For oncological data, we need a series of rules that have the following form:

if $antecedent_{11}$ and $antecedent_{12}$ ... and $antecedent_{1n}$ then
  $consequent_1$
end if
if $antecedent_{21}$ and $antecedent_{22}$ ... and $antecedent_{2n}$ then
  $consequent_2$
end if
...
if $antecedent_{m1}$ and $antecedent_{m2}$ ... and $antecedent_{mn}$ then
  $consequent_m$
end if

A gene is a rule, and an antecedent is of the form:
(coefficient, variable)
All null antecedent values indicates an invalid gene.

A combinatorial measure of the consequent values of the rules of the best chromosome is developed as the prognostic score.

Here we have m rules. Thus we could generate a population of a set of m rules, unlike classifier systems that have the benefit of online reappraisal. That is each individual or chromosome in the population has m genes, each gene being a rule. The fitness function is simple, test the chromosome with its set of rules, and establish fitness, relative to desired error (or some determinant factor), as in option 2 or relative to a series of already established rules, looking for better rules, as in options 5 and 6.

This has the risk of a multiplicative or an exponential difficulty, but should converge with fewer generations than a classifier system. Classifier systems avoid the multiplicative or exponential complexity by selecting m rules from a population of R rules, $m \leq R$. Each individual being a rule. An encouraging example of using genetic algorithms to generate classification rules (even for a medical task) is given by Kentala et al [12].

Encoding and decoding is carried out as in any other GA application based on desired values, and is considered trivial.

Here is a brief outline of the GA fitness function for rule generation:

Require: chomosome c
  $correct = 0$
  $total = 0$
  for all test data record **do**
    COMPUTE chromosome consequent value
    if chromosome consequent value == test data record antecedent value
    then
      correct++
    end if
    total++
  end for
  fitness value = correct/total

2.3 The fuzzy logic model for specifying genetic algorithms for evaluating oncological prognosis

The specfications are:
  if $avfitness_{pop}$ is **optimal** and $chromosome_1$ is **fit then**
    p_m is **high**
  end if
  if $avfitness_{pop}$ is **optimal** and $chromosome_1$ is **unfit then**
    p_m is **low**
  end if
  if $avfitness_{pop}$ is **sub-optimal** and $chromosome_1$ is **fit then**
    p_m is **low**
  end if
  if $avfitness_{pop}$ is **sub-optimal** and $chromosome_1$ is **unfit then**
    p_m is **high**

end if

$avfitness_{pop}$ is a measure of the average fitness of the population, while p_m is the probability of mutation. The fitter the chromosomes the lower the chance is of mutation, when the average chromosome is optimal, but if we are in a sub-optimal region largely, then lower fit chromosomes are encouraged to mutate in favour of highly fit ones, to encourage diversity (similar to Herrera et al [3] where a fuzzy model is used to monitor population diversity).

So there are seven fuzzy sets:

1. *fit* and *unfit* — two trapezoidal regions that qualify the fitness values, given maximum fitness, F_{max}, and minimum fitness, F_{min}, then the parameters for the two sets would be bounded by $(p_1(F_{max}, F_{min}) < F_{max}, \ldots, F_{max}, F_{max}+1.0)$ and $(F_{min}-1.0, F_{min}, F_{min} < p_2(F_{max}, F_{min}) < p_1, p_2 < p_3(F_{max}, F_{min}) < p_1)$ respectively. (p_1, p_2, and p_3, are user-defined linear functions that represent a slope of the corresponding trapezoidal.)

2. *low*, and *high* — a negative sloped line, and a positive sloped line respectively. If the ranges are 0.0 to 0.5, and 0.5 to 1.0, respectively then the equations of the two outermost lines are $y = 1.0-2.0x$, and $y = 2.0x-1.0$.

3. *suboptimal* and *optimal* — two trapeziodal regions identical to *unfit* and *fit* respectively though varied with the understanding that optimal if and only if fit, but unfit is a subset of sub-optimal: the area of the sub-optimal fuzzy set space is larger than for the unfit fuzzy set space.

These form the technical considerations.

3 Conclusion

Given the above technical considerations, the rulebase for the fuzzy systems in options 3, and 4, which forms the core of each's decision support system is generated with the c4.5 algorithm. A tree is produced by this algorithm, and the path from the root to each node, comprises a rule. A tree as a corollary to its definition has only one path from a root to any leaf, thus we have unique rules. The set of rules simply form the base outline of the fuzzy system, and improvements over and above the performance of the associated tree, is expected.

The variables accepted by each rule are degrees of membership of each relevant variable, that is fuzzified variables. An optimal collection of fuzzy sets is ensured by the evolutionary algorithm, that optimzes each fuzzy set.

The evolutionary algorithm in option 4 searches for optimal parameters of fuzzy sets. This is accomplished by evolving a population of chromosomes, comprising of all the parameters. Each chromosome is qualified by the fitness function which is the fuzzy system itself. The best chromosome is used to kit the fuzzy system, and the fuzzy system is thus ready to perform the necessary prognosis.

Further research to investigate experimentally these models is in progress.

References

1. Bäck, T. (1996) Evolutionary algorithms in theory and practice: evolutionary strategies evolutionary programming genetic algorithms. Oxford University Press

2. Cox, E. (1994) The fuzzy systems handbook. A practitioner's guide to building, using, and maintaining fuzzy systems. Academic Press, Inc., London

3. Herrera, F., Herrera-Viedma, E., Lozano, Verdegay, J.L. (1994) Fuzzy tools to improve genetic algorithms. IN: Proceedings of the Second European Congress on Intelligent Techniques and Soft Computing. pp. 804–809

4. Holland, J. H. (1992) Adaptation in Natural and Artificial Systems An Introductory Analysis with Applications to Biology, Control, and Artificial Intelligence. MIT Press, Massachusetts

5. Ichimura, T., Tazaki, E., and Yoshida, K. (1995) Extraction of fuzzy rules using neural networks with structure level adaptation – verification to the diagnosis of hepatobiliary disorders. Int. J. Biomed. Comput. 40, 139–46

6. Indurkhya, N., and Weiss, S. M. (1998) Estimating the performance gains for voted decision trees. Intelligent Data Analysis 2, http://www-east.elsevier.com/ida/browse/0204/ida00035/ida00035.htm

7. Janikow, C.Z. (1996) A genetic algorithm method for optimizing fuzzy decision trees. Information Sciences 89, 275–296

8. Kim, J., and Ziegler, B.P. (1995) Beneficial effect of intentional noise. IN: Chambers, L. ed. Practical Handbook of Genetic Algorithms, CRC Press. pp. 431–457

9. Kosko, B. (1992) Neural networks and fuzzy systems. A dynamical systems approach to machine intelligence. Prentice-Hall International Editions, Englewood Cliffs, N.J.

10. Lee, M, -R. (1998) Generating fuzzy rules by genetic method and its application. International Journal on Artificial Intelligence Tools 7, 399–413

11. Lim, T. S., Lok, W. Y., and Shih, Y. S. (1999?, forthcoming) A comparison of prediction accuracy, complexity, and training time of thirty-three old and new classification algorithms. IN: Machine Learning, Kluwer Academic Press. http://www.stat.wisc.edu/~limt/mach1317.ps. Appendix containing complete tables of error rates, ranks, and training times, http://www.stat.wisc.edu/~limt/appendix.ps

12. Kentala, E., Laurikkala, J., Pyykko, I., and Juhola, M. (1999) Discovering diagnostic rules from a neurotologic database with genetic algorithms. Annals of Otology, Rhinology & Laryngology 108, 948–54

13. Maguire, L. P., McGinnity, M., and McDaid, L. J. (1997) A fuzzy neural network for approximate fuzzy reasoning. IN: Ruan, D. ed. Intelligent hybrid systems. Fuzzy logic, neural networks, and genetic algorithms. Kluwer Academic Publishers. pp. 35–58

14. Mizumoto, M., and Shi, Y. (1997) A new approach of neurofuzzy learning algorithm. IN: Ruan, D. ed. Intelligent Hybrid Systems, Fuzzy Logic, Neural Networks, Genetic Algorithms, Kluwer Academic Publishers. pp. 109–129

15. Quinlan, J. R. (1986) Induction of decision trees. Machine Learning, 1, 81–106

16. Quinlan, J. R. (1993) C4.5: Programs for Machine Learning. Morgan Kaufmann

17. Quinlan, J. R. (1996) Improved use of continuous attributes in C4.5. Journal of Artificial Intelligence Research 4, 77–90

18. Takagi, H. (1997) Introduction to fuzzy systems, neural networks, and genetic algorithms. IN: Ruan, D. ed. Intelligent hybrid systems. Fuzzy logic, neural networks, and genetic algorithms. Kluwer Academic Publishers. pp. 3–33

19. Wang, L. -X., and Mendel, J. M. (1991) Generating fuzzy rules from numerical data, with applications. University of Southern California, Signal and Image Processing Institute, USC-SIPI REPORT #169

20. Wang, L. -X., and Mendel, J. M. (1992) Generating fuzzy rules by learning from examples. IEEE Transactions on Systems, Man, and Cybernetics 22, 1414–1427

21. Takagi, H. (1993) Neural network and genetic algorithm techniques for fuzzy systems. IN: Proceedings of the World Congress on Neural Networks. pp. II631-II634

22. Woodard, S. E., and Garg, D. P. (1997) A numerical optimization approach for tuning fuzzy logic controllers. IN: Third Joint Conference on Information Sciences.

23. Yuan, Y., and Suarga, S. (1995) On the integration of neural networks and fuzzy logic systems. IN: IEEE International Conference on Systems, Man and Cybernetics. pp. 452–7

24. Zadeh, L. A. (1965) Fuzzy sets. Information and Control 8, 338–353

Evolving Protein Similarity Scoring Matrices Using Differential Evolution

[1]Ketan Patel, [2]Andrew Tuson, [3]Andrew Coulson, [3]Shane Sturrock, [4]Robert Fisher

[1]Physical & Theoretical Chemistry Laboratory, Oxford University, South Parks Road, Oxford, OX1 3QZ.

[2]Department of Computing, City University, Northampton Square, London EC1V 0HB

[3]Institute of Cell and Molecular Biology, University of Edinburgh, Darwin Building, King's Buildings, Edinburgh, EH9 3JR

[4]Institute for Perception, Action, and Behaviour, University of Edinburgh, 5 Forrest Hill, Edinburgh EH1 2QL

Keywords: Protein Structure Prediction, Differential Evolution, Optimisation

1 Synopsis

The problem of protein structure prediction remains one of the major unsolved problems in structural biochemistry. The most successful method to date for predicting protein tertiary (3-dimensional) structure from the primary sequence data (of amino acids) is homology modelling based on alignment with similar sequences of known structure. The premier component utilised in this process is a scoring matrix that determines how similar one protein is to another.

The aim of this work was to improve upon the scoring matrices currently used such as the PAM250 matrix [Dayhoff *et al.* 72], in an effort to detect and classify proteins that are more distantly related to each other. To this end an optimisation approach was taken, using a type of evolutionary algorithm known as Differential Evolution. We shall show that it is possible to evolve both a better general scoring matrix and a matrix which is specialised to detect a specific class of protein.

2 The Problem

Protein classifaction requires the optimisation of a matrix to find proteins which have low sequence identity, but which have a high structural similarity. The matrix, *M*, is a 20 by 20 matrix of real numbers (although our algorithm recast these as integers), which represents the penalty of subsituting one of 20 amino acids with another. We do this for each part of the sequences which align, assigning further penalties to gaps in the alignment. Once these penalty scores are added up, this tells us how similar the two proteins are in terms of evolutionary divergence (if using the original PAM matrices). The matrix *M* is symmetrical about its diagonal and cannot have negative values along its diagonal (since if the two amino-acids at a point match exactly this should not invoke a penalty). Each element within the matrix was limited to the range of integers [-60, +20], due to using the sequence alignment program `sss_align` [Sturrock 97] for matrix evaluation. This constraint effectively narrowed our search space to only consider more sensible values for each matrix element.

This optimisation problem was recast as a minimisation problem *min z(x)* where *z(x)* is the objective function which tells us how effective the matrix is, and is a combination of cost functions. There are several flavours of evolutionary algorithm which we could have used for the optimisation, but eventually Differential Evolution [Storn & Price 95] was used for its simplicity and performance on continous search space optimisation problems.

3 Differential Evolution

Differential Evolution is similar to the original Genetic Algorithm [Holland 75] in that the general process is a simulation of the evolutionary process. A set of population members is maintained and operators are applied to mutate these members. The population is then ranked according to fitness and 'bad' members are discarded. This is where the similarity ends. DE uses a non binary representation, and uses a new form of mutation, and no crossover (although this can be added if desired). There are several variants of DE, but the one used in our experiments works as follows: for each member (scoring matrix) $x_{i,G}$, $i = 1,..., NP$, a trial vector *v* is generated according to:

$$v = x_{r_1,G} + F.\left(x_{r_2,G} - x_{r_3,G}\right)$$

The integers r_1, r_2 and r_3 are chosen randomly from the interval [1, *NP*] and are different from the running index i. *NP* is the number of population members and *G* is the generation number. *F* is a real and constant factor which controls the amplification of the differential variation. This vector *v* is then compared to $x_{i,G}$ and whichever is better is placed into the next generation G + 1. Since we were evolving a matrix of integers and the factor F is real valued, all calculations were rounded to the nearest whole number.

3.1 Design of Representation and Operators

The structure of a solution vector in any search and optimisation problem depends on the underlying problem. Our problem involves manipulating a matrix of integer values. The basic representation was thus a 20 by 20 array of integer values. The matrix has some constraints and so to cope with these the operators that manipulate the array (and generate it) will need to take these constraints into account. The main feature of the matrix is that it is symmetrical about its diagonal, and this was easily encoded into the operators, all we needed to do was to make sure that element $X_{i,j}$ equals element $X_{j,i}$ when generating the initial matrices. The other constraint was to make sure that all diagonal constraints were positive, this is easy when generating the initial population, but the move operators will change the elements, so a check was included to make sure that if a diagonal element was changed to a negative value, it was replaced by 1. The range constraint was also dealt with this way, the values were capped to either –60 or +20 if they were out of range. Addition and subtraction were implemented using matrix addition and subtraction.

4 Design of Evaluation Function

Evaluating a protein scoring matrix involves testing its efficiency at detecting proteins which are highly similar in structure, but which have a low sequence identity. This is a tricky task since to evaluate it properly one should use it to search for a variety of proteins from more than one database. However since we do not have time to do this for each matrix, we must come up with a fast way of assessing whether a particular matrix is good for the problem we are addressing.

There are two possible approaches to this problem. One is to use a direct database search, using the matrix to be evaluated, the results of this search could be used to score the matrix. This would probably have to be done more than once, since only one protein can be searched for at a time. A good representative sample of proteins would have to be used, in order to make sure that the matrix is adequate for all classes of protein. The other option is to use an analytical model for analysing the quality of a matrix. Several studies have been done on how to assess if a result from a search is statistically significant [Karlin & Altschul 93]. These techniques use a random model for proteins to predict how many 'hits' can occur by chance, when searching large databases. Given a non-random protein model (i.e. one that represents the proteins that we are looking for), and a set of scores, we can use the same technique to determine how good those scores are in the context of searching for that particular set of proteins.

After careful consideration it was decided that the former approach be taken. This was due to the fact that the analytical technique was not properly defined for gapped alignments (i.e. comparing protein sequences where some amino acids in one sequence has no correspondence with those in the second) and this is what the matrix will eventually be used for. Also, if the theory were properly developed there would be no need to 'evolve' a matrix, as we could derive it from the frequencies given in our 'ideal' model. Another point to consider is that the database search is what the final matrix is going to be used for, and so by using this as our evaluation function, we are evaluating the performance of the matrix under real-world conditions.

A full specification of the evaluation function is given in the thesis [Patel 98], but a brief description is given here. Firstly the matrix to be evaluated is used to search a database for a small set of proteins. Each protein used to query the database will have a set of homologues that the search is expected to find. The search will be done for each query sequence and the results will be parsed to see how well they match to the expected output. The search program returns a list of the matches it finds. This list is in order of significance. The highest match is not important because it corresponds to the same protein as the query sequence. So the first match will always be the same protein used for the search. We are more interested in later matches that correspond to the next most similar protein (according to the scoring matrix), and so on.

The search was done using the `sss_align` program. This program ranks the matches in order of significance, the most significant match being at the top of the list. The program returns the top 200 matches from the search (this value can be changed, but was kept at 200 for all our experiments). The best result would be to have all known homologues appear immediately after the highest match, but in practice they are often lower down in the list. By counting the positions between the highest match and the lowest match, we can score a matrix on its performance for that protein. This is then done for all the proteins in the training set, and the results are summed. If there are no matches then that protein is given a score of 400. If there is only one match then this is the same as the query protein. So it is still a bad result, but instead a score of 200 + the position of this highest match is given. This is because the `sss_align` program returns the top 200 matches, so if there is only one match and it is in position 200, then the score will be 400 (as if there were no matches).

The training set of proteins consisted of 24 proteins picked from a database called SCOP [Murzin *et al.* 95], which is organised by structure. This allowed us to pick examples from 6 different SCOP protein families. Since evaluating all proteins every time would be too expensive in terms of time, a subset selection scheme was used [Gathercole & Ross 94] to select a subset of the training set for evaluation purposes. This technique allows one to have a large training set, but then only use a subset of that training set for evaluating a solution vector (i.e. our matrix). The subset size was set at six proteins, out of a maximum set of 24 proteins. The SCOP database is organised by protein class, and there are six main classes of protein in the database. Therefore four proteins from each class were chosen to be included in our set of 24 proteins. This ensured a good sample of proteins from all the different classes. The subset selection model was also biased so that each one of the six proteins picked for evalution was from a different class. This would ensure that the matrix would remain as general as possible.

5 Results

Formative experiments were conducted to produce an appropriate optimiser configuration, and are detailed in full in [Patel 98]. The **F** value for the DE algorithm was set to 0.8. The population used was of size X, and run for Y generations in each case. The PAM250 matrix was used to seed the initial population, and the randomly generated matrices had their elements restricted to the range [-30, 10]. The parameters for dynamic subset selection were as recommended in [Gathercole & Ross 94]. Finally default gap penalties from the sss_align program were used.

Two sets of experiments were conducted. In the first set of experiments the aim was to evolve a *general* matrix capable of finding homologues to all proteins. When referring to matrices which were not evolved, the term *derived matrices* is used, and refers to the PAM and BLOSUM matrices used in the tests. In the second set of experiments the aim was to evolve a matrix which would be specific for a particular class of protein. The parameters for all experiments were kept the same.

5.1 Results for First Set of Experiments

The results for the first set of runs are shown in Table 1. These runs were seeded with the PAM250 matrix, and used the parameters given above. These results show the performance of the matrices with the test set of 24 proteins. The results for the training sets are omitted to save space and can be found in [Patel 98]. The mean score is shown for the entire test set. This was derived by totalling the individual component scores for each protein and dividing by 24. Furthermore a breakdown by each of the 6 SCOP classes considered is also given. This was computed by totalling the scores for the proteins in each class and dividing by the number of proteins in that class.

The test results show that only the matrix generated from run 5 is truly competitive with the PAM and BLOSUM matrices. This matrix performed better than the PAM120 and PAM250 matrices, but was outperformed by the

BLOSUM60 matrix. The run 5 matrix does however achieve better average scores than the BLOSUM60 matrix for SCOP classes 5 and 7.

Table 1: Test results for the general set of matrices

Matrix	Mean Score	Mean Score for each SCOP Class					
		Class 1	Class 2	Class 3	Class 4	Class 5	Class 7
PAM250	82.63	18.5	96	92.5	199	74	15.75
PAM120	79.88	49.75	115.5	94.5	151	24.5	44
BLOSUM60	73.21	50	90	57.75	120.5	95.5	25.5
DE Run 1	90.58	99.5	118.25	100.5	152	54.25	19
DE Run 2	97.63	115	120.5	118.5	156	67	8.75
DE Run 4	84.58	99.75	99.5	68	152.5	75.75	12
DE Run 5	76.25	53.25	90	71	160	60.5	22.75
DE Run 6	169.29	189.25	149.25	196.75	199	183	98.5

5.2 Results for the Second Set of Experiments

In the second set of experiments, matrices were evolved for specific classes of protein. This was done to investigate whether a matrix trained for a particular class of protein could outperform the general type of matrix (when used to detect proteins from that class). For the specific matrices the size of the test set was reduced to 12 proteins for each class.

Table 2: Results for SCOP class 1 experiments

Matrix	PAM250	PAM120	BLOSUM60	Run 1	Run 2	Run 3
Overall Score	552	601	564	519	525	774

For the class 1 matrix the test results (see Table 2) show that the matrices from run 1 and run 2 are better than the PAM and BLOSUM matrices. With this test data the run 1 matrix outperformed the run 2 matrix, but if the results over the training data (see [Patel 98]) are added to these test results, then run 2 is better overall.

Table 3: Results for SCOP Class 3 experiments

Matrix	PAM250	PAM120	BLOSUM60	Run 4	Run 5
Overall Score	601	612	656	1419	690

The class 3 matrices failed to beat the PAM and BLOSUM matrices (Table 3). This shows that the quality of results are dependent on the data set used.

The differences in performance between class 1 and class 3 can be rationalised as follows. SCOP class 1 proteins are composed entirely of alpha helices, whereas SCOP class 3 proteins are composed of both alpha helices and beta sheets. Therefore it was easier to specialise a matrix for class 1 proteins than class 3 proteins due to the relative richness of secondary structures found in both classes of protein.

6 Conclusion

Overall the results showed that the matrices evolved were competitive with the general matrices already used. One reason for this may well be that the assumption made by the PAM and BLOSUM matricies – that the evolutionary distance between proteins corresponds to tertiary structure – is in fact valid. This conclusion is biologically interesting in itself. That said, the variablity in results obtained between runs may indicate local optima, which means we cannot be sure whether DE has just failed to locate improved general matrices. Further work would be needed to ascertain this.

However the evolved matrices did outperform the PAM250 matrix on some classes of protein. Interestingly when we tried evolving matrices to only recognise a specific class of protein, these matrices did outperform the more general matrices for proteins of that class. This seems to imply that a set of such matrices intelligently applied could lead to a more robust and sensitive scoring system in the future.

The results presented here show that it is possible to use an optimisation approach for improving the amino acid scoring matrices used in protein database searches. We have also found that it may be more effective to use a set of matrices which are suited to particular types of protein, rather than a single matrix suitable for all proteins.

References

[Cartwright and Harris 93] H.M. Cartwrigh and S. P. Harris. Analysis of the distribution of airborne polluation using genetic algorithms. *Atmospheric Environment*, 27:1783-1791, 1993.

[Dayhoff *et al.* 72] M.O. Dayhoff, R.V. Eck, and C.M. Park. *Atlas of Protein Sequence and Structure*, volume 5, pages 89-99. National Biomedical Research Foundation, Washington, DC., 1972.

[Gathercole & Ross 94] C. Gathercole and P. Ross. Dynamic training subset selection for supervised learning in genetic programming. Technical report, Dept. of Artificial Intelligence, University of Edinburgh, February 1994.

[Holland 75] J.H. Holland. *Adaptation in Natural and Artificial Systems*. University of Michigan Press, Ann Arbor, MI, 1975.

[Karlin & Altschul 93] S. Karlin and S.F. Altschul. Applications and statistics for multiple high scoring segments in molecular sequences. *Proceedings of the National Academy of Science, USA*, 90:5873-5877, 1993.

[Murzin *et al.* 95] A.G. Murzin, S.E. Brenner, T. Hubbard, and C. Chothia. SCOP: a structure classification of proteins database for the investigation of sequences and structures. *Journal of Molecular Biology*, 247:536-540, 1995.

[Patel 98] K. Patel. *Evolving Protein Scoring Matrices*. MSc Thesis, Department of Artificial Intelligence, Edinburgh University, 1998.

[Storn and Price 95] R. Storn and K. Price. Differential Evolution – a simple and efficient adaptive scheme for global optimisation over continous spaces. TR-95-012, International Computer Science Institute, Berkeley, CA, March 1995.

[Sturrock 97] S.S. Sturrock. *Improved Tools for Protein Tertiary Structure Prediction*. PhD thesis, University of Edinburgh, 1997.

A Machine Process Cost Estimate Utilising Genetic Algorithms

J. G. Qi, D. J. Stockton, D. K. Harrison* and J. Ardon-Finch

Department of Mechnical and Manufacturing Engineering

De Montfort University

The Gateway, Leicester LE1 9BH, UK

E-mail: jgqi@dmu.ac.uk

*Department of Engineering

Glasgow Caledonian University

Glasgow G4 0BA, UK

Summary:
A major aim of manufacturers is to consider reducing the related machine process cost. A higher level cost estimate is normally taken into account as a guidance when establishing production plans and in addition help balance machine loading and minimise penalty costs. Practical machine process cost estimation relies heavily upon past experiential knowledge, which often leads to inaccurate estimates, and can make cost engineers incapable of achieving an estimation while the number of machines and operations increase. In this research, a genetic algorithm for estimating machine process cost is addressed, it is capable of providing a minimum machine process cost estimation according to the predicted production demand and available machine capability. The objective of this research is to provide an effective tool to assist a cost engineer for generating an optimal and accurate cost estimation in order to reduce unnecessary penalty costs.

Keywords: Cost estimation; Genetic algorithms; Machine process costs; Penalty costs

1 Introduction

As a result of the intense global competition there is now a very small margin of error for companies. Those wishing to remain competitive know it is crucial that the information they apply for decision-making reflects their environment as accurately and rapidly as possible. Costing information is one of the most important sources for this purpose, being used at all levels of company decision-making: strategic, tactical and operational.

With costing information playing such a vital role in decision-making, if these costing systems do not reflect accurately and rapidly the cost of machine process by products, machine loading will be unbalanced and at the same time penalty costs will be incurred.

Traditional machine process methods of cost estimation not only fail to reflect realities of the manufacturing environment, but they further fail to produce rapid and accurate costing information which can be fed upstream and downstream to improve design for manufacture, production planning and production costs.

Since the limitations of traditional cost methods were discovered, some alternate methods must be developed to demonstrate their ability for generating accurate and optimal production cost estimates. There are many techniques which can be developed and put forward as suitable replacements to traditional cost estimate methods. In this paper, we focus on developing a genetic algorithm which is considered as a higher level cost estimate in assisting reduce the related machine process cost, balance machine loading and minimize penalty costs.

The remainder of this paper is organized as follows: Section 2 briefly reviews genetic algorithms. Section 3 gives a description of the proposed genetic algorithm for a machine process cost estimate. Simulation results from a case study are provided in Section 4. Finally, Section 5 represents some conclusions of the paper.

2 Review of Genetic Algorithm

A genetic algorithm is a computational model that emulates biological evolutionary theories to solve optimization problems. A GA consists of a set of individual elements (the population) and a set of biologically inspired operators defined over the population itself. In terms of evolutionary theories, only the most suited elements in a population are likely to survive and generate offspring, thus transmitting their biological heredity to new generations [1].

For solution to an optimization problem, five components are typically required:

- *Initialization of the Population.* A method of initializing the population of chromosome is required. In general, the population of chromosomes is initialized randomly.

- *Encoding.* This is a way of encoding the decision variables of the optimization problem in a string of binary digits (1's and 0's) or other representations called a *chromosome*.

- *Evaluation or Objective Function.* This function is used to evaluate the given decision variables and return a value. The value of a chromosome's objective function is a measure of fitness of that chromosome.

- *Genetic Operators.* Genetic algorithms employ parent selection techniques that selects strings to create a new generation, where the fittest members reproduce most often. After the parent selection, the process of crossover, mutation and other operations are applied.

- *Optimal Parameters.* A set of parameters is predefined to guide the genetic algorithm, such as the length of each decision variable, the number of chromosomes, the crossover rate, the mutation rate and stopping criterion.

A GA optimisation application process is illustrated in Figure 1.

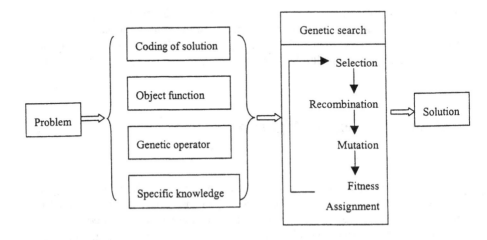

Figure 1. Problem solution using genetic algorithms

Genetic algorithms have proven to be an effective and flexible optimisation tool that can efficiently produce optimal or near-optimal solutions. Furthermore, the genetic algorithms do not need to make as many assumptions regarding the form of the objective functions as normally required by many other optimization techniques [2].

3 The Proposed Approach

3.1 Multiple Sequence Chromosome

In this representation, a large number of orders are broken down into smaller ones, the genes corresponding to the number of smaller jobs units are sequenced according to order numbers. This is called a sequence chromosome definition. Multiple sequence chromosomes allow the addition of further sequence chromosomes with a defined numbers of genes each related to the original orders sequence chromosome. The genes of the additional sequence chromosome describe the sequence by which machines should be considered when scheduling orders in the original orders sequence. A multiple sequence chromosome example is shown in Figure 2, which comprises 2 machines and 5 reduced smaller orders units.

3.2 Initialization

Initialization involves generating a set of possible solutions for the search algorithm. This initial population may be generated randomly or with some established heuristics. In our implementation, the initial population is created randomly.

3.3 Objective Function

The objective of machine process is to minimize the total cost of processing all operations.

When formulating constraints for the objective function, a penalty approach suggested by Goldberg [3] is followed. This approach transforms a constrained problem into an unconstrained problem by associating a cost, or penalty, with all constraint violations.

A penalty approach is adopted in this paper, therefore an objective function is finally constructed as:

Objective function = Production_cost+Penalty_cost

The genetic algorithm is initiated to minimise this cost objective function; which comprises the total cost of running the machines, plus the total penalty cost for exceeding the available capacity of machines. The relative cost of exceeding the available capacity per minute has to be set to a sensible value which reflects the severity of the constriants.

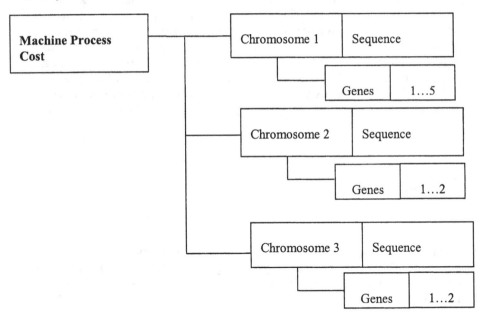

Figure 2. A multiple sequence chromsome

3.4 Crossover, Mutation and Adaptation

A basic operator for producing new chromosomes using genetic algorithm is that of crossover. Crossover produces new individuals that have some parts of both parents' genetic attributes.

Each chromosome consists of a number of genes. Each of these genes in turn comprises 16 bits. Thus each chromosome effectively consists of a string of bits. The crossover operator randomly selects two-bit position along the chromosome of the first parent and then exchanges bit information with the second parent in order to make an offspring. A simple example is shown below:

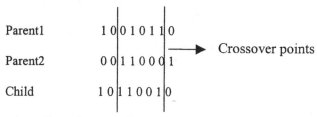

A mutation mechanism allows for a small number of genes to alter their internal structure in order to survive. A mutation operator plays a supportive role and runs in the background. The intention is either to explore new contexts or recover loss contexts of gene structures from the reproduction operator. It minimizes risks of discovering new gene structures by randomly changing gene strings. Mutation involves swapping the positions of two adjacent genes randomly selected.

Like mutation, adaptation is a random change to the value or order of genes within the chromosome. However, unlike mutation, the changes are only retained if they improve the cost (fitness) of the chromosome. As such, adaptation can be seen as a 'wise' mutation which is a deviation from the evolutionary selection process.

With incremental adaptation, each adaptation cycle works on the result of the previous cycle, regardless of whether it represented an improvement in cost. This will often produce better results, when the genes have a high degree of interaction in the way that they impact on the cost.

4 A Case Study

Consider the typical example of machine process cost in manufacturing. A factory has four machines A, B, C, D; these machines are of different ages and capabilities. Their respective maximum available capacity in a week is 1500, 4500, 800, and 1700 minutes. The products manufactured involve four operations O1, O2, O3 and O4. Some products require O1, O2, O3, O4, and others O2, O3, O4 and so on. The requirements for a week have been summed up as orders of

1400 units, 1200 units, 900 units and 900 units for operations O1, O2, O3 and O4 respectively. The times in minutes per operation and the cost per minute for each machine are shown in the Table 1 and Table 2 [4].

Table 1. The times per operation processed with different machines

Operation	Predicted weekly demand	Unit production time (minutes)			
		Machine A	Machine B	Machine C	Machine D
O1	1400	2	3	1	1
O2	1200	3	4	2	1
O3	900	1	7	4	3
O4	900	1	6	2	5

Table 2. The cost per minute for each machine

Resource	Cost per minute (£)	Available capacity (min)
Machine A	30	1500
Machine B	40	4500
Machine C	25	800
Machine D	20	1700

The problem is to decide how many units of each operation should be manufactured in each machine in order to fulfill the requirements at a minimum cost, without exceeding the capacity of the four machines. The obvious way of using genetic algorithms to solve the above problem is to use a number of numeric genes to represent the number of units of each operation assigned to each machine.

Simulation runs were carried out with XperRule KBS Package on a P3 550 128M computer. The advanced parameters are illustrated in Table 3. Which take few minutes to converge to the optimal cost. The simulation results are shown in Figure 3 and Table 4, and minimum and mean cost for optimised machine output are £275000 and £288350.8, this is the best solution achieved in terms of the machine process cost and the utilization of machine capability.

Table 3. The advanced parameters for optimal solution

Population size	50	Adaptation rate	0.5
Maximum number of generations	50	Adaptation cycles	2
First mutation rate	0.05	Inversion rate	0.2
Second mutation rate	0.5	In version starts at generation	11
Change from first to second at generation	11	Crossover rate	0.6

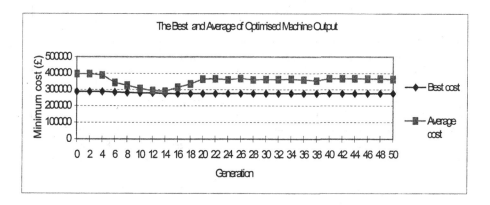

Figure 3. The results of the proposed Genetic Algorithm

5 Conclusions

The simulation results indicate that this new higher-level cost estimate scheme based on a genetic algorithm is an effective and efficient technique to tackle the problem of cost. The proposed algorithm has the potential for cost engineers to provide rapid and accurate estimates within real manufacturing environment, and an effective tool for production planning.

Further work will concentrate on the development of algorithm to be applied in a more complex manufacturing environment.

Table 4. The optimization report of machine output cost

Machine	O1	O2	O3	O4	Available Capacity	Used Capacity	Capacity Exceeded
A	0	500	0	0	1500	1500	0
B	0	700	350	900	4500	4400	0
C	800	0	0	0	800	800	0
D	600	0	550	0	1700	1700	0
Total	1400	1200	900	900			
Required	1400	1200	900	900			
Best cost : 275000 (£)					**Best average: 288350.8 (£)**		

6 References

1. Syswerda G. (1991) Schedule Optimization Using Genetic Algorithms. In: Davis L. (Ed.) Handbook of Genetic Algorithms. Van Nostrand Reinhold, New York, 332-349

2. Lee C. Y., Piramuthu S., Tsai Y. K. (1997) Job Shop Scheduling with Genetic Algorithm and Machine Learning. International Journal of Production Research, 35(4): 1171-1191

3. Goldberg D. E. (1989) Genetic Algorithms in Search, Optimization & Machine Learning. Reading, Addison-Wesley Publishing Company, MA

4. Anderson E. J. (1994) The Management of Manufacturing: Models and Analysis. Addison-Wesley Publishers, MA

Printing: Strauss GmbH, Mörlenbach
Binding: Schäffer, Grünstadt